CAGED
metal feathers

by
s. i. horvath

CYNTOMEDIA CORPORATION

Pittsburgh, PA

ISBN 1-58501-076-6

Trade Paperback
© Copyright 2004 Stephan Istvan Horvath
All Rights Reserved
First Printing — 2004
Library of Congress #2004105742

Request for information should be addressed to:

> SterlingHouse Publisher, Inc.
> 7436 Washington Avenue
> Pittsburgh, PA 15218
> www.sterlinghousepublisher.com

CeShore is an imprint of SterlingHouse Publisher, Inc.

SterlingHouse Publisher, Inc. is a company
of the CyntoMedia Corporation.

Cover Design: Melissa G. Hudak—SterlingHouse Publisher, Inc.
Book Design: Kathleen M. Gall
Cover Photograph: provided by author

All rights reserved. No part of this publication may be reproduced, stored in a retrieval system, or transmitted in any form or by any means—electronic, mechanical, photocopy, recording or any other, except for brief quotations in printed reviews—without prior permission of the publisher.

This publication includes images from Corel Draw 11 which are protected by the copyright laws of the U.S., Canada and elsewhere.

Printed in the United States of America

CAGED
metal feathers

by
s. i. horvath

*To my daughters
Becky and April,
and to my wife Beverly,
without whom this book
would not be in your hands.*

TABLE OF CONTENTS

PART ONE
Stones.. 1
The Whistler's Sons 4
A Goose in the Well 7
One Sunday... 13
Gigant 16

PART TWO
The Sky is Falling 25
Caged Metal Feathers 28
Split Peas 31
Peeling Potatoes... 35

PART THREE
Where Everything Grows 40
Bees in the Wall 47
Fishing 51
Prized Canvas 54

PART FOUR
Three Borders Mountain 65
Big Kadi... 76
Between Heaven and Earth 89
Bittersweet.. 99

PART FIVE
Flames of Anger... 112
Anyu.. 127
The Journey West 136
Seeds on the Wind....................................... 150

PART SIX
An Odd Decision... 168
Nixon 179
Coke.. 185
Green Skies... 190
Hell in Paradise 202

PART ONE

STONES

Among the meager stack of memorabilia from my childhood is a battered black and white photograph of two little boys standing in front of a picket fence. The boys are smiling; they are suntanned, barefoot, and blond. The older boy, nearly a head taller, is my brother Laci; the other is me. Not visible behind the fence and the verdant shrubbery is our home nestled among other, similar homes in the neighborhood of Sasad, the orchard-covered Hills of Eagles that lie between the peaks of Eagle Mountain and the great river Danube.

The following little story is from the summer predating the photograph, told over the years by my mother and godmother to anyone who would listen, often causing me embarrassment. Of course, in the telling and retelling the story did become somewhat embellished, in time congealing into the foundation of my character analysis according to which I was an independent cuss; one full of the adventurous spirit. On this, there was considerable agreement by all.

★ ★ ★

The boy watched in wonderment as the bee tried to turn around in the funnel-like cone of the morning glory, squirming under the fat little finger pressed against its back. The boy was toying with it.

The vines of the morning glory coiled around copper wires that stretched from the ground below the porch up to the eves. In the neighborhood of Sasad the purple-blue flowers signaled the onset of summer, and the nectar, nestled deep within, proved irresistible to the bees that were busy with the early day's task of making a living.

The bee finally made the turn, wriggled past the boy's finger and took to flight. The toddler didn't know how close he had come to being stung. For him the unfolding drama fit well with the happenings of the morning; he was unsupervised, Mother still asleep. He was exploring!

Mixed with the scent of flowers, the morning silence hung in the air, broken on occasion by the song of a bird. The hillsides were covered with orchards and vineyards in all directions, peppered with the weekend cottages of the better to do from the city, and older ancestral homes with their slate-tiled roofs. From the porch one could see a sliver of the city toward the east. Ten kilometers away, standing sentinel above the river and the city that lay beyond, the partly obscured Citadel on St. Gellért Hill commanded attention. Sun drenched and green with new growth, the hills of Sasad were at their best.

If one had to guess, the boy was about a year-and-a-half old, give or take a month. He stood on the porch completely naked except for the small blanket he clutched to himself. Ajar and painted forest-green, the door behind him opened into the family's quarters, its bronze handle, used by the boy to gain his freedom only minutes before, sparkling brightly in the morning sunlight.

Inlaid with sandstone blocks, the porch stood nearly a meter above the garden that surrounded the house. Two large steps led off it onto a walk. The steps were a formidable obstacle for a child the boy's age, but not impossible to conquer lying on his stomach.

The path below the porch connected the storage shed near the neighbor's fence with the pedestrian gate at the street. It was paved with white stones bedded into the dark soil that hardened after the spring rains, holding the stones in place with the tenacity of cement. The stones were of irregular size and shape, requiring an expert eye and an unlimited supply for a proper fit.

As good fortune would have it, the last criterium was easily met; all one had to do was to press a spade into the ground and almost certainly a stone would be there, especially when turning the earth for flowerbeds or vegetable gardens. After a good day's work, there would even be a surplus, piled into mounds for anyone to take.

Many of the houses had their porches and fences made of the stones. Bound together with cement, these structures were nearly indestructible. For some lucky city dwellers, working with the stones became a symbol of the good life, something to occupy time on a peaceful weekend. No one knew where the stones came from; their genesis remains a minor mystery. With each season the pathways in front of the summer cottages widened, new rows were added, runoff gullies were lined, all requiring stones. And still, the piles grew.

Once down the steps, the boy toddled past the glass-covered starter beds full of flower seedlings, on his way to the walk-through gate next to the big gate intended for carts and wagons. For the family, growing flowers meant extra cash. For the boy, the flowers and their scent was the way the world came.

Made of vertical wooden slats, the fence along the street was smartly reinforced with heavier beams at top and bottom. Only the underside of the blackened, weathered wood showed the green pigment that once covered it.

It was not an easy task to unlatch and open the gate, but somehow the boy managed it. Holding onto the handle, he glanced back at the house to see if anyone had followed. Satisfied, he toddled to the middle of the street and paused. After a tentative glance in one direction he chose the other, walking gingerly on the street's slag dressing, a painful task for his tiny, tender feet. A byproduct of the coal that powered the furnaces of the city, the slag had been spread on top of last winter's snow by Public Works.

Whenever he could, the boy stepped on the worn-down stones that broke through the slag surface, and on the clumps of grass that took hold here and there. They hurt less. Clutched in his little hand, his blanket trailed him, smoothing the dust.

The matronly, middle-aged woman stared at the child in front of her door, then burst into laughter. "Pista! How in the world did you get here?" she asked, sweeping him off the ground.

Holding the boy to her bosom now, she hurried along the deserted street toward his home.

★ ★ ★

The boy was myself, István, or as family and friends called me then, Pista, the second son of Gizella and László Horváth. The lady rushing me home was my godmother, Mrs. Deményi. The year was 1939, and the war was still far, far away.

THE WHISTLER'S SONS

Gizella brushed the flour off her apron and looked proudly at the boys. *They are good kids,* she thought. *If only László could see little Laci now, as he reads from the storybook to Pista. At only five, Laci is already an accomplished reader, and if it weren't for László pushing him so hard, he would probably want to read even more.* Little Laci could write his name by the time he was three, and at five, he had just about memorized his times-tables. *Definitely smart!* Gizella mused.

Turning back to the wood-burning stove, Gizella dipped the knife into the water to keep the dough from sticking and began slicing the dough into small, narrow slivers. She was making *csiplets,* just the way she had learned from her mother. As soon as the pieces rose to the top of the boiling water they were done, she used a sieve to skim them off the surface. She would add them to the sweet pea soup, one of the boys' favorites. Except for the noodles, the soup was ready, but Gizella hated to interrupt the boys.

When Gizella returned to the dayroom, she heard the boys arguing. Laci sounded bored and irritated. *His little brother's nagging to read aloud from the storybook is annoying him,* she thought. *Not only is his father constantly after him to improve his penmanship, Pista pesters him about everything.*

"I'm tired of reading," Laci said impatiently, snapping the book closed. "Why don't you learn to read?"

Pista started to sob. "I want to hear the hunter's story again."

"Like I said, if you want a story, learn to read!" Laci retorted.

Gizella couldn't let it pass. "Laci, Pista is only three years old, not a big boy like you," she told him.

"Don't care! He keeps bugging me! I have lots of homework, and Father will make me do it over, like last night. I hate rewriting the stuff over and over!"

Can't blame him, Gizella thought. *László is too hard on him; after all, Laci is just a little boy himself.* To Laci she said, "I know it's hard, but you know your father only wants what's best for you." She put the soup on the table and went to get Dodi; the baby probably needed changing by now. *Three boys, one after another it seems,* Gizella reflected. *It's hard to keep up with them.*

László, always working late, should be getting home soon, her patternless thoughts continued. *We need to spend more time together, but it's getting harder and harder with all these mouths to feed! I'll have to go back to work as soon as the baby gets a little older.*

★ ★ ★

László turned off the paved road onto Nagyszeben Trail, the narrow dirt path that paralleled the runoff channel. He had never figured to live in such rural area, but economically Sasad offered what they could afford. *Besides,* he thought, *Gizella likes it here. She is more connected to country living than I am. The truth is,* László sighed, *while I too feel more and more at home, I'd rather live in the heart of the city.*

The walk, edged on both sides with native shrubs and wild lilac, was just wide enough for two people to pass. Occasionally, a hand-drawn cart would negotiate it on the way to the markets, laden with fruits or flowers, but on the way back up, the way he was going now, the going would always be a challenge.

László picked up his pace and started to whistle one of his favorite tunes. Whistling Horvath, the neighbors called him. "Always whistling a happy tune," they said. *So let them hear one now,* he thought.

Nearing the familiar fork in the road, where Wide Road joined the trail as it passed through the runoff channel, László broke into yet another melody. His music echoed through the orchards, sweetly blending with the scent of flowers. The balmy evening matched his mood. Life was getting better. Only the news of the war intruded on his inner peace with a nagging sense of unease. *If only Prime Minister Horti would keep away from the Germans! Getting cozy with them may be expedient, but not likely good for Hungary,* László reasoned.

László pushed the heavy thoughts from his mind and concentrated on the song. The aria from Lehar's *Merry Widow* soared through the air, reaching clear, crystal-like heights and low tremolos.

The song ended just as he reached the crossing. Here, the channel flattened to accommodate the traffic off Wide Road. *This is where the neighborhood really begins*, he thought. He was nearly home now, home to see the kids and work with little Laci. *The kid is doing great, and if he keeps it up, he won't have to work like a serf when he grows up.* "As I do," László added wryly. *Not if I can do anything about it!*

★ ★ ★

The boys were busy eating, and the little one was dry. Gizella took the baby out on the porch and sat down with her back against the top step. The stone felt good against her aching back and suckling Dodi was easier sitting down. It was good to finally have a minute to herself, and even though the baby was nursing, sitting like this was being at ease.

The quiet evening made her think about how much she liked living here. Sasad was the perfect neighborhood for raising the boys. *A bit hard in the winter, to be sure, but winters are harsh everywhere. At least here the kids can play without having to worry about them every minute. No trolleys, busses, or trucks to keep them away from like in the city. Yes,* Gizella thought, *this is the right place for us!*

The sound of a familiar melody pulled Gizella back from her daydreaming. *László!* She could hear him from across the whole neighborhood. Gizella loved his whistling; László elevated whistling to the art of playing an instrument. *No,* she thought, *he sounded more like someone singing and playing an instrument at the same time.*

She buttoned the top of her dress and got up to greet him, helping the baby toddle all the way to the gate on the stone-paved walk.

A GOOSE IN THE WELL

Growing up there were times when my brother, Laci, pissed me off. Being older, he usually got to try everything first. One Saturday, Dad took him to work and showed him how to drive. Dad worked at a small salvage yard owned by a nice Jewish family. Not only did he let Laci drive all over the place, he proudly got his boss out of the office so he, too, could watch. Afterwards, when Laci stopped, they all applauded, Dad said.

Laci didn't waste any time bragging about his driving, either. As soon as the two of them walked through the door, he told everyone who would listen how he could do this and that! When I told him that if he could drive at six-and-a-half, I could do it at five, he just laughed. Like I said, he pissed me off!

I pleaded with Father to show me how to drive, too, but he just kept saying I was too little to reach the pedals. I told him I could, but he said, "No!" every time. But he must have tired of my nagging because he offered to take me for a ride.

"It'll be a long ride, too, because we'll have to go far away to do some work," he consoled me.

Until then I had only ridden on the *Electric* and the train, so I could hardly wait for the weekend. I had to get up really early in the morning to meet him at Small Bridge, the one we used to cross the runoff channel and get on to the Lake Balaton Highway. I could tell that Mom wasn't happy with the idea; we were in the middle of winter, and it was very cold. Mom said there was a chance the trip would be cancelled if too much snow covered the roads. I remember praying for a snowless weekend that night. Usually, I prayed for snow so we could go sledding.

When the big day came, early morning temperatures were

cold enough to freeze the water in our well ten centimeters thick. I learned of this when I overheard my mother tell my godmother about our trip.

"Pista," my mother said the morning of the trip. "If you want to go with your father it's time for you to get up and get ready. It's very cold and dark out there. Are you sure you still want to go?"

She sounded concerned. I think she had hoped I would prefer the warm bed and more sleep to getting up, but I guess I convinced her about wanting to go. Before letting me out from under the down covers, Mother set my clothes on a chair near the fire to warm them up. She must have been up for some time because the room was quite warm, and the side of the cast iron fireplace already glowed red.

After using the chamber pot, I cuddled up to her like I used to when I was little. She dressed me from head to toe, and as a last surprise, she put Laci's new hat, a warm, furry thing with flaps for the ears, on my head. "Remember, your dad will be looking for you under the light at the bridge," she said.

"Don't worry, Mom; I'll be fine," I told her.

She put a couple of hot stones in my pockets, and with much concern on her face, sent me on my way.

Even though the path was familiar, once I was outside our gate, alone, I had second thoughts about going on. The air was bitingly cold, and the snow crunched noisily under my every step. Each hundred and fifty meters along the trail there was a lamp affixed to a power pole, shining a small circle of light onto the ground. The sparkling white snow under the light accentuated the blackness of the night. This made the dark between the poles appear more scary and impenetrable.

Sometimes, as the snow crackled under my shoes, it sounded as if someone was following me. I stopped to listen, but no one was there. Unconvinced, I ran to the next circle of light, stopped, and listened some more. *If someone were following,* I thought, *he would be between home and me.* I had to go on!

Gradually, I closed in on Small Bridge where Father said he would be meeting me. I knew that I had to get there before him, for as my mother had said, if I wasn't there when he arrived, he would go on without me. *I can't let him think I stayed home,* I thought. *I'm not a baby anymore, I do what I promise.*

I reached the bridge and stood under the light just as we had agreed. There was no sign of Father. I waited and waited, tapping my shoes against the ground to keep my feet from freezing. The stones in my pocket were already cold, so I threw them into the runoff channel.

I was terribly cold! Moisture from my breath froze instantly to my shawl, and my nose and feet hurt. Even through the shawl the icy air was painful to breathe. I kept my gloved hands under my arms and hunched over in an attempt to stay warm. After a while the cold seemed to subside, and I felt strangely warmer.

I watched with renewed hope every time a truck approached, but each time it passed without stopping, I felt more anxious. In about thirty-five minutes five trucks had gone by, and I wondered if Father had forgotten about me. *No,* I thought, *he would not forget! I must have gotten here faster than usual, that's all. So now I must wait!*

Just about the time I was ready to give up and thought about going home, a truck pulled up, and there was my father, grinning from within. He opened the door. "Hi, Pista, hop in," he said, looking happy that I was there. When he saw I was too stiff from the cold to climb up, he reached over and helped me onto the seat. He slipped out of his greatcoat and draped it over me.

It was wonderfully warm inside the cab of the truck, but my hands and feet hurt so much, all I could do was cry. Father pulled over to the side of the road and took off my shoes and gloves and rubbed my hands and feet. Slowly, the pain subsided.

Once I stopped sobbing, Father explained that when he had gotten to the yard, he found the truck's engine frozen and could not get it started. He built a fire using rags soaked in used motor oil to warm up the engine, he said. That's why he was late. He showed me his hands; they were raw from cranking the engine, trying to get it started. He said, one time when he was cranking the engine kicked back, and the crank nearly broke his wrist. I didn't understand about engines kicking back, but I was happy to finally be with him.

The engine was so noisy; we had to talk very loud to hear each other. Once in a while we would hit a patch of snow and slide nearly sideways. I could see how much Father loved driving, and I knew when I grew up, I would love it too.

Father started to whistle as we flew by village after village. I was completely lost. "Look," he said, pointing over his left shoulder. "See that orange glow on the horizon?"

I nodded sleepily.

"That's the sun coming up; soon it'll be daylight."

I thought it was beautiful. It was the first time I remember seeing a sunrise.

Father awakened me at our destination and carried me into the house. We were met by Bálint-bácsi, who had a beard and a mustache. He and my father started talking about electricity. The lady of the house gave me hot milk and propped me up on the ledge of the fireplace on a furry sheepskin.

"I'm Bálint-néni," she said and smiled, "and this is my mother, Dobo-néni. Your father said your name was Pista?"

I nodded, thinking Dobo-néni was very old and that she wore funny clothes.

"You can lie down if you want to, but first, can I get you something to eat?"

I shook my head sleepily.

"Don't be bashful. You must be hungry after your long trip. How about some hot oats?"

"No, thank you. But I need to go to the bathroom," I said.

Bálint-néni glanced at her mother, who nodded. "Go with Dobo-néni; she will take care of you," Bálint-néni said.

Dobo-néni took my hand and led me to a room in the back of the house. The room had a fireplace, but it wasn't lit. The window was covered with lace curtains and had plants growing in the deep alcove. There was a carved bed with a large, wooden chest at its base; both were painted wheatflower-blue and had pretty yellow flowers.

Dobo-néni reached under the bed and pulled out a bedpan. "It's much too cold to go to the outhouse," she said. "Use this, then slide it back under the bed when you are done."

She noticed my discomfort.

"Don't worry," she said kindly, "I'll take care of it later." She left, closing the door behind her.

I was completely embarrassed, but I had to go very badly. I thanked Dobo-néni when I got back to the dayroom and snuggled up to the fireplace. The fireplace was similar to that of my grandparent's at their home in Ács. It had a ledge to sit on around the base and reached all the way to the ceiling. The ceramic tiles that covered it had pictures of animals painted on them. Best of all, it was warm.

Once in a while Father and Bálint-bácsi came in to warm up. While they drank hot tea with rum, I listened to their conversation. From what I could make out, they were going to draw wires from the electrical pole on the street to the house, then hook up the electricity for lights and things.

While Father worked with Bálint-bácsi, I was treated to a piece of breakfast cake and more hot milk by Dobo-néni.

Bálint-néni couldn't say enough about how much she liked Father's work. I thought it was peculiar that they would have electricity in their house before we had it in ours. On the way home I asked Father about it, and he said that the Bálints could because the power pole was close to their house, and had plenty of electricity. At our house, my father had rigged a bank of batteries to power our first electric light and our radio. Once a week, he had to take the batteries to work on a small trailer behind his bicycle to have them recharged. To explain electricity, Father had taught Laci and me how to build small electric motors out of shoe polish tins and wires he gave us. We were thrilled when at the completion of the project they actually worked.

About mid-morning, Bálint-néni ran in from the yard in a panic. It seemed a large, prized goose, in an effort to evade capture, had flown onto the rim of the well, where it must have slipped on the ice and fell in. The well was fifteen meters deep, Bálint-néni said, narrow at the top and wider at the water.

Soon, everyone was out in the yard, debating how to save the goose. I put my coat and hat back on and went out to see what they would do. For about an hour, everything that could be tried was, according to Dobo-néni. The closest to rescuing the bird came when Bálint-bácsi lowered a basket with a stone in it to make it sink, hoping that the bird was smart enough to get into it. Amazingly, Dobo-néni said, it did, but about halfway up it either slipped or jumped back out. Stupid bird!

Word of the calamity brought people over from around the neighborhood to help or commiserate. My father, who until now had kept to his work, approached the debating group, and after listening for a while, asked for a rope. He fashioned a harness from it and fixed it around his chest. In measured tones, he gave instructions to Bálint-bácsi and some other men, and then climbed up on the well ring.

"Laci, you mustn't go down there," Bálint-néni protested. "It's very dangerous! If you should fall, we probably couldn't pull you out fast enough to keep you from freezing. We had to break the ice with the bucket this morning to get water."

"I'll be all right," Father said confidently. "You men, take your time, Péter will tell you what to do, and when." He threw the free end of the rope over the well bridge's drum and gave it to the men. They wrapped the rope around their waists and backed away until the rope was taut.

"Péter," my father said to Bálint-bácsi, "I need you to stand by and direct the men."

Slowly, with Father straddling the bucket and holding onto the bucket chain, they lowered him out of sight with the well crank. Holding the rope taut, the men advanced toward the well, step by step.

I was kept away, but I watched and listened. Bálint-bácsi gave orders to the men handling the rope. He raised and lowered his arm as he spoke. "Slowly, ... slowly, ... a little slower." His arm stopped in mid-air with his palm toward the men. "Stop!" he said.

And so it went. In those days no one had flashlights and at one point they lost sight of Father in the darkness of the well. Everyone fell silent. After a long while, I heard my father's muffled yell.

Bálint-bácsi looked into the well. "He is swinging back and forth to get on a ledge," he explained.

Holding my breath, I watched Bálint-bácsi roll up the chain.

Row after row the chain wound onto the drum of the crank. When the bucket came into view, it had the frightened goose in it, wrapped in my father's overcoat. Cheers rang out from the onlookers, but I was panicking. What had happened to my father? Then, the bucket was lowered again.

"Careful! Don't let the bucket hit him," yelled Bálint-néni.

After what seemed an eternity, Father, with the familiar grin on his face, emerged from the well. Eager hands pulled him away from the rim, and everyone thanked and congratulated him. We were treated to dinner and, as a token of the Bálints' appreciation, my father was given another goose as big as the one he had rescued—in addition to the money he earned for the wiring.

We left after dark, and I remember looking at him admiringly all the way home. "Dad, was it real dark and cold down in the well?"

"Once my eyes got used to the dark, it was not so bad," Father said thoughtfully. "And while it was cold, I don't think it was half as cold as this morning, when you met me at Small Bridge under the light." He smiled at me. "Son, I'm very proud of you for being there!"

"Dad, Bálint-néni said if you'd fallen into the water, you would've frozen to death. You didn't look scared, but were you?"

He looked at me seriously for a moment, and then he laughed. "Only all the time," he said, grinning.

We were very late getting home, and my mother was upset! She said she had fretted for hours waiting for us—but she was very happy about the goose. Before falling asleep, I thought about all the people I knew and felt very lucky to be the son of a hero.

ONE SUNDAY

The three of us brothers were dressed for church in the best boys fashion of the day: white shorts, a pressed shirt with an open collar, kneesocks, and sandals. Each of us had a few coins in our pockets, intended for the collection at church, and a bit extra for ice cream to ease the hike on the way home.

Considered too immature to handle money, Sunday was the only chance we had to touch it, except of course for Laci, who was old enough to help out and go to the store for provisions. On those occasions, he would be given a list and money. He had to account to Mother for the leftover change on his return.

It was a warm, midsummer's day, not too hot, not too cold, the kind of day one waited for to spend time outdoors and experience nature. The hills of Buda were full of people from the city, painting the wood trims of their cottages, hoeing weeds, and gathering stones. Life was as it should be.

On this particular Sunday, the neighborhood bully, Jani, who was a couple of years older than Laci and, thus, pushing nine, was once again blocking our way demanding money to let us pass in front of his house. And once again, perhaps for the fourth time, we gave him what we had, fearing terrible retribution should we refuse.

After receiving his bounty and letting us pass, we resolved to avoid him the next time by circling the neighborhood the long way, which involved starting out in the opposite direction, then meeting up with the path along the runoff channel on the south side; quite a bit farther to go, but still better than getting robbed or being beaten up. We also debated whether or not to tell Father what was going on, even though Jani was quite clear about what would happen if we should tell anyone about his thievery.

Upon hearing our story, Father got very angry with us. His chest heaved, his face clouded with anger as he slammed his fist into his palm. "You mean to tell me that the three of you cowered before a brigand like Jani?"

Father went on and on, his nostrils belching fire. He promised to *let us have it* worse than any *young punk* could, should we yield to Jani's demands again. He was terrifying!

By next Sunday, we had a plan. We would fight back, and win or lose, let Jani know his marauding days are over!

As we anxiously passed in front of his house, Jani was nowhere in sight. I don't know about my two brothers, but I was both disappointed and relieved as we continued onto church unmolested.

It so happened that on the next day of the Lord, in addition to money, I also had my father's prized binoculars with me, having slipped them out of my father's normally locked desk drawer at an opportune moment. I don't quite recall the circumstances, but I do remember having a lot of fun with them; it's truly amazing how far things appear when one looks through binoculars the wrong way!

After church services and the obligatory stop at the sweet shop, Laci decided to linger on with friends, while Dodi and I headed for home. As usual, me and my young brother had a merry-old-time along the trail, perfecting our rock throwing skills on a nearly unlimited array of targets, which included the porcelain insulators near the top of the power poles and various bird nests.

As we passed in front of his house, Jani surprised us by waiting in ambush behind his gate. This had never happened before, him challenging us on our way home.

Too late to run, Dodi and I patiently explained we no longer had money, having given what we had to the usher at church, and that our next chance for riches would not come until the following Sunday.

"No problem," Jani said. "Go home and tell your mom that you'd lost your money on the way to church, and you want to go back and give the money to the usher like you should've done in the first place."

Boy! I can just see Father buying this one, I thought.

"Then," Jani continued, "I'll accept the money instead of beating you up, and everybody will be happy!

"And just to make sure things go right, I'll hang onto those binoculars in the meantime." Jani's face broadened into a confident grin. He put his hands in his pockets and rocked back and forth. He had us, and he knew it.

I don't know what came over me. It could have been the fear of Father's wrath if I behaved cowardly once again, or the fear of Jani keeping the binoculars and having to deal with my father about that. Whatever it was, I unexpectedly swung at him with the binoculars. The heavy instrument made solid contact with his head above the left eyebrow. I heard the lenses inside the binoculars make a sickening noise, the kind made by breaking glass, which infuriated me even more! Now, no matter what happened next, I would have to account not only for having the binoculars in my possession, bad enough under any circumstance with Father, but also for damaging them.

Jani, surprised and bleeding profusely, didn't know what else to do but run. I lashed out time and again as he shielded his head with his arms, cowering from my blows. Dodi cheered me on. I pursued him relentlessly until he ducked into safety behind his gate.

I have no recollection of Father's reaction, but never again did Jani challenge us. From that day on, messing with the Horváth boys was asking for trouble. "They might fight like cats and dogs among themselves," people would say, "but if you get sideways with one, you'd better be prepared to take on all of them!"

GIGANT

It was customary at our house that on Sundays, Mother would start preparing the holiday meal early while my brothers and I went off to church. Father, who almost never went to church, would read the paper and do the crossword puzzle. He had this unique style of printing block letters into the squares of the puzzle that I admired, and eventually emulated. I suspect my fascination with words started with watching him do crossword puzzles. I would sit next to him, awed by him knowing a word that would fit in both directions. Occasionally, he would compliment me by asking for a simple word, never letting on that he likely already had what he needed.

From time to time, Mother did accompany us to church, but for her the weekends were the only time she had to catch up with the house. After my younger brother Dodi grew out of diapers; Mother returned to work to help support our growing family.

Working in those days meant five eight-hour days during the week, plus a half-day on Saturdays, leaving precious little time for anything else. The five-and-a-half day work week applied to work and school alike. Those were the working-class realities of life in 1940s Hungary, and probably the rest of Europe.

This particular Sunday restlessness filled the air, the kind of vague unease one didn't quite know the source of, but could feel nonetheless. All through the night we heard airplanes, not just one, which by itself would have been unusual, but many. In our neighborhood the nights were usually still, save for an occasional barking dog or the screeching of an *Electric's* wheels against the rails; sounds that traveled far on certain nights.

Mixed in with the overnight comings and goings, something very big and noisy flew over the house, its powerful engines thundering over the hills and rattling our windows. Nothing I'd ever heard compared with the ominous sound.

On Sunday mornings, something very unusual had to happen to draw Father away from his coffee, his paper, and his puzzle. This morning he addressed us before we left for church; "Boys, I can't imagine what the ruckus was about last night; ask around and see if anyone knows."

By the time we covered half the distance to the highway, we could hear a rumbling. The ground shook and the noise became louder as we neared Small Bridge at the highway's edge. A cloud of dust hung over the whole area, and the air was heavy with the smell of burnt petrol.

A dense pack of onlookers lined both sides of the pavement. We wriggled our way through the crowd, only to see one vehicle after another rumble past us, all emblazoned with the German cross insignia. There were tanks, too, and trucks pulling light artillery.

Marching along the edge of the highway were foot soldiers, each loaded down with a weapon and a heavy backpack. Long-handled hand grenades and ammunition pouches were clipped to their belts. The line extended as far as the eye could see.

Motorcycle soldiers with red armbands zipped by, waving red disks at the end of wooden handles, apparently directing the flow of traffic.

The onlookers seemed bewildered. When I finally squeezed to the front of the line, a lady pulled me back. "Careful!" she said. "A tank nearly ran us over." The noise was so deafening I strained to understand her. A big truck equipped with front wheels and tank-like tracks careened toward us just as she finished warning me. She and another bystander yanked me away. "This is no place for children!" the bystander shouted angrily. Dodi and I moved to another spot.

We watched for a long time, but Laci eventually found us and made us head back home. Father met us halfway up the road. "I started to worry about you," he said. "What's all the racket?"

We told him what we had seen. He listened intently, and for a moment it seemed, he didn't believe us. "Their mother's saint-hood!" He finally exclaimed.

Even though we did not understand the implications of what was happening, the way he spoke, and the fact that he used the expression Mother considered near blasphemy, we knew it was something bad.

"We are supposed allies," Father muttered. "What are they doing occupying a friendly country?" After questioning us all the way home, he rushed into the house to try the radio, which was set on one of the two possible stations that always played classical music. We followed him excitedly. He expertly tuned in the other station. Budapest One was broadcasting the usual Sunday fare: a church sermon. There was no news on either channel.

This was one of a few times I've seen my father flustered. He switched channels back and forth, grumbling. Finally, he bolted into action. "Come boys," he said, "I want to see this for myself!"

Dragging Dodi along by the hand, we followed him up a neighboring hill, from the top of which we could see a portion of the highway and Budapest's second airport that was part of the grasslands on the far side. In normal times, this airport had little activity even on weekends, and at most only a handful of small planes called it home. Nearing the top, we anxiously anticipated the view.

Spread out on the tarmac below was a scene one could only find in a Jules Verne novel. Two-engine cargo planes lined the fence between the highway and the runway. People, looking like ants scurried about, unloading cargo. But my attention immediately focused on something else.

Dominating the paved runway was a giant plane of such dimensions that all else was dwarfed by it! It had eight engines, and wings so long that they would hang off a soccer field at both ends. The nose of the plane's fuselage was hinged open and a tank was rolling out of it.

"My God," Father gasped, "it's the *GIGANT!*" After listening to more oohs and ahs from us, he explained that he had heard rumors of this plane before, but never believed it actually existed. "With technology such as this, nothing in the world can stop the Germans!" he said quietly, his wide-eyed expression matching ours.

We rushed home and anxiously tried the radio again. Still nothing.

Father spent the rest of the day with my godfather, Deményi-bácsi, and two other men from the neighborhood. This group usually met for a game of cards, but today, playing cards was secondary to the day's events.

Throughout the day the broadcasts went on as if nothing had happened. Finally, on the evening news, presented as a *by-the-way*—the announcer mentioned something about Hungarian troops conducting joint exercises with the forces of the German Reich, and that *officials* speaking for the government said that the exercises would continue for an indefinite time.

★ ★ ★

I was not quite six years old at the time, but even today, so many years later, I can still remember the awe that filled me on that fateful day.

In a couple of weeks, life once again settled into routine in German-occupied Hungary. The news, which was now back on its regular schedule, took on a different tone. Hungarian leaders assured the population that the war was near its end. We heard many speeches, and the reports of German triumphs became a regular feature. But I could tell the adults were scared. They stopped explaining things about the war. "You're too young to understand," became the refrain to our questions.

My father was drafted, then excused from the service. The combination of a childhood injury that left his left arm forever frozen at the elbow, coupled with his Head of Household status, having three young sons and a wife to support, was impairment enough to earn him a pass. When after the war someone asked him about his lucky exemption, he explained: "I faked weakness in my injured arm at the induction office. I knew that a soldier who can't hold a rifle is useless."

More and more people were conscripted and sent to the Russian Front. The age for military service was lowered first to seventeen, then to sixteen. Eventually, I saw something else had changed. Hungarian Jews were ordered to sew the six-pointed Star of David onto their clothing. While I did not understand the significance of this, I heard the grownups argue a lot about it.

My first knowledge of the Jews' plight came from Father's concern for the Goldberg family for whom he worked. Father brought them to our home a few months after the German occupation and carefully coached us to tell anyone who would ask that the Goldbergs were family from Ács, the small village near which my grandparents had their tanya, a Hungarian word for a small holding.

In the confusion and bureaucratic chaos that existed in Hungary prior to the arrival of the Second World War, this was an effective cover story, certainly good enough for our nosy neighbors.

After staying with us for a few weeks, the Jewish couple left. Father said they had made arrangements to leave the country. Only God knows if they survived the horrors that followed and made it to safety.

That very summer my brother Laci was sent to vacation at Ács with my grandparents. A month after his arrival, a decision was made to extend his visit indefinitely. The war was closing in on Hungary, and my parents may have reasoned that he was safer there, Ács having no military value as far as they knew. Much of what went into their decision to send Laci away is still unknown to me at this writing. When I asked Laci, who now lives in Prescott, Arizona, he couldn't clear it up, either. My guess is that our parents were uncertain about *how to best protect us. Leaving Laci in the country was a possible way for them to hedge their bets.*

Later that summer, father and I left our home in Sasad to visit Laci at my mother's urging. She hoped, knowing her parents generosity, we would be sent home with food, which became more and more difficult to come by in the capital since the introduction of rationing. In those days few people had telephones, and arrangements that would require but a few minutes today took extraordinary effort.

★ ★ ★

Father worked on his bicycle for days on end to prepare it for our journey. He fashioned a small, flatbed sidecar out of welded steel that could be folded against the frame of the bicycle when not in use. Like most of his inventions, the contraption functioned flawlessly.

Finally, the day came for us to leave. The sidecar became my space on the bicycle. Mother had a pillow for me to sit on, and Father showed me where to keep my feet and grip with my hands. We left while it was still dark. The ride on the sidecar was very bumpy; I had to hold fast to stay on board.

At about the edge of the city, the Vienna Highway we were traveling on became very crowded. Jews, in rows six across, wearing yellow armbands and the Star of David on their chest, were being herded toward the west. Kilometer after kilometer the Jews, men, women, and children, filled the highway. German soldiers carrying submachine guns marched on both sides of the column, and armed men on motorcycles sped by at regular intervals. Occasionally, trucks, also filled with Jews, interrupted the lines, perhaps carrying Jews who could no longer walk.

When a vehicle approached, the column would be herded off the road until it passed. We often had to leave the pavement ourselves to give way to the speeding motorcycles and oncoming traffic. My father labored mightily to keep us going.

The farther we got from the city, the more ragtag the Jews' column became. The soldiers constantly yelled to keep the lines moving, and the Jews pleaded for water, food, and rest. I wondered what they might have done to be treated this way. Certainly, it must have been something awful, but I still felt very sad.

At one point, Father asked me to reach into the rucksack and toss some of what we had into the crowd. I understood that we did not want to be seen doing this. There was a commotion when the sandwiches Mother made were snatched out of the air, but the soldiers did not see us. All day we struggled along, never reaching the head of the marching column.

We arrived in Komárom, a larger city on the south shore of the Danube, after dark, still twenty kilometers from Ács, and spent the night at my uncle's house.

Early next morning, after the usual barrage of messy kisses, we were off to Ács. En route, the Vienna Highway was empty except for us and, occasionally, a farmer's horse-drawn wagon. The Jews must have been marched across the Danube-bridge to Czechoslovakia at Komárom, or possibly they had been herded onto trains.

"We were looking for you yesterday," Grandmother said matter-of-factly when we arrived. She was a tall, large woman, very intimidating. She had braided her hair into a twist and piled the plaits on top of her head. This made her appear even taller.

"The highway was full of Germans and an unending column of Jews," Father explained. "We had to ride on the shoulder much of the time. I hope the going will be better on the way home."

We sat down at the kitchen table while my grandmother prepared a midday meal of sliced tomatoes, yellow peppers, sourdough bread, and a link of homemade, smoked sausage of lean pork finely seasoned with paprika. A typical meal in the country. We ate ravenously.

"So," Grandfather asked when the edge of our hunger appeared to have been sated, "how goes life in the big city?"

Father cut another slice of the rich bread and piled the fixings on it. "Life is more and more difficult," he said. "There are long lines in front of every store that still has some food to sell. But compared to what we saw on the way here, it's not so bad. I didn't realize this was going on," Father continued, appearing deeply disturbed. "I thought the Germans were more civilized; I was even sympathetic toward some of their grievances, but this is inhumane!"

"They say the Jews will be resettled in Russia after the war," said Grandmother, "until then, they'll be kept in labor camps in Germany, and in Poland."

"According to the news, the Russians are retreating without much of a fight, and the German army is on the outskirts of Moskva," offered Grandfather.

"Something doesn't ring true to me," Father said. "If the Germans are having such an easy time, how come more and more people are being drafted?" Father's question hung in the air.

"And why is it that the Allies can bomb all the way to Berlin, according to the BBC, when supposedly they have been 'knocked out of the sky,'" Grandmother added.

"I didn't realize you had a radio," Father said, "without electricity and all. I thought you just had the crystal-detector set I made for you, which could only pull in Budapest-One."

"Actually," my grandfather said as soon as he could interrupt, "after going to the market on Fridays, we spend a couple of hours at Joli's house to visit. We listen to the radio there."

This is grown up talk, I thought and excused myself. I went looking for Laci. I found him throwing pebbles into the well at the edge of the property.

"You can't believe how boring it is here," he lamented.

"At least, you have plenty to eat," I replied.

Laci shrugged. "I'd rather starve. You know how Grandma is; I'm up with the chickens and go to bed with the chickens. And in between, I get to feed the damned chickens!"

"But Grandpapa always has something neat to do." I said.

Laci sighed. "At least, they don't make me constantly redo my homework, like Father. And I can read all I want."

Two days later, Father and I were back on the bicycle, now loaded with foodstuffs, pushing hard toward Budapest. Father was determined to reach the capital before dark, so once again we had an early start. Past Komárom the road was again crowded with unending columns of Jews, still being marched toward the west.

"Father, what have the Jews done to be treated this way?"

"As far as I know, son, nothing. Some say the Jews have all the money and own all the businesses. They say that they are poor because the Jews cheated them, so the Jews have to be tossed out of Europe."

"The Goldbergs were nice," I ventured.

"Yes, son, the Goldbergs were nice people."

Toward early afternoon we came up on a particularly sad looking group in clear need of help just to keep walking. While we passed, one of them staggered away from the others. A soldier shoved him back into line yelling what sounded like obscenities. There were cries for rest. When the soldier moved on, Father tossed a loaf of bread into the crowd. Just as the bread landed in eager hands, a soldier Father had not noticed sprayed a line of bullets over our heads.

"*Verboten! Verboten!*" the German yelled harshly, letting go of another volley into the dirt directly in front of us. A cloud of dust erupted, and I could hear the bullets ricochet away. I was terrified and started to cry. My father raised his arms over his head, and we nearly crashed into the roadside ditch. The soldier continued to yell and made menacing motions with his gun, ordering us to move on.

Once back on the pavement I glanced at my father. His face was ashen and his ever-present grin was gone. "Sorry about the scare, son, some people go crazy in wartime," he said.

We rode in silence the rest of the way, reaching Budapest at dusk.

PART TWO

THE SKY IS FALLING

We watched the bomber trail smoke as it circled, slowly elongating his circle toward the west and tightening it toward the east.

A small cloud of white smoke materialized out of nothing near him, then another, and another. With flack bursting all around, he completed orbit after orbit, moving slowly away.

At the edge of the sky, a new squadron moved into view, locked in formations of three, the lead plane followed by one at each wingtip. Perhaps a hundred twenty in all. Then, there was a narrow swath of clear sky before yet a new armada of planes approached. This pattern repeated without end, covering the sky from horizon to horizon.

Kovács-bácsi, a neighbor from across our street joined us as we watched the formations overtake the stricken bomber from the rear, opening their tightly packed ranks as they flew around him, and closing up once they have passed.

Wave after wave.

The pattern formed by the planes around the burning bomber looked like an eye, the bomber's smoke-trail formed the iris, and the planes around him were the eyebrows and eye socket. A giant eye in the sky!

"I wonder where they are from?" Kovács-bácsi asked, his head tilting skyward at an awkward angle.

"Most likely they are American, from a base in England," Father speculated. "They're too high to make out the insignias, but they are Allied planes, that's for sure. Germans wouldn't fire on their own."

More flack appeared. The sky became an exquisite tapestry of death as each lethal burst gave birth to a tiny, white cloud in a sea of deepest blue.

Around and around the bomber flew, smoke spewing from its wounded wing. The smoke blackened from time to time, then bleached to white, then blackened again.

As the column flew by, the ones nearest to him seemed to have dipped their wings as if to say a final farewell, but they were too high to see for sure. Like ants crossing the roadway, they came and went out of view.

Then, they were gone.

"My guess is he'll make it," Kovács-bácsi said, turning to go, lifting his hat to say goodbye. I watched him, wondering why he came over. He had never done that before, we usually saw him only on his side of the fence.

"Bye!" we said in unison after him.

I lifted my eyes back to the sky. Left to himself, and still bleeding smoke, the wounded bird continued his dance of death. Slowly, forever slowly, he swam across the dangerous waters of the speckled sky toward his nest in some distant land.

He was small now, barely visible, the setting sun glancing a gleaming spark on him only once in a while. Then he, too, was gone.

★ ★ ★

The sky stayed bottomless blue without a cloud for several days. One could hardly imagine a more peaceful setting. The hillsides basked in the warmth of the late-day sun of the Hungarian fall. Many trees had already shed their leaves, and the others were painted in brilliant colors. Reds, yellows, oranges, in all possible permutations. The walnut trees dominated the spectacle, towering over the red peach trees of the hillside.

This evening, several neighbors joined us to watch a dogfight over the Danube. Called by the woeful sounds of air raid sirens, the action was staged with a masterful hand directly in front of us. The setting sun illuminated the swirling madness from behind us.

Every detail was exposed, down to the puffs of smoke trailing the planes as they fired their guns. Strings of pearls from Hell!

Planes turned and twisted everywhere. From our perspective it seemed a miracle that the pilots could avoid crashing into one another. The sound of powerful engines thundered between the hills as the planes pulled out of their dives and arched for the sky. New fighters joined the melee as we watched, coming in from great heights. The air screamed over their wings as they dove toward the others. *Stukas!* I recognized them. Their guns rained a deadly staccato on the ones below.

"Look!" Dodi said, pointing toward the sky with his tiny finger.

"One of them got hit!"

We could see black smoke pouring from one of the planes. The Stukas closed in for the kill. A blast of fire severed one of the wings, and the plane started spinning in a spiral toward the earth. Like a giant corkscrew made of black smoke tipped with metal, the plane wound its way toward the ground.

"The pilot jumped," Ruzics-néni, our next-door neighbor shrieked.

"He's out, but his chute hasn't opened," said her son without emotion. He hobbled forward on his one leg to see better, clanking the worn tips of his crutches on the stone floor of the porch.

That tiny black dot trailing the plane couldn't possibly be the pilot, I thought, but then I saw a tail form above him, and moments later his deploying parachute.

The pilot floated through the air, swinging gently from side to side, his chute spinning slowly above him. A Stuka dove at him but missed. The chutist appeared motionless. The Stuka came back around, firing his gun as he neared. Part of the parachute collapsed, but the rate of descent seemed unaffected. After a long minute, the pilot and the spinning canopy of his chute disappeared behind a row of trees.

Two more planes were downed; no one jumped free from either one.

★ ★ ★

The chutist's plane fell to earth about two kilometers from our house, near Wide Road. Its mangled fuselage became a plaything for children after the war. Later, when I became a pilot and parachuted for sport, I often wondered what had become of the downed pilot. I never learned whether he had survived, but I always hoped he had.

CAGED METAL FEATHERS

The air raid sirens sounded again, whining their song of urgency, but no one ran for the cellar. The grownups crowded onto the porch, abandoning their labor to fortify our cellar, waiting for the bombers. I guess if the bombs came closer, we could just run down to the cellar. Mom said we're too far from any target up here, in the hills of Buda.

The moonless night was darker than I had ever known before. Not a single light flickered in the city below. Soon a distant rumble broke the evening's silence. The dissonance of laboring engines reverberated from the nearby hills, from the valley, and even from below. The porch seemed to resonate under our feet.

Breaching the blackness over the city, a brilliant shaft of light pierced the dark, searching for a target, roaming aimlessly across the sky. The show had begun.

Other searchlights joined the hunt, crisscrossing one another, creating whimsical shapes. Then we could see tracer bullets marching in succession, looking for their quarry. The staccato of the anti-aircraft batteries that belched them forth reached our ears seconds later.

The sirens started up again.

The bombers were nearly over the city now, and we could hear them unload their cargo. The bombs gave out a low whistle that was barely audible at first but grew louder as they neared the ground. I could see the explosions and felt the ground tremble under my feet. The sound followed the flashes as thunder follows lightning.

"Did you see that?" one of the adults asked of no one in particular. "Must've been the gas factory!" Another pillar of flame rose to answer him.

Secondary explosions lit up the sky, now filled with towering smoke columns glowing red. The unearthly rumble of exploding bombs fused with the earth's motion. The windows rattled rhythmically as one detonation followed another. The sky was ablaze, red with the blood of the convulsing city.

"Carpet-bombing again," the quiet voice of a woman asserted.

"Just like last night," said someone else.

Carpet-bombing? I wondered what she meant. Carpets were soft and expensive; we had one from Persia in our bedroom. *Father, why would anyone want to bomb carpets?* The question formed in my mind, but I didn't want to ask because it sounded stupid.

I suddenly realized that the detonations had stopped. The drone of the engines, and the sound of the aircraft batteries became more distant. The ground stopped moving, but I could still feel the low rumble in my chest. The sky to the east continued to glow red, lit by fires raging in the city.

"God help us," Ruzics-néni moaned, "God help us all!"

From that night forward, we lived in the cellar because of the nightly raids. We shared the cellar with about twenty others, women and children, and a few older men. Under Father's direction all the windows were fortified with sacks filled with dirt, blocking out all natural light. Though it was very dark below, Father said the sandbags would stop shrapnel and bullets from coming inside.

Everyone was assigned his or her own space, even us kids. We had to keep it clean, organized. The worst part was that we were no longer allowed to go topside without supervision, and the adults insisted on "school." We were also kept from watching the planes, the part I missed the most. In all, life below was very boring.

One day, a dive-bomber dropped a bomb that fell into Jani's orchard behind their house. It was the kind of bomb that made everything burn. Luckily, no one got hurt.

"I'm sure it was just an accident," Father said. "A mistake!" he added with emphasis.

But I was scared, because bombs continued to fall nearer every night. When we could hear one hit the ground, we knew the impact point was close. The grownups debated how close, and where. The nearest crater was in the middle of Big Grassy Field, about a kilometer away. I heard it coming before it hit. It sounded like someone screaming, but you could tell it was a bomb. Father drew me a picture to show me what they looked like. Bombs have a pointed nose and a fat body, and tail fins. The fins direct them to the target and make them spin. "Just like the feathers of an arrow," Father explained, "only they are inside a sort of metal cage, to keep the air flowing against the quills."

After the stray bomb that fell in Jani's garden, we started to get under the beds when the bombers neared. We had laid straw and empty burlap under ours. I hated lying there because the straw poked through the bedding and made me itch, but Father said it was better than laying on the ground. Sometimes we waited so long for the bombers to leave, I'd fall asleep no matter what was going on outside.

I don't remember how it started, but for several nights I woke up screaming. My nightmares seemed so real, several minutes had to pass before I could feel safe. In the dream there was this terrible, faceless monster that wanted to kill me. The monster would chase me, claws reaching, jaws snapping at my heels, barely missing me. Should I let it catch me, it would devour me alive! The terror of the monster closing in inspired me to inhuman efforts, allowing me to lift off the ground, out of his reach; never to safety, just far enough for his claws to miss me. This frightful game would go on endlessly, and I would wake up completely exhausted, drenched in cold sweat. Mother said I had the worst scream she had ever heard.

The sound of heavy bombers awakened me. I slipped under the bed and lay on top of the straw, listening to the approaching bombers. Soon, the sound of distant explosions drowned out the drone of the engines. The detonations rolled toward us, each louder than the one before. I buried my face into the pillow and started sobbing. I didn't want to cry. This wasn't different from the other times, but I couldn't help myself. My body shuddered with every impact.

Then, I started hearing the incoming bombs. The ground shook. Dishes fell off the shelves and shattered on the floor. People began to cry. A plane flew over us, very low, and the next instant the earth seemed to blow up. It was deafening. I could hear my little brother's screams over the explosions. Mother's soothing would not quiet him.

My teeth chattered so hard my jaw hurt. Over the ear-splitting noise of the explosions I could hear it coming. Only a low whistle at first, the sound quickly grew. It was right above me.

"It's going to hit us!" I screamed though my clenched teeth, knowing that this was the one, I had only moments longer to live. I smashed my face against the pillow. My mind's eye rose through the ceiling and watched the bomb's caged metal feathers spin with sinister precision, guiding it toward me, the hellish sound of the air ramming through the cage, growing louder and louder, the shrill of death deafening. "MOMMY!" I cried, "I don't want to die!

"Mommy, Mommy, I don't want to … die!

"GOD … HELP ME! I'm sorry for all my sins …

"… Please, please …, I don't want to die … .

"Our Father who art in Heaven, our Father, our Father …"

And then the world ceased to be, and I felt the monster's ice-cold fingers tearing at my flesh! I lay under my bed, cold, shuddering out of control, listening to my chattering teeth, shivering, in the warm pool of my urine.

SPLIT PEAS

The stranger unbundled the load from the bicycle sidecar. The peasant looked on, glancing at the treasures nonchalantly, having learned that a shrewd man never gives his hand away. The pair of boots sticking out from under the burlap made his heart jump. He hadn't seen a pair as fine in years and thought that these city folk didn't seem to know when they had it good.

The city man laid the burlap next to the sidecar and started to unload—gloves, hats, a fine blouse, then a set of assorted tools, followed by bedding that looked brand new. The boots came out next, along with a heavy, somewhat worn overcoat.

"So, what do you think?" the man from the city said, sounding anxious. "I would entertain trading for any foodstuff you might have, potatoes, grain, whatever."

The peasant looked disinterested. "Well, we don't rightly have much of anything ourselves. Certainly, nothing extra," he said cautiously, " 'cept maybe some peas that I couldn't plant in the spring on account of the flood. Nothing else."

"I'd consider whatever you have," responded the stranger hopefully. "We're in poor shape in the city when it comes to food, with the war and all. How much do you think you could spare?"

The peasant didn't answer, but reached down and picked up the boots. *By the sound of him,* he thought, *I could drive whatever bargain I wanted.*

"I also have a bit of money—" the stranger continued.

The peasant spat on the ground. "Money!" he said disdainfully. "Money has no value around here! Last week's thousand won't get you a hundred's worth today, and that if you're lucky!" He raised the boots to eye level. "I think we could spare maybe twenty, twenty-five kilos of peas for this," he said.

"Only twenty-five?" the city man asked. "That pair was expensive, and I only wore them three or four times. My boss gave them to me as a Christmas present last winter. "How about making it fifty kilos, and I'll throw in these tools? They would surely be of use around here, and as you can see, they are worth more than fifty kilos by themselves." He pressed the point. "Why, if you had these made by a shoemaker, you'd—"

"All right, all right!" the peasant stopped him, raising his hand. "Fifty kilos for the boots and the tools, but that's all I can spare," he said, shrugging apologetically. "Now, if you could fix a motorcycle, that would be worth something."

The stranger's eyes brightened. "You have a motorcycle? What kind is it?"

"It's an old Indian from America. My brother left it to me, God bless his soul. A stroke took him last fall," he explained. "It's in the shed out back if you want to see it."

László pressed hard on the pedals, struggling to keep moving. He barely made it up the last hill, pushing the heavy load on foot, the rim of the sidecar's wheel nearly touching the pavement as the tire flattened under the heavy load. *More precious than gold,* he thought, glancing down at the sacks of peas. He picked up his pace.

The peasant gave him all he could carry in exchange for fixing the motorbike. László practically had to force the rest of his goods on him, the man was so grateful. There was only room for the four sacks of split peas on the flatbed of the sidecar; otherwise the peasant would have given him even more.

László turned off the pavement and rolled the bicycle across Small Bridge onto Nagyszeben Trail, heading home. "Now comes the hard part," he muttered under his breath as he got off the bike and started pushing. "But one way or another, I'm getting up this hill!"

He started a song of his own design, whistling the tune when he exhaled, and using the intake of air as some sort of percussion.

★ ★ ★

We had been living in the cellar for nearly seven months without a break. In the last two of those months the front moved back and forth over Sasad. One time we were in German territory, the next Russian, but most of the time we were in "no man's land."

The actual fighting between the warring parties was much more fierce at Wolf Mountain Cemetery five kilometers away, especially in the cemetery itself, but from time to time, our house came under mortar and small arms fire. The sandbags outside had made the cellar safe so far, but no one knew what the next day would bring.

While the war raged outside, we had our troubles within. In addition to the effect of siege conditions on our nerves, an early spring's thaw brought about heavy snowmelt, which in turn flooded the cellar.

One morning we awoke to water up to the second step, and rising.

A hasty brigade was formed by the grownups to bucket the water to the outside, even though they said that the expelled water would probably seep back into the cellar. In a way, the emergency served a greater purpose: giving people something to do.

The planks of wood that once kept wine barrels off the ground were enlisted to create a walk between the beds and the cellar's steps. The bucketing went on for days, until a cold spell froze the ground and stemmed the flow.

Our dwindling supplies of split peas were among the casualties of the flood, soaked completely before anyone knew that we had a problem. With no other recourse, the women spread the wet peas on top of the beds during the day in an attempt to dry them. Soon the peas developed a mold similar in color to the peas themselves, making the peas smell even worse then before.

I didn't know it at the time, but we were among the lucky; many had nothing to eat.

★ ★ ★

We had been eating only split peas for the last three weeks. The peas were cooked in plain water to a consistency of baked beans, salted, and consumed. Everyone complained, but there was no choice.

None of us kids wanted any of it. At mealtime, two women held me down while my mother stuffed the foul mush down my throat, all the while pleading with me not to spit it back. "If you don't eat it, you'll die," she gravely said.

Yesterday one of the men out on a foray for food spotted a dead horse in the runoff channel. The horse was shot up badly and had started to decompose, but after inspecting it, the man thought the side on the snow would still be good. It had been too late to do anything about it yesterday, but this day Father and the man went back to get some of the meat off the carcass, and sure enough, they came back loaded down with meat. Soon the smell of peas mixed with the smell of cooking meat. I gagged with every spoonful, but I ate.

★

PEELING POTATOES

I awakened to silence! The cellar was cold and damp as usual so I snuggled closer to Dodi to share his warmth. Not a sound! *Was I still alive?* I felt warm and dead people were cold so I must be. I held my breath and listened for the distant rumble of artillery or the sound of small arms. *Nothing! Where did all this silence come from?*

All around me, people were awakening as if on cue. I heard one after another ask, "What's happening?"

"Maybe the Germans gave up," someone opined.

"Or maybe the Allies did. You've heard about the German's secret weapon."

A third entered the conversation, "If it's as terrible as they say, the Allies may have been forced to capitulate."

I lay motionless, listening. The discussion that followed seemed to change no one's mind. Small children responded to the animated chatter by crying. The debate slowly changed from guessing, to choosing who would go topside and find out what was going on. Who would it be this time?

One of the older men volunteered, and after getting help to open the heavy hatch, he climbed up the stairs. Everyone fell silent, waiting. I rolled out of bed and walked barefoot on the cold plank to the corner of the cellar where the bucket was behind a hanging blanket. I had to urinate. Overhead, I could hear the creaking of the veranda door as the old man opened it and left the house. More silence.

In what seemed only a few minutes, the old man returned. "Russians!" he said, as soon as he stepped on the first rung, "Russians are coming up the road."

The muffled conversations resumed and filled the cellar. No one knew what would happen next. Our neighborhood had been under constant siege for the last two weeks with gun battles raging every day, the Germans on one side, the Russians on the other. Back and forth. After a while one could tell the weapons apart even from the cellar; a heavy gun here, a mortar there.

The men closed the cellar's door. And now, there was silence.

The Russians were coming and no one seemed to like the Russians.

Hours went by, then suddenly, there was a commotion above, and we heard people talking. The sound of boots clanked hard against the floor overhead. There was more talking, but I couldn't make out the words. Doors were opened, then banged shut again. Then, all of a sudden, one of the heavy wooden doors of the cellar inched open, and someone with a deep voice shouted through the gap. *"Stoy!"* Then, the door slammed open against the wall. I shuddered and felt like peeing again.

The dark silhouette of a large man appeared in the opening. Gun in hand, feet apart. *"Davaj, davaj!"* he shouted, his voice echoing off the far wall of the cellar. No one moved. More figures appeared behind him.

"Davaj!" he shouted once more, banging the stock of the gun against the cellar door for emphasis.

The ones closest to the stairs made a tentative move toward him. One by one, we climbed the stairs and crowded onto the veranda. The children cried. An older woman had to be helped. We were terrified.

The soldier had a long, unhemmed coat that nearly touched the ground. A round fur hat with rabbit ears and a red star covered his head. He was old, unshaven, and looked dirty. He held his submachine gun on us while several others, similarly equipped, stormed down into the cellar.

Once they searched the cellar, presumably for hiding Germans, one of the soldiers addressed us: "Don't afraid, don't afraid," he said in badly pronounced, poor Hungarian. They all seemed to defer to the older soldier, who watched us silently with a broad grin on his face. He said something to the one who spoke to us in Hungarian.

"Drink," the soldier translated, "we want drink."

One of the women pointed back down the cellar. A soldier took her arm, and the two of them went below. We heard the soldier laugh heartily, and soon they were back on the verandah with the woman, carrying a bottle and a glazed metal cup. I recognized the cup; we all had used it to drink from the water bucket.

"*Davaj!*" he ordered her, still laughing from his belly.

She poured from the bottle into the cup and offered the cup to the older soldier. He tossed the contents down his throat, coughed, then smashed the cup against the ground, spewing the remaining liquid, and denting the cup. He yelled something angrily while the soldier who escorted the woman down the cellar couldn't stop laughing. The others joined in.

"Alcohol," the translator said once he could control his laughter. When no one moved, one of the soldiers stood guard while the others rummaged through the house. Soon they returned with the can of denatured alcohol we kept for our small, single burner camp-stove in the storage room. Cheered by the find, the Russians passed the can around, taking swigs one after the other until the can emptied.

We spent the night back in the cellar, and the next morning one of the women was ordered upstairs to cook breakfast. When she returned, she seemed in shock. The Russians had a smallish chicken, and eggs. Only God knows where they had come up with these things. We had not seen meat since the dead horse a couple of months earlier. And eggs? Well, let's just say they didn't come from anywhere in Hungary. As for many, many days before, the rest of us ate split pea mush.

Father was known in the neighborhood for his mechanical talents. If anyone needed something of this nature, and if it could be done, the Whistling Horvath could do it. So they said.

One day, weeks after the occupation, a drunken Russian took Father to another house where he put an alarm clock and a wristwatch in front of Father and demanded that he should fix his wristwatch using parts from the alarm clock. Father checked the watch and saw that the spring was broken. He tried to tell the Russian that what he asked was not possible, but the drunkard insisted.

When Father got this far in telling the story to us cellar dwellers, he raised his arms with the palm of his hands toward us in his familiar, "you've got to be kidding!" gesture we kids knew well. "He wanted his wristwatch fixed, and that was that!" Father said.

Everyone in the cellar laughed.

"Please try to imagine the conversation between us, neither speaking the other's tongue, and you're getting the picture. Fix a wristwatch with parts from an alarm clock indeed!" Father said with a mocking nod, and resumed. "And under the duress of a drunkard aiming a submachine gun on me!"

More laughter.

"You can now appreciate the finer points of black humor," Father added indignantly.

"So, what happened?" someone asked.

"The soldier got very frustrated when I explained that I couldn't do what he asked. He tossed the alarm clock into the corner of the room and sprayed it with bullets. Thank God, his buddies rushed in and wrestled the gun away from him. I then walked back here."

★ ★ ★

I was asked to draw water from the well by a Russian, so I did.

When I entered the kitchen, I saw a soldier sitting at the table, spreading toothpaste on a slab of dark bread. He was squeezing it out of the tube, spreading it with a pocketknife. When I told Mother about it, she said that that these men were Mongols, and they would not know about things like toothpaste.

Barbarians or not, for the most part these frontline soldiers were kind to us and harmed no one in our group. Their replacements, on the other hand, were a different story.

Replacing the frontline troops was a well-organized, well-disciplined horde of young thugs. Their uniforms were clean and pressed, and the hems of their overcoats were not frayed. They wore side arms instead of the submachine guns we named davaj-guitars.

It was these young officers' routine to collect women to peel potatoes at their mess hall. "Kartocska, kartocska," they would explain, imitating the peeling process with their hands as they rounded up the women. There was no appeal, no choice given, if you were chosen, you had to go. A young woman from our cellar was also taken. When she returned, she sobbed uncontrollably.

She was chosen again and again. Some in our group consoled her, and others shunned her. I didn't understand what was going on and when I queried my mother, she told me it was grownup stuff and I shouldn't ask any more questions about it.

Since I was just a young boy when these events took place, "peeling potatoes" had no special meaning for me. Years later I understood the dreadful fate of those women.

A month later, the front moved further west and the Russians left with it. With our rooms vacated, we could move back into the house. We had been living underground for many months by this time, and now it was time to return to the surface and the light of day.

PART THREE

WHERE EVERYTHING GROWS

The modern notion of vacation had not yet penetrated rural Hungary, often resulting in friction between us boys and Grandmother. When we came for our summer or winter vacations, she saw a lot of work added to her already busy day, and it was only natural for her to want to make use of the extra hands. A set of tasks particular to the seasons and the time of day had to be done. Of course, all we wanted to do was play. As a result of this conflict of interests, on most of my visits I spent considerable time kneeling on kernels of corn facing a corner, atonement for some mischief or dereliction of assigned duty.

★   ★   ★

"István," my mother called up from the platform, letting me know what she had to say was important by using my formal name. "Conductor-bácsi will tell you when it's time for you to get off the train.

"Don't wander around, and behave! The train is not a playground. Your grandfather will meet you at Ács, and if you don't see him, the note in your pocket—"

Fortunately the train began to move and Mother's instructions could not be endlessly repeated. I was five years old, and this was the first time I traveled on the train by myself. Of course, I wanted to spend the entire trip at the window and was thrilled at the thought that no one would be along to tell me otherwise.

The train was filled to capacity with travelers. An older-néni took a liking to me, and I had a difficult time getting away from her incessant questions without appearing to be rude. Finally, the train pulled into her station and she got off. But not before planting a wet kiss on my cheek. In what seemed only a few minutes, conductor-bácsi came and took me and my bag to the door of the railcar.

Grandfather greeted me formally, a kiss on one cheek then the other. His handlebar mustache was longer than I remembered. "How are you, Pista? How was the trip? You've grown since I saw you last! Traveling by yourself, are you?" Then, he asked me how the rest of my family was and led me off the platform to his bicycle. He was a man of few words.

Grandfather peddled the sixteen or so kilometers between Komárom and Ács in about an hour. The road followed the straight lines of the acacia trees, leading through fields of sugar beets, wheat, and corn. Occasionally, a small stand of trees and fields of hemp would break the monotony.

Grandmama was waiting for us at the gate. She lifted me off the bicycle and looked at me measuringly. "You're getting tall. I can see that you are fed well," she said without smiling, and she gave me a hug. "Come, I fixed you a meal."

As we finished the evening meal, Grandmother parceled out the coming day's chores. "Pista, tomorrow morning, I want you to take the ducks to the pond at the crossroads. The little ones hatched a few days back, and I'm sure they would enjoy a swim."

"Yes, Grandmother."

"When you get back," Grandfather broke the silence that followed, "I'll show you how to graft a peach tree. I got cuttings from the neighbor, and after a year or so, we should have peaches as good as he.

"Would you like to do that?"

"Sure would," I assured him, hoping all the while that being with him would save me from another one of grandmother's chores. Grandfather loved for me to watch him work. With great patience, he would show me how to do things while he explained why he did what he did.

Grandmother woke me at sunrise and helped me get the ducks and geese out on the road. With sleep still in my eyes, I started herding them along the wagon tracks. After the rains the day before, I knew the pond would be at least knee deep and looked forward to wading in it.

The birds lined up in the wheel ruts, the little ones trailing their mother as if on a string. I followed barefoot, carefully avoiding their droppings but otherwise enjoying the fine dust squishing between my toes. One of the great things about being at Ács was the complete lack of stones, quite unlike Sasad where we often stubbed and bloodied our toes.

As the birds and I slowly progressed toward the pond, a fast-moving carriage caught up with us from the rear. I immediately tried to shoo the birds off the road, but the rut was too deep and the smaller ones had difficulty getting up on the ledge. Finally, I got all of them out of the way, except for one goose. The stupid bird would not get out of the rut. In a last ditch effort, I caught up with it, and tossed it to the roadside with a twirl. The bird flew through the air end over end and landed in a heap.

"That was a cruel thing to do!" from behind me came the powerful voice of the driver. "What's your name, boy?"

"My name is István," I said, "and I didn't mean to hurt him," I continued, not realizing the bird was dead.

"Whose fowl are these?" the driver continued his bellow.

"My grandmother's."

"What's your grandmother's name?"

"Veres-néni," I said, already fearing the worst.

"I think you best turn around and go home. On my way back I'll tell your grandmother what you have done."

"But," I started crying, "I just wanted to clear your way, sir." I picked up the lifeless gander and spoke to it. "Come on little goose," I pleaded, but nothing helped.

I got the rest of the birds back to the yard and walked into the kitchen with the dead bird in my arms to face Grandmother.

"What in the world happened?" she demanded.

"All I wanted to do was to let a carriage go by, and he wouldn't get out of the rut," I told her sobbing.

I spent the rest of the day doing chores and kneeling on kernels of corn, facing a corner of the kitchen under the watchful eyes of Grandmother.

Next morning, Grandfather handed me a small basket with a bundle of folded, wet burlap in it. "Bring this along," he said, and started along the path toward the orchard at the top of the hill. Once there, he carefully examined a branch of a smallish, bitter almond tree, one in a row of several I had "helped" him plant the year before. He pulled out a knife from his pocket.

I watched him make an incision on the tender bough, cutting through the bark, forming the shape of a cross. He carefully slipped the blade under the bark and peeled it back from the tissue underneath.

"Hand me a cutting; it's wrapped in the cloth," Grandfather instructed me.

I complied. He shaped the cutting, which, as far as I could tell was only a piece of bark from the peach tree with an unopened leaf nodule, into a wedge with his knife. He then slipped the wedge into the slot he had cut on the bitter almond branch, wrapped the whole assembly with a sliver of a wet cornhusk, and tied it off. After watching him graft a couple of trees, he let me try my hand, mess up, watch some more, then try again.

By midday, we had all the trees grafted, and I had forgotten the entire business with the gander until I saw Grandmother, who had lunch waiting for us.

★ ★ ★

Growing up, I had never considered family ties very important. Perhaps because the family was always there, a safety net for its members, strong and vibrant; I took its many gifts for granted.

My maternal grandfather, Lajos Veres, was a larger-than-life figure in my childhood. He was hardworking, unfailingly honest, and good-natured. During the many visits we had with one another, not once did I hear a cross word about anyone or anything come out of his mouth. He weathered life's ups and downs without ever claiming misfortune or blaming someone else. He possessed that basic goodness which often characterizes people connected with the land. If only more people were like him our world would be better.

Grandfather came from the stock of Hungarians that inhabit parts of the new Slovak Republic, fair skinned, blue-eyed blondes with a stocky build. While he grew up on a farm very much like the one he retired on, for much of his adult life he managed a hemp processing plant in the small city of Komárom.

Sometime before the marriage of my mother, his eldest, he bought land near the village of Ács, between the Vienna Highway and the Danube. The soil there is not much more than alluvial sand, deposited over the ages by the periodic flooding of the Danube, but given care it will grow just about anything.

Quietly, Grandfather went about creating his dream. He planted wheat to make bread, grew corn and potatoes, and started a vineyard and an orchard. By the time of my first recollection, his beloved Tanya, country place in English, was complete. His orchard was the finest in the area, and his vineyard made wines of distinction.

Not large enough for mechanization, the Tanya required every task to be done either by hand or by simple hand operated contrivances such as butter churns and things similar. Life here was not all that different from the life of country folk in Central Europe as far back as feudal times.

On the northwest corner of the property stood an old country home, built two, possibly three, centuries before. The house had an earthen floor and a thatched roof lain over massive beams. Its walls were fashioned from adobe nearly a meter thick, born of the clay common to the area. Below the east end of the house, a basement provided the principle storage for all manner of goods, including a modest collection of wine casks, the largest of which held Grandfathers' prized red, pressed and fermented from the grapes he grew.

To keep the few animals, simple agricultural equipment, and grain out of the weather, Grandfather erected a support building near the house. He also built an outdoor oven for baking bread and pastries. This was a large structure, set just inside the fence next to the pedestrian gate, rising the better part of a meter above the ground. A graceful dome covered the hearth, backed by a tall chimney to lead off smoke and to provide draft for the fire. I remember the wooden *paddle he used to slide the dough into position and retrieve the baked goods. Grandfather carved it out of the native, stone-hard acacia that surrounded the Tanya. It had an elegant shape perfectly suited for the task, and a gleaming, smooth finish. He made simple tools into functioning works of art.*

★   ★   ★

Once, visiting the Tanya on winter break, I helped Grandfather cut a couple of thick branches from a nearby acacia tree. We took the branches out to the field and placed them on the ground, bark still attached. We spent the rest of the morning wheelbarrowing dung from the cow-pen and piling the foul-smelling stuff onto the branches. The pile grew and grew, giving off steam in the winter air.

"I'm seasoning the wood," Grandfather explained.

When I returned the following spring, Grandfather was spreading dung over last year's potato field, fortifying it for the new crop. I put on the pair of old pants and rubber boots and trotted out to see him. After exchanging greetings, I offered to help. He silently handed me the pitchfork and watched me fill the wheelbarrow. When full, Grandfather attached a rope harness he had around his neck to the handles, stood upright, then wheeled the laden wheelbarrow through the soft earth to the point of deposit.

When I attempted to relieve him, I dumped the contents after only a few staggering steps, unable to balance the load with my best effort.

We worked until the pile of manure was gone. Near the bottom I came across the two lengths of acacia we had buried under the dung last winter. The wood looked awful; foul enough for me not to touch it.

Grandfather picked up the shafts and carried them to his workshop. Here he quickly made a jig, wooden pegs driven into holes in a thick board, outlining the shape of an open S, and to my amazement, bent the thick shafts into the jig with what seemed little effort.

"Soaking them all winter under the dung heap made the wood

easy to bend," he explained. "I don't know what, but something in the juices coupled with the heat from the fermenting manure makes wood pliable. This is how my father made sections of wagon wheels for his carriages."

I guess my great-grandfather was a carriage maker, I thought.

"We'll leave them to dry, and when done, they'll come out as hard and inflexible as before, but in the shape I want," he said.

"What are they for?"

"They'll be the handles of a new wheelbarrow."

A few days later, I watched him take the shafts out of the jig, and as he had said, they were once again hard as bone. Using his drawknife, he shaped the shafts into the form he wanted. Under the rotten bark the wood was beautiful, golden in color with the darker grain following the new shape. When done, the wood reminded me of snakes, smooth as silk to the touch.

★ ★ ★

The Tanya was my immediate family's connection to rural life. Except for the war years, the extended family gathered here around the second week of each December.

The festivities kicked into high gear with the slaughtering of a pig, especially fattened for the occasion. The men would be busy with the butchering under Grandfather's supervision, while the women heated water to scalding temperatures to remove the hairs and the outer-layer of the pig's skin. No part of the animal was wasted.

Everyone had a special duty, even the children. The evening meal was prepared while the various parts were hung in the smokehouse for flavoring and preservation, all the while Grandpa's favorite red wine would be served, keeping me and my brothers busy making trips to the cellar. We would draw wine with a wine-steal, an especially shaped gourd used for this duty. Of course, getting a mouthful in the process was completely unavoidable, and Laci and I made as many trips to the cellar as possible.

The merriment lasted days on end, until several hundred kilos of meat were completely processed. All the while the clans reconnected, plans were made for the coming year's visits, and once again we became a close-knit family. After all the chores were done, all the hugs given and kisses spent, we scattered with the wind, carting away provisions that would last through the winter.

When in 1998 I returned to Hungary for a visit, my aunt Aranka turned to her grandson at the dinner table: "Anti, this is your Uncle István," she said, "the one who twirled the goose by the neck and tossed it into the air to get it off the road."

The boy looked me over with widened eyes, and I saw a recognition that wasn't there before.

Aranka laughed. "His father had told him the story; he heard it from your grandmother. As you can see, you are something of a legend."

BEES IN THE WALL

No question about it, Gyuszi was one of the neatest guys I grew up with. Here I mean neat in its colloquial sense, the way one would describe something good, though the real meaning of the word could also have applied to him, if not more so.

Gyuszi was the lone son of a small-time homebuilder who, in addition to building very nice houses, had been found of some fiscal irregularity and spent several years in jail. One would have to apply two basic truths to his situation. First, as a capitalist, Mr. Nagy was an enemy of the People; after all, he was caught red-handed practicing free enterprise. And second, the People's Republic thought nothing of eliminating competitors on trumped-up charges.

Being years older than most of us kids in the neighborhood, Gyuszi was a natural role model. Well-dressed, well-read, and well-mannered, Gyuszi could carry on a conversation with anyone, in any setting. Area parents trusted him; they knew that their prodigy would only learn something appropriate in his company. In addition to his academic acumen and willingness to spend time with us lesser mortals, Gyuszi also presented himself as a gentleman to all. In other words, I admired and envied him, all at the same time. I was not alone. Years later in the New World, my brother, Laci, paid Gyuszi the ultimate compliment, naming his youngest son after him. It would not be an exaggeration to say that all who knew Gyuszi liked him.

The Nagy house was located where Wide Road crossed the Runoff Channel, right about where Father would begin whistling his last song on the way home. Bordering their property to the north was a fenced-in orchard that had hazelnut bushes that were, shall we say, planted a convenient proximity to the street. These very bushes are responsible for my lifelong addiction to hazelnuts.

On the west, the family's property touched a large, grassy field for which the Hungarian language has a single word: *rét*.

Our *rét* was created by God to be the center of juvenile life. No neighborhood child five years older or younger than me could have grown up without having had a meaningfully joyous or depending on ones perspective, tragic experience, connected to this magical place. It was here a friend of mine and I pulled down our shorts to show Erzsi, the youngest sister of neighborhood bully, Jani, "ours," after she had agreed to show us "hers." And it was the *rét* that witnessed blood running down her sister Ilona's legs years later, in the presence of a dozen of us adolescent boys.

The *rét* saw me fend off ten consecutive penalty shots taken at a makeshift goal from the legal distance prescribed by the rules of soccer, a fete much talked about at the time by the younger enthusiasts of the game. Need I say more? To us, the *rét* embodied everything that was good in the world, nay, the world itself.

Soon after starting middle school, I spent a lot of time with Gyuszi; trading stamps, discussing books, and the like, but mostly, designing and building model airplanes. For purely economic reasons our interest in flight centered on gliders, a less expensive genre of model building. Gyuszi, who started on this hobby some time before, became an indispensable mentor in teaching the basic skills. Under his patient tutelage, I quickly learned how to shape balsa, bend wood, and make modeler's cement from strips of cellulose film and acetone. Once completed, we covered our creations with onion paper and launched them from the end of a string like a kite, hoping that they would be caught in a rising column of air and carried off to distant lands.

To cope with this last eventuality, we glued a typewritten note with our name and address onto the fuselage. (Somehow, to have one's name printed with a typewriter signified something very official.) The note on my creation read: *Horváth István, Budapest XI, Nagyszeben-ut 46sz, Hungary.* I asked Gyuszi to add *Hungary,* so if the glider flew into another country, the finder would know where to return it. Sounds ambitious, I know, but believe it or not, some of these fragile little flyers did end up soaring hundreds of kilometers, riding thermal currents. None of mine ever did, but I knew the chance was there.

It was during one of these building sessions that I noticed bees entering and leaving a hole in the middle of the south wall of Gyuszi's house. Created by a bullet during the war, the hole had a diameter of approximately two centimeters. A closer examination revealed a clear and present danger to all, a hive in the wall, and I promptly informed my companions of the calamity.

Most of the homes of the period were double-walled structures, an outer layer of bricks and an inner layer of bricks, with airspace for insulation in between. The bees had taken up residence in the space so provided. Due to the scarcity and expense of building materials, many of the houses that suffered damage during the war were repaired only to make them livable, as in this case. The hole had been plugged and finished from the inside, but repairs to the outer wall were left for a time when resources became more available.

Once the hive was discovered, a heated discussion followed as to how best dispose of the problem. Our first method, to spray the bees with water from a hose, only resulted in pissing the bees off. No one got stung, but it took over an hour before we could approach the hole again.

Finally, a plan to burn the buggers out won favor, and to insure success, we decided to use gunpowder, an easily acquired commodity, to do the job. Please understand that by now, several years after the war, most of us kids were gunpowder aficionados. I learned about handling explosives from my father who led a demolition squad after the war, and who saw to it that the three of us boys would not become casualties of ignorance, as many of our contemporaries had.

We knew all the varieties of gunpowder used in the war, what they looked like, and what they did. For example, the "macaroni" powder we found in large artillery shells. This long, tubular gunpowder filled the body of the shell lengthwise and was ignited with a faster, hotter burning, black powder placed between it and the ignition cap. The combination of these propelled an explosive-laden bullet, weighing as much as a hundred kilos, for up to ten kilometers. There were dozens of varieties in the unexploded ammunition that was all around the neighborhood, with which we played.

But back to the bees!

We carefully loaded a bundle of macaroni, and a small pouch's worth of black into the hole. The care we took had more to do with the bees than the explosives. I lit a strand of the long powder at one end, shoved it into the hole, then scrambled to join the others at our pre-selected safety spot. Just in case.

We waited. The time the burn should have taken had long past. No smoke, no burn, no nothing! The bees seemed to enjoy our failure, entering and exiting unruffled.

Disappointed, we added an extra packet of black and tried again. We held our breath as the macaroni burned toward the wall. Long seconds passed as the flame made its way into the hole, and then:

"Bang!!!!!!!!!!!!!!!!!!!!"

Bricks flew in all directions amid the white dust of pulverized plaster! The explosion rocked the entire neighborhood and reverberated from the nearby hills. Miraculously none of the windows were blown out, but a large, gaping hole appeared in the south wall. There were no signs of the bees.

"His mother's sainthood!" Gyuszi said with great emphasis, the motion of his head punctuating the words.

"His mother's sainthood!" Our wailing chorus echoed him. We watched as Gyuszi apprehensively entered the dust-filled house.

When he reemerged, Gyuszi dusted the white plaster from his jacket, holding his usual stoic expression. Fearing the worst, we looked at him for some clue as to the extent of the damage. After what seemed an eternity his face broadened into a grin. "His mother's sainthood!" he repeated, shaking his head. "Let's get to work."

"You and I will mix the cement," he said to me, "and you," Gyuszi pointed at our two companions, "get the house cleaned up."

By the time Nagy-néni came home from work, the wall was finished. True, the plaster was not quite dry, and the color of the paint was slightly off, but it was finished nonetheless. She paused and looked at the wall on her way in from the street, but said nothing.

We waited anxiously.

Once inside the house, she finally exclaimed: "You, wonderful boys! How good of you, especially without being asked, to fix that ugly hole and repaint the wall." Then she added, "I'll make something special for supper, and when I see your parents I'll tell them that they can be very proud of you." With that, Nagy-néni hugged Gyuszi tenderly and wiped her eyes.

Needless to say, none of us boys volunteered to correct her impressions. For all I know, Mrs. Nagy never learned about the bees.

FISHING

I was about fourteen and not very happy about being sent to the Tanya for my vacation. There were too many better things to do in the city. Alas, family finances being what they were, I did as I was told. And so, armed with several books, I was anxiously awaiting three weeks of boredom. As soon as I could negotiate the terms of engagement with Grandmother, I started spending as much time at the river as possible. Summers were always hotter in the country and a body of water nearby made living there more endurable.

★   ★   ★

One afternoon, on my way back from the river, I ran into a bunch of country kids from a nearby settlement. Soon I began meeting up with them to go fishing and swimming in the Danube. Much to my grandmother's distress, each day I looked forward to being with them instead of awaiting her beck and call.

While the cast of characters changed, as country kids had to work, I made fast friends with some of them. Others teased me mercilessly, mocking my city ways and general ineptness about country living. The routine would go something like this:

"So, Pista, do you know how to ride a horse?" one would ask.

Before I could answer someone else would butt in, pretending to be me. "A horse, hmm ... let's see ... no. We only have electric horses in the big city."

Laughter would follow, then the first speaker would add, sounding resigned: "No matter, he probably wouldn't know which end to feed anyway!"

More laughter. If it hadn't been for one girl, Mari, I would've given up on them, but being around her made the tormenting bearable.

Days later, while fishing across Mosquito Island off a platform I had fashioned by weaving the tall reeds together, a contraption that swayed about, but kept me out of the mud, Mari showed up. The last time I saw her I had nearly gathered enough courage to ask her to see me without her pestering horde of friends, but had chickened out at the last minute. Now here she was, standing on the shore by herself.

"How's fishing?" she asked, smiling.

"Just a couple of catfish," I replied, returning her smile. "You can join me," I continued, "the reed will hold your weight, just stay toward the center." I felt elated that she showed up.

"A clever job," Mari said, referring to my platform.

"Thanks! Is anyone else coming?" I asked, hoping that my glee over her solo arrival didn't show.

Mari shook her head. "I didn't tell them where I was going," she said. "Besides, I don't like all the teasing," she added.

"I can handle it," I said, using my most confident voice.

Mari eased herself down next to me and dangled her legs. I

busied myself with skewering a worm onto my hook.

"It's pretty hot, isn't it?" Mari said. "Let's swim over to the other side of the island where there's no mud, and lie in the sand."

"What about the current?" I said apprehensively. "I was there with the fishermen yesterday. The current is swift out there."

Mari shrugged. "I've been there many times, the current is okay. Don't be a city boy!" she coyly added.

I hesitated. "Okay, but promise, if the current is too strong, we'll turn around."

Mari laughed and unbuttoned her dress. "It's a promise," she said, dropping her dress around her ankles, standing before me completely naked, not even attempting to cover up. She was still laughing when she dove into the water.

Speechless, I followed her with my shorts on.

We made it to the far side of the island without trouble and lounged on the sand. Her body was tanned everywhere. She had small breasts and golden hair around her privates. I had difficulty carrying on a conversation; all I could do was ogle. I think Mari enjoyed my discomfort.

On the way home I tried to figure out what to make of Mari's behavior. When Grandfather asked me to join him for our usual evening stroll to the well, I was more than happy to oblige. We walked in silence. At the well, while he was wheeling up the bucket, I found enough courage to talk to him about the day's events.

He listened, then cut through my carefully crafted nonsense.

"You're close to becoming a man. Maybe Mari would have let you take advantage, but are you ready to be a daddy?"

I felt my face turn red as I protested. "It's not what I was thinking about, Grandpapa! I just … you know …"

Grandfather looked at me, a playful smile dancing in his wheat-flower-blue eyes. "Well, Pista, that's what I would've been thinking about!"

★

PRIZED CANVAS

I became politically active in my early teens. It was my time to examine the communist precepts I had been pressured to accept, and test them against the truths I learned from people I trusted. One particular thing about being young is one's sense of indestructibility. We often take risks unacceptable to more mature people.

Tempted by the dangling carrot of an all-expenses-paid vacation on the shores of Hungary's inland ocean, Lake Balaton, I attended a rally hosted by the district chapter of the Communist Party. The purpose of the rally was to promote enrollment into the Young Socialist Movement, a precursor to regular party membership. The recruiters scoured neighborhood schools to find meritorious students of humble origins, meaning students from the working class and not tainted by having parents from the intelligentsia or, God forbid, connected in any way to the hated, old world aristocracy. I fitted their target profile perfectly.

★   ★   ★

The presenter's words bounced off the walls of the nearly empty auditorium as I listened to him wrap up his spiel. As usual, I sat in the front row by myself, all the others, perhaps a couple dozen, occupying the rows behind me in a haphazard pattern.

A persistent question kept rattling around my mind. How was it right to nationalize private property, in this case a former chateau, "for the good of the people," then grant its use to yet another privileged group, namely the Communist Party, which was basically what the presenter was saying? I couldn't keep quiet.

"*Elvtárs!*" I interrupted, raising my hand, using the Hungarian equivalent of *Comrade* as I addressed him. "I thought you said that the chateau had been reserved for the exclusive use of the Csepel Ironworkers Union members and their families."

The balding, round-stomached man with the five-pointed red star pinned to his lapel smiled at me, then scanned the rest of the auditorium. "That's right, young man, and other, deserving members of society," he paused for emphasis, "like all of you."

Going against the alarms in my brain, I stood up. "Why then, comrade, were those workers' vacations cancelled last August in order to accommodate Communist Party officials and their families?" The question's final words faded into stark silence. I shrugged off the displeasure in the presenter's eyes and continued.

"I know a family whose vacation request was denied to accommodate party officials, this after months of planning. Who would we be displacing should we sign up?"

A hushed hubbub filled the auditorium. Some in the room were familiar with my special talent for this kind of disruption, the inappropriate questions that could not be ignored. *You idiot,* I chided myself as I took my seat, *forget the Lake Balaton vacation; you've just become an undesirable!*

That evening, as I leafed through my papers for the next day's classes, I found a scribbled note in my briefcase. Someone must have slipped it there while I wasn't looking. The note challenged me to *act* if I really meant what I was saying and told me to look for instructions behind a loose brick on the corner fencepost of my school. Given all this, who would not look?

I carefully observed the area around the fencepost without seeing anything out of the ordinary. I strolled by it between classes and on the way to and from the electric trolley station, all the while suspiciously scrutinizing every passerby. Many scenarios played out in my head, all having to do with the fear of being set up.

After a couple days of doing this, I finally checked. To my surprise, the loose brick was there, complete with a space suitable for hiding a note or a small object, but the cavity was empty. Though paranoid about being caught, I returned again and again only to find nothing.

I was about to dismiss the whole incident, thinking a prankster had had me, when I found a note. The instructions were simple: Go to the townhouse behind the Turkish baths in ÓBuda, look under the staircase for a stack of handbills and paste them around the neighborhood.

That evening, under the glow of city lights, I did go around this old Buda neighborhood, plastering handbills onto portals and poster-pillars everywhere. The handbills called for new elections, stating that the elections that put the Communist Party in charge were rigged, and called upon the people to rise and rid themselves of the "Fat Soviet Leach" and its "Hungarian Lackeys." While I perspired from fear, ducking into one doorway after the other, it felt good to actually do something against the puppet regime.

At first, this cloak-and-dagger business seemed a game, exciting, to be sure, but not particularly dangerous. I was wrong about the risk. Distributing handbills with anti-state, anti-revolutionary "lies" was regarded as subversive, punishable by imprisonment and even deportation to Siberian labor camps. People were imprisoned for things more innocent than this, like listening to Radio Free Europe, or the Voice of America.

Even political jokes were forbidden. One of Hungary's beloved comedians was convicted of anti-revolutionary activity after he rode a bicycle with a red handlebar onto the stage, complaining that it always pulled to the left. In Hungarian, steering and government are the same word, differentiated only by context.

Soon after the handbill assignment I received another instruction, this time to steal a truck tire from a Russian supply depot across town. This, I finally realized, was the real thing. Should I be caught, I'd be sent to a labor camp for a long, long time. After thinking it over, I realized that since the instructions did not specify the size of the tire, the point of "liberating" it, to use a favorite Russian euphemism for stealing, had to be a final test of trustworthiness, and to see if I would be willing to take significant risks.

I rode the Electric to the area of the supply depot several days in a row and observed all I could. With every visit, I became more convinced about the impossible nature of the assignment.

A sentry in a guard tower, allowing for an easy overview of the surroundings, guarded the depot. A tall brick wall, with pieces of broken glass embedded into cement along its top, enclosed the yard on three sides, while a three-meter-high chain-link fence capped with strands of barbed wire separated the depot from an open lot along the back. The lot still had rubble and discarded materials left on it from the time of the Second World War. Lights placed at strategic intervals on top of tall, metal poles illuminated the yard at night. *A slim chance of penetrating this fortification,* I thought.

Nonetheless, I was determined to rise to the challenge and made several journeys to the depot, all the while racking my brain for a solution.

Rising skyward across the street, a six-story tenement house offered the only hope to get an unfettered look of the comings and goings inside the depot. *If I could somehow get to the roof, I would have an unobstructed view*, I thought. I climbed the stairs past the last floor, and after kicking free a locked clasp that barred entry into the attic, I made my way to a pigeon window inset into a gable overlooking the depot.

I saw nothing that offered a clue as to how I might accomplish the task. The only thing of value I learned was the location of the tires, which were in a pile behind a stack of steel drums, under a lean-to. Now at last I had all the information, but still none of the answers.

★ ★ ★

"What's up, Istvan?" Mr. Kocsis, my physics teacher asked when we met in the hallway. "You seem preoccupied lately."

"Ah, nothing. I'm working on a problem that does not appear to have a solution," I said, wishing I could talk with him more freely.

"Many seemingly unsolvable problems have solutions," he said. "You just have to change the premises. Let me know if I can help." He smiled and patted me on the shoulder as he opened the door to his next class.

"Good luck!"

I wondered wryly if he could solve my problem. Guards, fences, bright lights. Good luck, indeed! Still, what about changing the premises? What premise could I alter that could make stealing the tires possible?

Darkness fell over the city, and slowly the lights came on. *Just another evening in Budapest, the Pearl of the Danube,* I thought, *still a beautiful city, even after the war and all the bombing.*

The Electric was crossing the Danube, carrying me toward the Russian supply depot. Clutched in my hand was a brown paper bag that contained a piece of wood one half-meter long, cut from the handle of a broom; a length of heavy copper-wire and, attached to the wire at one end; a spool of thread.

On arriving at the scene, I casually strode to the open lot then ducked out of view from the street. There, carrying power to the supply depot was the solution to my problem, the electric lines cutting across from the street. I took the heavy wire out of my bag and with shaking hands, unraveled the thread. I bent the wire into the shape of a J, made a few practice swings, and tossed it up to the power lines.

The J caught on the top wire and flung against the one below. A bright flash and the sound of an electric short issued, then all went dark inside the yard. With my heart pounding wildly, I attempted to retrieve the cable, but it was firmly stuck. Finally, I pulled the J to the nearby pole, and by yanking the hook against the insulator, jerked it free. Relieved, I ran back along the chain link fence until I was between two fence posts, directly across from the steel drums on the other side. I pulled up on the fence and jammed the piece of wood under the bottom strand to create a small gap. Moments later I was inside!

I lay flat next to the petrol drums and listened. Over the pounding of my heart I could hear the guards yelling angrily, but a ways off. I sprang to my feet and grabbed one of the tires, rolled it to the fence, and pushed it out onto the lot in front of me. Once on the other side, I kicked the piece of wood out from under the fence and tossed it across the lot. The two minutes this took was an eternity.

Moments later the conductor looked at me quizzically as I climbed on board acting as if traveling with a heavy tire was the most natural thing in the world.

A day after executing my assignment and delivering the tire to the designated spot, I finally met the person responsible for the notes. He came out from under a doorway as I was bounding down the steps at school and stopped me.

"I'm Lajos," he said nervously, "I found the tire."

I recognized him. Lajos, a second year student from a nearby university, frequented my favorite coffee house near the Turkish Baths at the foot of Palace Hill.

"How about meeting me at the Bathhouse Café for a chat," he continued.

"István," I said, extending my hand. "I have another class. Would five be okay?"

Lajos nodded.

The entry to the café led from street level down a narrow, marble-stepped stairway into a different world. Down below, small smoke-filled rooms featured brass fixtures and beveled mirrors, dark stained woods, and crystal chandeliers.

On an average day, the café's clientele would include the usual college crowd, there to argue endlessly over the day's important events; members of the arts community; and retired, old intelligentsia for whom the café had become the last refuge of a forgotten, gracious way of life for which Budapest had been known before the war. As in the old days, waiters and waitresses in black suits and starched white shirts tended to the needs of the guests who sat on bentwood chairs around small round tables with rose-colored marble tops.

Lajos was already there when I arrived. After listening to my experiences while "liberating" the tire, he began telling me about an organization called Hungarian Indians. "Ours is a loosely-knit group," he said, "mostly college students."

"I'm in high school," I countered.

He ignored my comment. "We are dedicated to letting people know the real truth about this regime and the Soviet occupation and to exposing the lies we are told every day." He paused with an expectant look, and when I stayed quiet, he fidgeted with his cup and saucer.

"We do acts of sabotage," he said with the kind of emphasis that compelled a response.

I looked around, feeling a tinge of discomfort upon hearing the word *sabotage*, but said nothing. If this was a trap my responses must not implicate me.

Apparently Lajos could not deal with the vacuum of my

silence and continued. "Let me start at the beginning," he said. "Many Indians used to be members of the *Cserkész* movement, which was the Hungarian chapter of the International Boy Scouts, a Christian Youth Organization formed in 1908 by Sir R. S. S. Baden Powell."

I nodded. "My father was a *Cserkész* before the war, and for a few months before it was disbanded, so was my brother."

Lajos' voice took on a more philosophical tone as he corrected me. "Actually, the *Cserkész* was prohibited by the government in 1948, on the basis that it was a bourgeois, counter-revolutionary organization, there to serve only the ruling class."

"I think any organization that teaches Christian values would be an enemy to this bunch," I ventured.

"We were all too young to understand what was going on, and unfortunately the adult population hardly paid attention. They were too busy staying alive and rebuilding the country's infrastructure."

I nodded.

"When the order to disband came, a teacher by the name of Kovács, our leader's father, found himself in an untenable position, having already made arrangements to spend two weeks camping with his students. Arranging this had been difficult, and he thought the students would be disappointed if the outing were cancelled.

"Kovács went through with his original plans, but called the group Indians to prevent the authorities from taking action against them. The successful outing was repeated the following year."

"None of this explains the political context you've been talking about," I said. "What does scouting in the woods have to do with plastering anti-socialist leaflets around the city?"

Lajos looked a bit exasperated, but instead of commenting, he ordered another espresso for each of us. Once we were served, he continued. "Mr. Kovács was asked to bring the group under the auspices of the Communist Pioneer organization, but he told them that he was not interested. After repeated and unsuccessful efforts to convince him failed, one day Mr. Kovács did not come home from school. He simply disappeared. Neither the police nor party officials could find him."

"Aha," I said, "so his son continued his father's work!"

Lajos shook his head. "He was too young. But later he started collecting friends. That's what the Hungarian Indians are, friends motivated by a single purpose. In a country where people disappear for telling the truth, there's a lot of work to do!" Lajos paused, letting me digest the information.

"What brought you into the organization?" I asked.

Lajos hesitated before answering. "Three years ago, during my last year in high school, my father was arrested for diverting building supplies earmarked for public housing into private use."

"Was that true?"

"No! His boss, a good party member, framed him. It was he who did the diverting. Long story, but the boss got a vacation home on Lake Balaton, and my father was sent to a labor camp in Siberia."

As we talked, Lajos became more relaxed. I explained that it was my beliefs that fueled my discontent. Our "liberated" country struggled under Soviet occupation, the fruits of our labor filled long trains heading toward Russia every day. And while we were told we had freedoms, any attempt to exercise them landed us in jail.

Lajos stood and extended his hand. "I have to go," he said smiling, squeezing my hand heartily. "Welcome to our group! Remember, if they should catch up with you, we don't know you!"

As if I would claim them if the situation was reversed, I thought.

★ ★ ★

At one of our rare meetings, Lajos told our small group about Fall Camp, a gathering of Indians from across the country. From our group, only Lajos had been to camp before. After hearing about the wonderful times he'd had, we all wanted to go, but alas, we had no money even for the bare essentials needed to spend two weeks in the wilderness. We might come up with enough foodstuffs, but more costly items, such as a tent, were out of our reach.

Béla, an ever-clowning, jovial college freshman suggested that we should steal a tent from the Russians. "Hey, Russian trucks have enough canvas to cover half the city!"

While we laughed, the suggestion to obtain the materials needed, and at the same time be a thorn in the side of the Russians, stirred our excitement, and we made plans to investigate the possibilities.

Unfortunately, the idea had to be scrapped because it seemed all the canvas on the Russian trucks had *CCCP* and other Russian words printed on them, making them unsuitable for our purposes. The source of the material would immediately be known if found in our possession. We all understood the predictable consequences.

Weeks went by and I had almost forgotten about Fall Camp, when unexpectedly I received instructions to meet cell members in Aquinkum. The rest of the instructions were puzzling: wear your swimming trunks under your clothes, and bring sandwiches.

We met late in the afternoon at the Aquinkum Museum of Antiquities, where we sat in a circle in one of the bathhouses built by the Romans two thousand years before. Joining us was Gergely, whom I met for the first time. Lajos explained the plan.

After eating, we proceeded toward the shore of the Danube along a warm stream that originated at a cluster of nearby hot springs. These were the very springs used by the Romans to heat their sandstone houses and fill their elaborate marble baths. Once at the rivers edge, Gergely collected our clothes.

I had no fear of swimming in the Danube. The water was dark and cloudy with sediment, but not too cold, and the current wasn't excessive. We swam the few hundred meters to Mosquito Island, one of many Mosquito Islands on the Danube, without trouble. Accompanied by the sucking sounds of our steps, we made our way through the underbrush, stirring up clouds of the pesky insects for which the island was so aptly named. As we waited for our mission to commence, we were tormented mercilessly by their growing hordes. By the time we finally slipped into the murky waters again, I was itching from head to toe, covered with the telltale bumps of their bites.

The current turned swift as soon as we left the protective lee of the island. We swam silently, working just enough to stay afloat, letting the water carry us. I was cold. Slowly the sky turned dark and the lights along both shores appeared more numerous and brighter. From this perspective, submerged to my chin, I began doubting that I could reach either side.

We drifted endlessly. I felt numb from the cold and hoped that swimming harder would warm me up. My teeth started chattering.

"Pista," Lajos called out, "Are you all right?"

I answered affirmatively and made my way closer to the group.

"From this point on," Lajos said, "we should speak as little as possible. Sound carries a long way on top of the water." As if underlining his statement, an Electric rang its chimes on the Pest side of the river, sounding as if it was only meters from us.

Slowly, we made our way toward a dark stretch on the western shore. Only from a short distance could I tell that what we were closing in on was a small island. Before rounding it, Lajos spoke again. "If any of you thought about pulling out, this is the time and place. Once we get between this island and the mainland, we are committed."

No one pulled out.

The sheltered waterway between the mainland and the island served as a marina for all sorts of craft. This was an area off limits to civilians, guarded heavily by armed Russian patrols. We quietly swam between the tied up barges toward the docks.

As we cleared the shadows of the last barge, we became more exposed. We could easily have been spotted; the lights were bright enough to hurt my eyes, which had become accustomed to the darkness out on the river. Silently, we closed the last few meters to our goal, the gunboats, where we assembled in the shadow of the gunboat farthest from the guard shack and the lights.

Even under the canvas cover one could see the outlines of the machine gun that dominated the center of the gunboat, giving the vessel a lethal appearance. The boat was about eight meters long and had a long engine protruding from its stern.

We gathered silently around it. With numbed fingers and teeth chattering from the cold, I began undoing the knots that held the heavy canvas in position. I saw the others do the same.

Finally, the tarp was free. We slowly pulled it off the boat and into the water. The friction between the heavy canvas and the body of the boat made a loud, raspy sound, growing louder as the tarp picked up speed and submerged. As we slipped under the surface with the tarp, I felt the weight of the material pulling me down.

The cooler temperature of deeper water quickly rose along my body. At the limit of my protesting lungs, I kicked as hard as I could to stop from sinking deeper. Near panic and desperate for air, I finally broke the surface. One by one, my fellow conspirators' heads popped up around me, gasping for air. We struggled to hold onto our prize as the river slowly carried us away.

After drifting for about a quarter of an hour along the western shore, we waded onto land and dragged the boat cover out of the water. Lajos ran off and returned with a small party of men. Gergely was there with our clothes. While we dried, the men folded the canvas and loaded it onto a small, three-wheeled truck, completely filling its bed. We dressed and shook hands with little discussion, anxious to put as much distance as possible between the boatyard and us.

The small truck belched blue, oil-laden smoke as it sped away, bouncing on the cobblestones of the avenue. I looked at the undulating patterns made by the lights on the dark waters of the river and felt elated. Like pesky mosquitoes, we had stung the Russian beast and made it itch. In our small way, we were heroes, one and all.

PART FOUR

THREE BORDERS MOUNTAIN

After a long flight from the New World and a couple days of visiting family, I'm seated on a mostly empty Electric on my way to the gliderport at Three Borders Mountain. It's early. Among the few passengers is a middle-aged man sitting across from me. Dressed in a business suit, he looks up from his paper now and then and glances in my direction. His expression has that universal this-is-a-weekday-morning-in-the-big-city look I know all too well. I'm here, in part, to break out of the same rut.

The Electric's wheels screech against the rails as we round the curve away from West Station, opposing the morning rush-hour traffic. The roadway is crowded with tiny, Russian-made cars, all belching blue smoke from their two-cycle engines.

The streetcar lumbers through a malachite-green tunnel of ancient chestnut trees. As we move away from the city fewer and fewer people get on and off. I slouch down on the hardwood slats and relax. The crowns of the trees become a green blur as the Electric's wheels cross the rail seams faster and faster. "Click-ity clack, click-ity clack," the wheels sing. With my eyes closed, I can almost believe I'm speeding through a time tunnel, being transported from the present to the 1950s. In my mind's eye I can see myself, nearly fifteen, weighing one hundred twenty-five pounds on a five-foot-eleven, still-growing frame. My blondish-brown, always-in-need-of-trimming hair is blowing in the wind as I lean out of the streetcar, full of anticipation and excitement.

The Electric comes to a halt with a jerk. We are at Cool Valley, the end of the line. After disembarking, I look around to see if anything has changed since I was here last, twenty-five years ago. The station, nestled in a natural depression and surrounded by verdant forest, still looks the same. If something is different, I cannot tell.

The few buildings around the platform house a coffee shop, the underground public bathrooms, and a gift shop trading mostly in tobacco, magazines, and scenic postcards.

Toward the south, I can see the Cool Valley Station of the Pioneer Railroad. This children-run rail system winds through the surrounding forests, connecting one beautiful valley with another. The narrow gauge rails tunnel through mountains and fjord streams on their way to Wolf Mountain, the railway's highest point.

As a child of ten, I, too, have worked on this railroad, having earned the privilege with good scholarship. Most of the jobs, including conductors, telegraph operators, ticket agents, and signal men, are handled by children between the ages of ten and fourteen, smartly uniformed in the best tradition of European railways. Only the train operators and station managers are adults.

In the summer months the train carries thousands of sightseers, in the winter skiers crowd the cars on their way to the slopes and lodges. The Pioneer Railroad makes the picnic grounds of Budapest, a metropolis of three and a half million, accessible.

During the walk from the station to the edge of the airfield on a winding trail, I'm filled with the same anticipation and anxiety I felt the very first time I made this trek.

Even before reaching the edge of the gliderport I hear the sound of an engine. "Must be the winch or the cable-puller." I find myself speaking aloud. As I clear the last line of trees, the panorama I know so well unfolds before me. Nearest to my right and almost hidden by the trees is a group of low-slung buildings, just as I remembered. The forest, mostly poplar and softwoods, continues toward the north and forms a silver-green wall against the pale blue sky. This living wall edges the eastern boundary of a large, grassy field that hosts what we called the Lower Deck.

Dominating the view to the north stands Three Borders Mountain, separating the green, southern plateau from the

Danube basin. The mountain's exposed granite cliffs are dappled with the dark shadows of canyons and crevices.

Ahead, the foothills hug the base, and as the ground rises in a crescendo to form the crest, the mountain reaches its highest glory, a nearly level ridge that stretches unbroken for fifteen kilometers. Only a shallow dip toward the center, one that always reminds me of a pouting lower lip, alters its ruler's edge. I stop and stand in awe of its magnificence.

From my vantage point I cannot see the hangars at the top, but I know they are there, hidden by distance and trees. My eyes continue their sweep westward to where the ground rises to form a line of smaller, brownish hills. These hills parallel the western boundary of Lower Deck, flattening outward into rolling grasslands and merging finally with a distant, bluish mountain range.

As I complete my survey, an involuntary shudder runs through my body. I'm back, back to my mountain of dreams, a pilot with thousands of hours of flight-time, standing where flying became real for me. I sigh and turn. It's time to meet Commander Fehér.

I feel lucky to have had flying as a dominant interest in my life. While other fascinations have come and gone, flying, in one way or another, has played a vital role in determining what I studied, where I worked, and even where I lived. My life bridges the time between aviation's pioneering days and the high-tech space flights of today. It's a good feeling to be connected to both worlds.

My first memory of trying to fly comes from the time I was three years old. I stood on the bank of the Runoff Channel, facing into a strong wind with my overcoat spread, jumping off to the bottom. I jumped and climbed back up time and again, enjoying the sensation of the wind caught in my "wings," imagining that the pressure against my overcoat extended my fall.

The open cockpit, primary glider rested on its skid atop a small hill with its wings parallel to the ground. Behind the cockpit the fuselage resembled a tapered, wooden ladder standing on edge. Cables from the wing tips and struts supported a conventional tail section. When viewed from a distance the glider reminded one of a giant dragonfly.

The wing lost its balance and dipped to the ground. The young pilot, only a boy, swore. It was his job to keep the wings balanced with the ailerons, but the wind was barely a breeze at the moment, and the ailerons were ineffective. Cursing the insufficiency of the wind, the pilot stared straight ahead, knowing that the next time the wing dropped he would have to give up his seat to the wing tip man. He concentrated with deep furrows between his eyes.

The wing tip man, responsible for leveling the wing at the pilot's command, sympathized, but was also glad. Three times down for the wing and you had to give up your turn! Those were the rules.

Struggling with eminent ruin for a couple more minutes, the pilot finally lost control. The other boy rushed to the cockpit and helped him get out. The pilot cursed again, but dutifully strapped his replacement into the cockpit and walked to the wing tip.

The new pilot grinned as the wing was raised to balance on his thumbs-up signal. This new pilot was me.

★ ★ ★

Sweat poured off my face and burned my eyes, but I couldn't wipe because we were double-timing up the hill, carrying a glider on our shoulders. It was very hot and my shoulders were raw in spite of the cushion I had fashioned from a folded towel. The three of us, Gergely, Jenö, and me, were assigned to bring the glider back to the hilltop.

I was exhausted. The glider weighed around 115 kilos, nearly three times my weight, and this was our tenth retrieve. Except for a short break for the latrine, we had been at it since sunup and there were still a couple of hours to go. We rotated after each retrieve, moving clockwise from the left strut to the right, then to the tail, which was the easiest to carry. Jenö was sulking because we told him to shut up and take his turn under the wings like the rest of us. We were tired of his whining.

The "A" hill we operated from stood twenty-five meters above the valley floor. Once airborne the glider would fly straight about five hundred meters before skidding to a halt. Each 'flight' took roughly twenty seconds, the time logged until the wing touched the ground.

There were operations going on all around us. Each operation had a glider, a support crew of students, and a flight instructor. The tasks were also similar: instruct, launch, fly, observe, then retrieve. Only the difficulty level changed, with the more advanced pilots flying off taller hills. There were A hills, B hills, and a C hill that was only used when the wind was strong enough and from the right direction for ridge soaring.

From the top we could see a B hill operation. From there, the pilot had enough altitude to make shallow turns before landing. I could hardly wait to be good enough to fly from there, but not this day. It was bloody hot under a cloudless sky.

After placing the glider into takeoff position, the three of us crowded around the water bucket, brought up here with great effort from across the Lower Deck to quench our thirst. I snared the aluminum cup out of Gergely's hand, the tail man this time, and drank greedily. I passed it on to Jenö, who in turn gave it back to Gergely. We let the water flow freely from our mouths, down our overheated bodies, desperate to cool ourselves before the next retrieve.

Between fills I watched the glider we had just brought back up being readied for the next slingshot. The tail was anchored and the Y shaped bungee cord hooked into the nose as soon as the pilot was strapped in. Three crews on each arm of the y began moving down the hill, stretching the bungee for the catapult. I took one last gulp before the wing tip was leveled on the pilots command. By the time the instructor ordered, "Release!" I was already running down the hill with Gergely next to me, and Jenö, as usual, trailing behind.

The glider passed us about a meter off the ground, the intent pilot arching forward in the open cockpit. He'll be judged on the straightness of the flight, and that will include the skid mark after touchdown. I lengthened my stride. *Tomorrow it'll be my turn to fly*, I thought, gritting my teeth.

★ ★ ★

In the two years since I started flying, I slowly closed the skills gap between my brother, László, and myself. Laci and I are very different people: he, the serious wage earner and I, the forever-romantic poet; however, we both share the love of flying.

This particular morning the wind blew from the south, the weather condition we had both been waiting for and, in my case, dreamt about for weeks. We had been signed off by our instructors to make our C badge attempts, the achievement of which would give us an internationally recognized standard for piloting gliders.

I don't remember having been more impatient. We had both worked tirelessly for this day; all we needed now was the opportunity. The last crucial requirement, the clearance to catapult from the top of Three Borders Mountain, in itself a badge of acceptance into the rarified circle of elite pilots, lay tucked safely in our pockets. From the top, given a strong wind from the right direction, one could easily stay aloft for the required sixty minutes using ridge lift.

So, here we were, speeding toward the gliderport on the Express Electric at the break of dawn, holding our breaths that the south wind would still be blowing when we reached the mountaintop.

At the Electric's terminus, we unexpectedly spotted the gliderport's first morning shuttle, apparently delayed. We ran for it. The large, military style truck was already loaded to the rafters with those arriving ahead of us. People were sitting on the benches, on the truck's bed, and on each other's laps. We were pulled on board. Pepe, our driver, protested, but no one wanted to get off. We crammed in closer until he could finally close the tailgate. As the shuttle wound its way up the mountain, somebody started a song, and everyone joined in. Each verse eased my anxiety.

At the top, Laci and I quickly ran to the launch assignment board posted in front of Hangar Five. Flight Commander Pálinkás assigned takeoff position seven to Laci, and I would follow at number eleven. Both are lucky numbers according to lore. We grinned and hoped that the superstition would hold one more time. After the launch assignments, we joined the crews to get the first gliders to their assigned catapults. Every team wanted to be the first to the flightline; it was a matter of pride and competitive spirit.

With southerly winds the big catapult in front of Hangar Three became the primary launch platform. The gliders were lined up in takeoff sequence. Number One, a high-performance glider with a closed-in, bubble cockpit, was rolled onto the pad and readied.

The pull crew was given last minute instructions on how to handle the steep drop-off in front of the catapult. Catapult Three was notorious for injuries; the pull crew had to run down on a nearly vertical slope, stretching the shock cord to its maximum. After the glider released and the tension on the shock cord ceased, there was nothing to stop them except a line of shrubs and trees.

The first four gliders were launched in quick succession into a diminishing wind. The last one barely made it past the aptly named Must Land Peak, and the pilot, instead of tucking in close to the ridge to benefit from the lift, continued straight ahead. He lost altitude so rapidly that he was forced to land on the Lower Deck with a straight in approach. I knew the Lord of the Ants, a name we gave the commander, wouldn't like the pilot's decisions and that he would get a talking-to before the day was over.

The takeoffs were temporarily halted. There was no point in launching when the ridge didn't hold, because the gliders that landed on the Lower Deck would have to be brought back to the top on our backs, about an hour and a half's worth of steep climb on a rock strewn, winding road. Tough enough without carrying a glider. Even the light, primary gliders needed five people, with a relief crew of another five, and frequent stops to rest. As many as thirty people were assigned to bring up the heavier, high-performance planes, so whenever the weather permitted, these would be towed aloft behind a power plane. Only the best pilots were allowed to attempt the inevitably treacherous crosswind landings on the Top's skimpy runway.

In the meantime, like most weekend days when there was ridge soaring, the Top was filling up with onlookers. People from all around Budapest, which was just out of sight past the east end of the mountain, came to see the gliders. It was amazing how far the gliders could be seen when soaring above the crest. One of the side benefits of ridge soaring was the closeness of the planes to the spectators, sometimes only a few meters away. It made for quite a show to have a graceful, long-winged glider swim silently by, seemingly suspended in space.

Two more gliders had to abandon the ridge, and only one made it back to the landing strip in front of Hangar Five. Not a good sign! Only Number One was still soaring. Laci and I watched him admiringly as he maneuvered around the outcroppings of the ridge, very close to the trees. Having the ridge to himself he positioned as he liked, taking advantage of the best lift.

The wind seemed to have freshened again, boosting Number One even higher. On the next pass the pilot made it to the best section of the ridge and disappeared behind a crag. Because of a turn-back in the slope, this part of the ridge was out of reach at lower altitudes.

Encouraged, the flight commander decided to resume launching and a mad scramble to ready the planes ensued. The two gliders ahead of Laci gained altitude immediately and headed out along the mountain. Just then Number One re-appeared, returning from the east end of his run. He was very high, at least a hundred meters above the heads of the crowd.

The primary glider Laci would be piloting was lifted onto the launching ramp. Laci's face showed quiet determination, but no anxiety, as he was strapped in. He gave the sign and the wing was leveled.

I waved to him. "See you on the mountain!" I yelled.

"Pull," the launch-captain's command rang out, and the pull crew disappeared from view as they began their run down the steep incline. The shock cord stretched to nearly twice its original length before the order to release finally came. The lightweight primary responded like a stone hurled from a slingshot. There was an *ooh* and *ah* from the direction of the crowd as Laci used the force of the catapult to gain altitude in an ambitious climb.

"Don't overdo it!" I whispered, and just as if he heard me,

Laci smartly lowered the nose to avoid a stall and turned out on course. I saw his timer, who was also mine, start his stopwatch.

The quickness of the next three launches caught me by surprise.

The pull crew was already up after Number Ten's catapult before I realized that I was next. Willing hands strapped me into the cockpit as I listened to the line manager's warning.

"This is not an A hill launch!" he said, as if I needed to be reminded. "The acceleration is tremendous. You must prevent the stick from lurching back; you could do a backward loop right into the mountain!" he continued. I gave him a hurried nod to let him know I understood, and raised my thumb to level the wing. I was ready!

Even though I expected it, the force of the catapult surprised me.

My body slammed against the bulkhead pad at about three Gs, hard enough to bang my head and make my ears ring from the impact. Like Laci before me, I used the power of the catapult to climb before lowering the nose and turning onto the ridge.

The ground quickly dropped away, and I found myself looking across the top of the mountain where I could see the silver ribbon of the Danube in the distance. I had a moment's glimpse of the spectators lining the walk along the edge of the ridge, then I was alone.

I had never been this high before. For an instant, I experienced a pang of fear. "Focus on the task," I heard my own voice urging me from afar, besting the sound of the rushing air. Regaining my composure, I scanned the horizon for Laci and spotted him as he was about to make his turn at the west end of the ridge.

From my vantage point he looked to be very low, tucked in close to the cliffs and just above the treetops. He had almost reached the spot where the ridge formed a bowl, which funneled the wind into a vertical chimney. This was the best place to find lift on marginal days, we were told. Sure enough, I saw him gain altitude rapidly and watched him make a shallow turn back toward the eye of the wind.

A shadow crossed my face. When I looked up to investigate, I just about soiled my pants. One of the high-performance gliders was overtaking me with a vertical clearance of only about five meters! This was the nearest I'd ever been to another plane in the air. I was scared to death! I tucked in closer to the mountain to increase the distance between us. By this time he was next to me, slowing down and descending to my level by deploying a sliver of his dive brakes. I recognized him! It was Géza, one of the Silver Badge hot shots. I knew him to be a personable man in his early-twenties; I'd attended one of his lectures on wave lift. I watched him grin as he closed his dive brakes, his mirrored sunglasses glinting in the sun. He left me in the dust. "One day," I sighed, and focused on the task at hand: staying up.

The combination of him lingering at the bowl in search of lift and the extra altitude I had gained from the force of the catapult allowed me to catch up with Laci. I found myself looking almost directly down at him as he headed back toward the east. I made a shallow, downwind turn to follow him.

After we slid past Must Land Peak, with Laci slightly ahead and below, I watched him gain altitude dramatically, almost as if he were in an elevator, and all of a sudden I found myself looking at his belly from below. Slowing down would let me stay in the lift longer, but if overdone the slower speed would result in the loss of control. Among the pilots this was called *milking it*, one of the more serious don'ts on the list of DO NOTs!

Nonetheless, slowing rapidly closed the vertical distance between us. Just as I had reached his level a dozen or so meters behind, I realized that Laci, if possible, was flying even slower. To keep from having to go around him, I pulled back on the stick even more. I immediately experienced the first signs of a stall.

Better be careful, the trees are only meters away! I heard my inner voice say. I'd always relied on my inner voice whenever there was danger, and now it was screaming! I lowered the nose for more speed and started to overtake Laci. I was between him and the mountain. Not a good position when the crest is slightly higher than either of us, not to mention the fact that the ridge rules specifically disallow it!

Luckily, Laci began his turn toward the west. Now it was his turn to lose altitude, and lose he did. I started a turn to follow, but instead of continuing it, I rolled into a shallow left to complete an

S turn, again prohibited by ridge soaring rules.

I was still in modest lift when I turned away from the ridge and looked for my brother. I spotted him scraping the rocks, still a fair distance from the Bowl. His white wings looked like a butterfly over a sea of green. He was very, very low! *Unless he gets some lift,* I thought, *he'll be forced to land!*

In the next minute or so, I, too, would have to cross the gap from Must Land Peak to the Bowl, and though I was considerably higher, I wondered what my fate would be. No matter, the rules compelled me to follow, even into a down.

And the down did come! The glider dropped as if in a free fall, and to make matters worse, I had to lower the nose to gain enough maneuvering speed to be able to steer away from the rocks. I squeezed against the ridge, praying that my instructor's comments were true: "The wind cannot go through the mountain, therefore it must rise to go over it, and when it does, we call it lift." His words played in my head as I kept losing altitude.

I inched closer to the cliffs, and I was rewarded with a soft rise. As the rocks slowly receded, I continued to follow the contour of the ridge, about half a wingspan away. The sensation was that of riding on the top of a wave, rushing toward a rocky shore. Out of eminent danger, I knew if I could reach the Bowl I'd be all right, so I relaxed my death grip on the stick and looked for László.

As if by magic, László appeared, coming right at me at about the same altitude. He must have gained altitude rapidly after reaching the Bowl while I had struggled to stay up. We waved to one another as we passed, him slightly above. Two thumbs up.

I scanned the ridge for other gliders. Two were ahead and below me, and I spotted a third just as he was about to land on the Lower Deck. It appeared no one had immunity from the vagaries of lift.

Oops! The glider shuddered. *"That's the start of a spin,"* I scolded myself. *Stick forward, reverse rudder! No more of that!*

Later, at the east turn just above Lower Deck, Laci must have spotted the Land Now sign because he obeyed and went in to land. I missed the signal, and when I returned from the west turn point, red flares following one another in quick succession greeted me. I was about to turn back when it dawned on me that the combination of the white *Must Land Now* shapes below and the incessant red flares may have been meant for me.

Moments after touchdown, Opitz, the presiding instructor, walked up to me and said, "It's too late today, but Field Commander Pálinkás wants to see you and your brother first thing next weekend."

When I asked why, he shrugged. "I'm sure you'll find out!"

Commander Pálinkás kept us waiting for nearly an hour. Once we were inside his office, he read us the riot act. "You two may believe that you are hotshot pilots because you outlasted senior pilots and better planes on the ridge last weekend, but you should know that if you ever fly recklessly again, I will personally see to it that you are grounded for good! Is this understood?"

We nodded silently.

"I didn't hear you!" Pálinkás bellowed. "Was that understood?"

"Yes, sir!" we said in unison, standing at attention.

"Now get the hell out of my sight, and be advised that you are grounded for the next six months!"

We were devastated! Still, in spite of the grounding, both László and I were awarded our C badges with identical flight times of one hour and forty-seven minutes. We had become pilots.

BIG KADI

The grounding collapsed my world. It wasn't that it was unjustified but the least I wanted was someone like Chief Instructor Opitz to tell me that I had done a good job flying under marginal conditions. Okay, perhaps at times I was pressing, but not outright dangerous. I think grounding us was Pálinkás' way to send a message to others. At the time, I had no idea that it was Chief Instructor Opitz who called the commander's attention to the two Vöcsöks on the ridge. While his motivation was to express his pride in his young students, alas, the attention resulted in our grounding.

I spent the first few days feeling sorry for myself, cursing the commander. Having been awarded the C in spite of the grounding had eased the pain somewhat, but six months! His mother's sainthood! It might as well have been an eternity.

There were a number of things I planned to do while grounded, one of these was parachute jumping. Knowing how to bail out of a plane had high value in performance flying, so why not. *That's it,* I resolved, *I would attend every workshop, every evening course possible until my flying privileges were restored.* I'll show them! *By the time I'm allowed to fly again—*

Two weeks after the grounding I was back at the gliderport, working with the crews. I spent the day moving gliders between the landing strip and the flightline. This was not as hard as doubletiming up a hill with a glider on your back, but by the end of the day I was sunburned and exhausted. Without a payoff, such as a well-earned flight, it was perversely laborious.

As was our custom, those of us who stayed for the weekend spent Friday and Saturday evenings sprawled around a campfire. The fire was lit as soon as the planes were tucked away and everything was readied for next day's operation. There were a good number of new cadets spending the weekend at the gliderport. The cadets knew that I had to have done something seriously wrong to be grounded. When the inevitable questions about the grounding came up, I simply said that I was grounded for unsafe flying. Now that I was a C badge pilot, I had certain responsibilities toward the younger cadets. So I told them the entire story: stalling close to the mountain, not following ridge rules, and generally ignoring procedures.

During the storytelling I often pointed to the dark mountain looming to the north of us and, as pilots do everywhere, used my hands to illustrate what I was talking about. I had them listening intently. Except for a couple of older kids, none of them had ever been higher in a glider than five meters. For them, I was the reincarnation of the notorious Red Baron.

After a while we followed another tradition and sang. When I sensed that the atmosphere was just right, I screwed up my courage and played a couple of tunes on my harmonica. Recognizing one of the tunes, the group joined in. It felt good to be able to play well enough for people to enjoy it. As the evening wore on, we fell silent. One by one the cadets left for the bunkhouse.

I was staring into the fire, mesmerized by the dancing flames, when Chief Instructor Opitz sat down next to me.

"Good work today, Horvath! Not only with the planes, but also with the new cadets."

"Thank you, sir."

"Are you going to be here next weekend?"

"Yes, sir, bright and early."

"What would you say if I assigned you to apprentice on the winch?"

Until that moment, I had never even considered the possibility. To be a winch operator carried not only prestige, but also a lot of responsibility. Not only was the operator trusted with the most expensive piece of equipment we had, he was also responsible for the lives of the pilots he towed aloft. In the past, I would have said no, but now I jumped on it.

"I would like that very much, sir! Who will I be assigned to?"

"Zoltán," Opitz said. "He's our best and the only one authorized to conduct training. Be here at six o'clock next Saturday. I'll let Zoltán know your are coming." Opitz got to his feet.

"Thank you, sir," I called after him. He raised an arm in acknowledgment and kept on going toward the barracks, slowly swallowed up by the dark.

★ ★ ★

When Zoltán arrived Saturday morning, he found me with rag in hand, wiping the dust and grime off our biggest winch, the twelve-cylinder Cadillac we affectionately called Big Kadi.

"Good morning, sir," I greeted him, putting the rag aside.

"Morning, you must be István. And please drop the sir bit, and just call me Zoltán." He smiled and extended his hand.

While we worked to hook Big Kadi to the truck and get her set up at the end of the field, Zoltán introduced me to the winch's components. Once set up, the winch stood on four legs, the front ones a bit longer than the ones in the back, all slightly spread for better stability. This gave the winch the appearance of a large animal sitting on its haunches. The wheels used for transporting the heavy machine were jacked off the ground.

On each side of the engine toward the front there was a large spool equipped with a cable feeder that directed the cable back and forth between the lips of the spool as the winch reeled the cable in. Each cable feeder had a guillotine, enabling the operator to cut the cable in case of an emergency just by pulling a lever.

Big Kadi was powerful. Her twelve in-line cylinders were capable of three hundred horsepower. She could pull a two-place glider up to pattern altitude, the height needed to properly plan and execute a safe landing, in about forty seconds. A metal cage protected the operator from the falling cable ends, which were the heavy metal rings used to hook up the gliders.

Zoltán, a good natured, no-nonsense man in his early forties, spent the rest of the morning showing me how to tow. By midday, he was talking me through the use of the throttle. A combination of power and clutch allowed the operator to control both the speed and the force with which the cable reeled in. Once the glider obtained safe altitude and started its extreme angle climb, the throttle had to be eased off to prevent the cable from breaking.

Cable breaks were common and very dangerous. The cable weakened from being dragged on the ground after every tow, and when it broke the whiplash could maim anyone in its path. Fortunately, we went through the whole day without incident.

By day's end, I had performed a dozen or so tows supervised by Zoltán. In all, it was a very good day, and that evening, I had a lot to talk about by the campfire.

A small group of us were standing around, debating some of the points presented by Géza in the program, when he walked over and asked, "So, what do you guys think? I'm hoping that you found the workshop valuable."

Gyözö, a senior club member who also sported a Silver Badge on his lapel just like Géza, said, "The part about not using country roads for landing made sense, thank you! But I've—"

He was about to continue with something else, but Géza rested his arm on my shoulder and turned us away.

"István, how about joining Veronika and me for an espresso tonight? My treat."

When I nodded, he continued, "I would like to talk to you about crewing for me for my Gold distance flight. Opitz thought you might be available."

"I would be glad to," I said without hesitation. Géza was a rising star in our Association of Flying Clubs. Rumor had it that he would probably be the one replacing Pálinkás after his tour of duty with the Army Pilot Corps.

"Good," he said with a pleased expression. "I have to visit with a few more people, so why don't you and Veronika take off. I'll meet you at the café in a few minutes."

"Okay!" I said and turned to look for Veronika. I spotted her at the lectern and walked over to join the group that gathered around her.

She was deeply involved in conversation, something concerning wing loading and its effects on optimum speeds, which has to do with the heaviness of the plane versus its wing area. It was technical stuff, but it so happened I had just finished a class dealing with the same subject, so I wasn't lost.

I watched Veronika's animated, engaging style as she fended off challenge after challenge. She used her hands to describe the effects of wing loading on the glide angle, the standard by which a glider's performance is measured. Her face was slightly flushed, and her eyes danced as she spoke. I was unable to take my eyes off her. Finally, when someone else took the lead in the discussion, I pulled her aside and relayed Géza's plan for the evening.

"Oh, yes," Veronika said, "we talked about asking you to crew with us."

On the way to our favorite coffeehouse, Veronika and I hung

onto the overhead straps of the Electric. We chatted about Géza, his career in flying and how he and Veronika had met, while swaying to and fro, absorbing the motions of the streetcar. Her simple, red dress with large, white polka dots was a pleasant change from the flight coveralls she usually wore. As we stood facing each other, Veronika's heavy, chestnut-brown hair swayed in rhythm with the train's motion, revealing one eye, then the other. I found myself completely captivated.

At each stop, more people piled into the Electric, cramming us closer together. I tried to maintain space between us, but it was no use; our bodies were pressed together by the crowd. I felt my face turn red when a lurch brought us even closer. I hoped she wouldn't notice my discomfort. Her face brightened into a smile, causing dimples to form at the corners of her mouth. She lifted her chin, her golden-green eyes looked unflinchingly into mine. Our lips were barely apart.

"Trains!" she said.

"Sorry," I said clumsily and felt heat spread through my body. I detected a faint scent of lilacs.

"These cars are getting too crowded," she repeated simply and continued, "Our plan is to head out toward the Tátra Mountains, past the river Tisza. Géza hopes to connect with a fast-moving cold front and take advantage of the atmospheric instability—"

I could barely focus on what she was saying and was glad when we arrived at the coffeehouse, the always-noisy meeting place where I didn't feel so exposed.

Veronika and I were already on our second cup when Géza finally joined us. He restated his invitation about crewing and promised to help me get ready for my Silver flights in return. I was very excited about having been asked, especially about crewing with Veronika.

★ ★ ★

I fell into a more or less routine schedule for the rest of the year. School, along with evening workshops and parachute training occupied my time during the week, and work at Three Borders Mountain filled my weekends.

At the gliderport I'd been given the privilege of assisting Opitz with novice students and, at his discretion, working with Géza, who was apprenticing to become a flight instructor. I was now almost the exclusive operator of the winch on Sundays, a development much appreciated by Zoltán. My schedule was very busy and satisfying.

In late November, our parachute training moved from the classroom to the jump tower in Uj-Pest, a sprawling urban center featuring pre-fabricated, high-rise condominiums built in the "Nouveau Socialist" style. These drab tenement neighborhoods gave silent testimony to the utterly bankrupt ideology of socialism.

One didn't have to be afraid of heights to experience queasiness, even at first glance the jump tower looked intimidating. It was about fifty meters tall and guyed with steel cables, not unlike a radio tower. Jutting out at the top was what appeared to be a crane holding a giant ring. Across from it a heavy cable stretched all the way from the top of an elevator shaft housing to the ground.

I was used to heights and did not experience undue fear standing at the edge of cliffs, but on the way up the tower I felt queasy and beads of sweat formed on my brow. In a glider this would feel low to the ground, but here—

This last phase of the training called for three slides and three simulated jumps from the top. To do a slide, a fully outfitted trainee carabined onto the steel cable and leapt into space at the jumpmaster's command. Once in the air, the slider accelerated to nearly free-fall speeds until he reached the belly of the wire. The belly would slow him down, giving him enough time to plant his feet. The impact velocity, along with the heavy gear, simulated the field conditions a chutist would encounter on landing.

When my turn came, I was determined not to show fear. On the jumpmaster's command I leapt, folded my arms across my chest—and fell!

I watched the ground come at me with frightening speed. For a brief moment I panicked! I stiffened my muscles to prepare for impact. Then, in the last possible moment, my fall flattened, and I was able to plant my feet and roll.

"How did it go?" one of my fellow trainees asked with a voice of forced nonchalance when I got back to the top.

"Nothing to it," I lied, "Just remember to reach for the ground and roll on contact in one continuous motion."

"Looks pretty extreme from here," said another, also waiting for his first slide.

"It's not as scary as it looks," I encouraged them, mentally readying myself for the next slide.

While this little exchange was going on, one of the girls hyperventilated near the elevator shaft. Her hands were locked onto the railing, and she was not about to let go. The slides had to be halted until she could be pried away from the railing and returned to the ground. She kept repeating, "I just can't … I just can't …" all the way down.

I know many of us on the platform felt exactly the way she did, but we somehow managed. Two guys and all the girls failed to make any of the slides. They were rescheduled for additional training. I later learned that only one of them, a girl, actually jumped. The others had dropped out.

I returned to the tower to complete my jumps the following week. The jumps were more pleasant and involved being harnessed to an already-open parachute, pulled up to platform level, then dropped to float to the ground. On the way up, the parachute was held open by the giant ring I saw before. The ring was equipped with a release mechanism that allowed the chute to fall free.

Back at the mountain, I slowly became the youngest member of the "insiders" group that included Commander Pálinkás, his second in command, Chief Instructor Opitz, and the gliderport's mechanic and the driver of our shuttle, Pepe. Apprentice Instructor Géza, Veronika, and I were the non-staff regulars. We also had some irregulars, like Éva Pálinkás and Zoltán, but for the most part, we were the core.

Without question, Pálinkás was the unchallenged leader. He would ruthlessly cut down any threat to his supremacy. His authoritarian style was simultaneously quick, intimidating, and charming. Except when he drank.

One time, the party secretary from the local People's Committee decided to close down operations to force the placement of additional heads of cattle on the gliderport's property. Pálinkás was enraged! When the Secretary started citing "The Public Good," he and his escorts were met with a stream of expletives.

Pálinkás, a party member himself, did not hesitate to point out that the gliderport operated under a special directive of the State, connected to National Defense, and no "local yokel" would be allowed to impose limitations to the gliderport's mission or interfere with its operation.

"So get the hell off my airport and tend to your (expletive) cows!" he yelled, without any fear of retaliation or concern about who might be informed of the exchange.

He was a person of average height with a slight hint of a bulge around the waist. I guessed him to be about forty, quite old compared to the rest of us, except for Opitz. He loved flying and cursed the day he had been promoted to head the Three Borders Mountain operation, the duties of which, according to him, kept him from the skies. When he got to fly the World War II Russian biplane we used for towing gliders, he wore a brown, age-cracked leather jacket over his flight suit. He added a white shawl and a bomber's cap with goggles to complete the image of a flying ace.

Second in rank, and the sanest among us, was Chief Instructor Opitz. Unlike Pálinkás, Opitz never took a drink nor tried his charms on the female cadets. In his earlier life, he had been a professor of aerodynamics at one of the universities. Though soft-spoken, his calls about flying matters were rarely challenged. He stood with a slight hunch and talked with his hands. Every once in awhile he would put his arm on my shoulders and call me István instead of Horváth. He would usually follow this with a new assignment, one that required even more of his trust than the one before.

Pepe, our intrepid mechanic and driver, constantly bragged about his talents. Once, he claimed, he had rebuilt the engine of the truck we used to go up and down the mountain, and still had a satchel full of nuts and bolts left over.

"No one else," he said with a straight face, "could redo an engine with that many parts left over and make it run!" He feigned surprise at the laughter that usually followed. I was never quite sure whether or not to believe him. Pálinkás sometimes called Pepe a "Big Dumb German," but Pepe never took offense. His long blond hair and blue eyes complemented his ever-present grin. His obvious good nature disarmed everyone around, and only his reddish nose attested to the one weakness he had: drinking.

Blending in with the greatest of ease was Géza, the rising young star among the top pilots of local clubs. Géza had a special gift; he made everyone in his presence feel more important. This was not a cultivated skill; he came by it naturally, making it even more effective. In Géza's presence, Pálinkás was the best leader who ever lived. Around him, I felt appreciated and the equal of all.

When Géza talked to you, you felt as if you were the only one in the world whose opinion mattered. This, and a genuine talent for flying, elevated Géza in everyone's eyes and moved him along the career path. By the age of twenty-three, he was the youngest Silver Badge pilot in the country, and despite his youth, he had the AFC's (the Association of Flying Clubs) support to eventually replace Pálinkás.

The AFC's high regard for Géza grew even more when he persuaded the parents of a young female cadet to drop their complaint against Pálinkás, a complaint they had launched out of some misunderstanding that had arisen from an unsubstantiated claim of their daughter. I had heard the tale, but couldn't figure out what actually happened. Géza would never say.

Veronika, the only girl in the group, if we don't count the mysterious Mrs. Pálinkás, was, at twenty, three years older than I. She was a quick study and fine young pilot, able and willing to work any assignment. Veronika's relationship with Géza clearly made her blossom both as a pilot and as a woman. The word was that sometime in the near future they would be married.

From the time of our ride on the Electric, Veronika and I spent a lot of time together, usually discussing flying. Also a holder of the coveted C badge, and having earned it in a thermal, she was in fact ahead of me in flying skills. With the backing of all who mattered, she could become the first female Silver Badge pilot in the country.

The only problem with Veronika was her good looks. She had that mysterious power over men some women are born with from the dawn of history. Adding to her allure was the fact that she was quite unwilling to wield this, relying instead on solid work and keen intellect.

Veronika was a skillful communicator, and more often that not, she would prevail in a debate. One evening, while cadets, instructors, and seasoned pilots sat around the campfire, Szeles, an assistant instructor, started a heated discussion about the wind's effect on thermaling.

Szeles was not well liked by the inner circle because, while he fell under the direct supervision of Opitz, he often bypassed Opitz and solicited orders directly from Pálinkás, thus raising havoc with the chain of command. For some reason Pálinkás was unaware of being manipulated, and Szeles used this to get out of some of the hard work the rest of us had to do. Emboldened, at times Szeles openly challenged Géza, making no secret about wanting to replace him as Opitz's number one assistant.

"I would argue," Szeles said on this occasion as he addressed the cadets by the fire, "that as the glider turns into the wind its speed drops, and as it turns downwind its speed increases in direct proportion to the speed of the wind." With his ill fitting, oversized flight suit hanging on his tall, bony frame, Szeles glanced around, hoping to catch some assenting nods.

"You can actually see this when you watch a glider thermaling on a windy day." Szeles continued. "If you observe carefully, you'll see that the glider's path is not a circle but an elliptical orbit."

Veronika, who had been staying out of the discussion until now, took up the challenge. "Actually," she said, "for the glider, wind does not exist. Its speed is relative only to the air."

"Not so," countered Szeles, happy there was a taker. "When going downwind he is moving with the wind, but when he turns around he moves against it; and at that moment his speed is slowed. Right?"

"Feri," Veronika called him by his personal name, "I will need your agreement, as far as you care to give it, to help me make my point." She smiled at Szeles.

"Of course," Szeles replied, as saying no would have showed weakness.

Veronika continued. "Please visualize a very, very large, completely enclosed railroad car." Veronika's expressions and body language added emphasis to her every word. "This box car is so large that an entire field, one as big as the Lower Deck, could fit into it. Can you imagine it?"

When she paused to allow for his response, her face melded into a disarming smile. She looked at Szeles, her green eyes alive with the light of the flickering flames, inviting him to speak, subliminally asking, "Let me know what you're thinking."

"I don't know what a giant railroad car has to do with the speed of a glider thermaling on a windy day," said Szeles, suspecting a trap.

"Stay with me!" Veronika smiled. "Imagine that the train starts moving, faster and faster, until it's over fifty kilometers per hour."

Szeles reluctantly nodded, indicating his comprehension.

"The train's motion represents the wind relative to the ground."

Veronika continued, pausing to get his assent. "Now a glider is towed into the air off the field in the boxcar, it releases and catches a thermal. In the meantime, the train just keeps roaring along."

Veronika glanced at the circle of observers and spread her arms. "Would the pilot even know that the train was in motion?" Her eyes stopped on Szeles. "No! His plane wouldn't be affected," she concluded quietly. She was beautiful, her sinuous body exuding confidence, the fire adding to her glow.

Veronika made her point brilliantly. We voiced our pleasure with muted laughter and clapping hands, enjoying Szeles' defeat. For once, he had gotten what he deserved.

Szeles knew he was checkmated and didn't smile. "I don't see what a boxcar has to do with flying gliders," he repeated defiantly, and started out for the barracks.

Géza stepped in front of him. "Feri, I thought you presented your point well," he said kindly. "We all learn from these discussions, so thank you for making us think."

"I still don't see what—" started Szeles, but Géza stopped him. They walked away from the fire together.

I focused my attention on Veronika as she peered into the dark after them. *Lucky guy!* I thought.

Veronika turned toward us. "What about a song?"

★ ★ ★

In retrospect, it was not accidental that Éva Pálinkás, a woman with considerable charms over men herself, would hate Veronika. Once, when Éva joined our after hours party, she and the commander got into an argument. They were behind the closed doors of his office, but Éva carried on loud enough for us to hear from the clubroom. I believe that she delighted in embarrassing the commander.

"… And if you think you can just waltz in at three o'clock in the morning, you have another thing coming!"

"But dear—"

"Don't 'but dear' me! Just make up your mind where you want to spend your nights: here with your whores, or at home with me! And if you can't, I'll make it up for you!"

And so it went for some time, culminating in Éva Pálinkás storming out of the commander's office, her perfectly groomed head held high and her heels determined to punch holes in the linoleum floor. She never acknowledged our presence. The deafening sound of the outer door slamming shut was followed by our embarrassed silence.

The next thing we heard sounded like Pálinkás kicking a chair against the wall. A few moments later he emerged with a bottle of Scotch whisky in each hand. Pálinkás looked at us squarely. "Let's party!" he said without conviction.

He never made home that night.

BETWEEN HEAVEN AND EARTH

The fall of 1953 came and went. In early January, the parachute team finally got the call to execute our first jump. We met at a small grassy field east of Budapest, and after a short briefing by the jumpmaster, we boarded a Douglas DC-3 Dakota. Full of anticipation and excitement, our troop sat on the floorboards as the two-engine taildragger lumbered across the field to an eventual takeoff.

The door of the DC-3 had been removed, and the wind and the noise of the right engine blasted through the opening. It was a mild winter, and except for some northern exposures, the ground below was snowless. The lowlands between the two great rivers of Hungary, the Danube and the Tisza, often stayed snow free until late in the spring when artic storms from the North Atlantic would strangle Europe with bitter cold. Now, the plowed-over, tree edged wheat fields below us only had melted snow glistening in the furrows.

I guess I will always hold in awe the view of earth from above, and this time was no exception as I strained to see over the jumpmaster who sat between the open doorway and me.

"Hold up, Horvath," the jumpmaster yelled with a grin, "I don't think we're high enough!"

As we reached our target area, the jumpmaster got to his feet and made his way to the cockpit, gripping the steel cable overhead hand-over-hand.

From my position, I could see the pilot shaking his head and the jumpmaster listening intently. When he returned to the cabin and settled back on the floor, he cupped his hands around his mouth and yelled. "As of now, the jump is canceled due to stronger-than-acceptable winds." He showed no emotion in response to the cacophony of expletives that greeted the news. After the troop settled down, he continued, "The pilot will make another run in a few minutes, and the situation will be reassessed."

I never considered this possibility and felt an emotional letdown. What could possibly change in a few minutes? For all practical purposes this Saturday was shot, and I would once again have to prepare myself for the jump. *Nuts!*

When the hook up and stand by to jump command came I was truly surprised. *One should never lose faith,* I thought. With my anxiety revved up anew, I stood and clipped the carabiner of my static line onto the cable. We lined up in a row over the centerline of the Dakota. "Jump!" The jumpmaster pointed to the first in line. One by one the jumpers exited the aircraft. When it was my turn, I followed the person in front of me without appearing hesitant, but I was glad no one could read my thoughts.

A split second after the Dakota's tail assembly passed me, I felt the tug on the static line and I was yanked out of my spread-eagle position by the deploying parachute. I looked up at the canopy in wonder. I had accomplished yet another dream.

The rapidly diminishing noise of the engines was replaced by quiet. A soft, cool breeze fanned my face from below as I swung back and forth, riding on a giant aerial swing. I was, suspended between heaven and earth, looking across space to my nearest companions.

The last of the jumpers were still piling out of the receding aircraft, each looking like a flower bud bursting into bloom. Below me, the white canopies of the jumpers who preceded me were scattered through the sky, looking motionless as they floated silently.

Slowly, the ground began to rise and the leafless trees grew taller. I was positioned perfectly above the target area, drifting toward the middle of the field. The first jumpers were making contact with the ground. I could tell the direction of the wind from my drift, and I maneuvered to face into it. For a minute more I enjoyed the unearthly sensation of floating in mid-air, then the ground began to accelerate toward me, and I prepared for landing. Remembering the scary slides from the tower, I stiffened my muscles, pulled hard on the harness above my shoulders, and with my feet together, landed. There was no need for the over-the-shoulder roll; I stood erect in the soft, plowed field with my arms raised toward the sky—celebrating.

The next moment I was yanked unceremoniously onto my back. *You idiot!* I scolded myself as I was dragged through the mud across the furrows. *You forgot to collapse your chute!* I rolled to my stomach and tugged desperately on the lower lines. Eventually, my muddy tobogganing came to a stop, and I drudged back across the field toward my companions, clutching the gathered parachute in front of me. Even across the decades, I can hear the laughter.

★ ★ ★

On the last Sunday of January, I was instructing a group of fresh cadets on one of the A hills when a runner from the lower deck office sprinted across the field to deliver a message from Opitz. "Replace yourself and come to the Top as soon as you can," the message said.

It was a windy day without clouds, the kind of day when keeping the wing level was easy even for new cadets. I liked what I was doing, working with a group of students, getting them started with the basics.

It took a while before I could replace myself with someone qualified. Not knowing what the message was about, I asked the office to have Pepe pick me up and take me to the Top. Generally, the use of the jeep was reserved for official business only, but the message sounded official enough.

I found Opitz in Pálinkás' office, talking with the commander.

When I entered, I overheard Pálinkás saying, "I don't like it, but if that's your judgment—"

When we got out of the building Opitz turned to me. "You have been cleared to fly with me. We are going to make an attempt to get into the wave." He said this as if he were talking about his morning coffee.

I could hardly contain my excitement as Opitz and I prepared a side-by-side two-seater called *Coma* for flight. This tadpole-looking, high-performance glider held most of the Hungarian two-place records. It was equipped with oxygen and was highly maneuverable. I was excited just to get a flight in it, let alone to fly it into a wave.

We were catapulted from the platform in front of Hangar Three, and with Opitz at the controls we quickly gained altitude. It was a privilege to watch a master pilot ply his art. Not once did

I see the yaw string, a simple length of yarn attached to the outside of the canopy to show the direction of airflow, stray from dead center. A testament to his flying skills.

He relinquished the controls at two thousand meters, twice the height of the mountain. I carefully followed the pattern set by him, and we were soon above the rest of the gliders, except for two single-seaters who had a clear performance edge over us.

At about twenty-five hundred meters, Opitz pointed to the lenticular cloud (so called because it is shaped like a lens) to the south of us. "The wave is at the leading edge of that cloud. That's where we are going."

"But that means we would have to fly through the lee of the wave, doesn't it?" I tried to sound intelligent.

"Yes, it does, but given our position we do not have a choice. Check your harness and tighten it up. It'll be a rough ride!"

Full of anxiety, I did as instructed. From Géza's workshop on wave lift I remembered the warnings about the incredible forces pilots would encounter under the umbrella of the wave. This area, called the rotor, is named after the characteristic motion of a cigar shaped roll cloud. If ventured into unprepared, the turbulence could rip off the wings.

As we glided away from the ridge toward the likely direction of the wave, I mentally checked off the safety equipment in the cockpit. Opitz must have guessed what I was doing, because when I glanced at him, he had a broad smile on his face.

"That's right!" he said, turning serious. "It is exactly what we should be doing right now!"

"What happens if we fail to make contact?"

"We know the wave is there because of the lenticular clouds. We also know forces in nature tend to balance: big ups come with big downs, and vice-versa. The worst thing that would happen if we don't make contact is we could be forced to make an off-field landing."

The price of approaching the wave from a downwind position became evident as I watched the variometer needle drop below zero. Considered to be the most important instrument on board a glider, the variometer shows the amount of lift or sink at a given moment. Ours moved from lift to zero, then from twenty-five meters per minute down to fifty meters, then to a hundred. The needle finally pegged, registering our rate of sink at over five hundred meters per minute.

Opitz took back the controls and responded to the heavy sink by gradually increasing speed to limit the amount of time we would spend in the descending air mass. This was a gutsy move: if we did not make contact with the upside of the wave, he had committed us to a certain off-field landing. I watched in quiet desperation as the altimeter unwound. The lenticular cloud looked as far from us now as it did from above the mountain.

We were nearing redline speed when Opitz finally raised the nose to slow us down. Lucky that he did. The falling elevator we had been riding turned into a raging torrent of updrafts in quick succession, hitting us with a force that made the glider groan, bending the wings upward as if our plane was a flimsy toy.

As quickly as the lift had come, we fell into the void again and experienced several seconds of free-fall. At the bottom, we slammed against solid resistance and were boosted upward hard enough to force my head into my knees and crush the air out of my lungs. *So this is the dreaded rotor,* I thought.

Scissors of ups and downs raged against us. As our glider alternated between stalling and screaming speeds, the maelstrom torqued our wings up and down in rapid succession. I held my breath. This was the perfect formula for disaster.

I felt warm blood running down my shins, broken open from slamming against the underside of the instrument panel. I glanced over to see Opitz's face. His expression betrayed nothing. I was glad to have him at the controls.

Then came the eeriest moment of the flight. From the screaming sounds of the past minutes, we slipped into smoothness and silence. The variometer that moments ago had pegged on maximum ups and downs, now showed a needle's width above zero, climbing perceptibly even as I watched. We reached the upside of the wave, an area so smooth that our craft seemed to become motionless.

Opitz read the instruments aloud and asked me to write the

time and the numbers down. "Altimeter, eight hundred meters; lift, twenty-five meters per minute and climbing; speed, forty-two kilometers per hour." He then leaned against the backrest. "Istvan, take over. You and I have just become two of a handful of pilots in the world to fly in a mountain wave. It's one thing to theorize about something and quite another to have your assumptions verified!" he added.

I realized for the first time that Opitz had an emotional side to him. He spoke with the reverence one reserved for church.

"Géza and I mapped the likely pressure profile of the wave, but until now it's all been just theory. Now it is real."

If it weren't for the fact that we were strapped inside a tiny cockpit, I think he might have gotten up and danced.

We slowly climbed through three thousand meters and put on our oxygen masks. Except for the occasional popping sounds of structural contractions caused by the increasing cold, we were motionless and climbing. Our lift now registered just over two hundred meters per minute, and we were nearing the level of the lenticular cloud. The cloud turned out to be of several layers paralleling one another, and as we climbed past them, we could see blue sky between the layers.

We soared without speaking, in complete awe.

It was bitterly cold. Frost started to cover everything inside the cockpit from the moisture supplied by the exhaust ports of our masks. Opitz opened the side vent before the spreading frost completely obscured our vision, and while the temperature dropped noticeably, the canopy slowly cleared.

We gradually had to increase our speed as we climbed higher and higher to stop from drifting backwards relative to the ground. We registered eighty-eight kilometers per hour as we passed through seven thousand meters. I pointed to show Opitz that our variometer was resting near zero. He nodded to indicate he understood, tapped the sluggish altimeter, and motioned for me to execute a shallow turn to leave the wave.

I looked around for the last time from this exalted altitude and took in all I could, hoping to remember it forever. The lenticular cloud, now well below us, started to turn bluish-gray on top, blending into blood red at the leading edge. As the winter sun neared the horizon the undulating mountains and forest below us slowly disappeared into the mist.

I waited until we were well clear of the area of the rotor before I started our long descent. I thought it most decadent to work at losing, instead of gaining, altitude. Even with dive brakes deployed, it took us nearly thirty minutes to reach pattern altitude.

Once we dropped below twelve hundred meters, Opitz put away our masks and turned off the oxygen. I set up a large, sweeping pattern for landing at the Top.

Back on the ground, Opitz, with his characteristic penchant for understatements, wrote *Wave-Flight—seven thousand two hundred meters* into my logbook. I later learned that if we had a recording barograph with us during the flight, we would have set a new Hungarian altitude record for two-place gliders, besting the old mark by a staggering two thousand meters.

The atmospheric conditions that create mountain waves were not well understood in the 1950s. Wave formation requires sustained, uniform wind velocities, such as found in the jet stream.

It is believed that when the winds bounce off several mountain ranges in succession the airmass begins to oscillate, one bounce amplifying the next, thus forming the wave. The shape of the wave is not unlike the shape created by a length of rope when it's whipped up and down at one end while the other end is held steady. It is estimated that mountain waves, also know as clear air turbulence among pilots, may reach 100,000 feet above sea level.

Two youngsters helped me set up the winch that morning, the cable Puller and the flagman. Having a flagman at the winch was in response to an unfortunate incident in which a student, who had been in the process of hooking up the cable to a glider, was inadvertently dragged on the ground by the winch. Fortunately, other than having the you-know-what scared out of him and losing some skin, he was all right. Opitz figured that having to give two instead of one confirmation of readiness improved safety. I was glad for the company.

Today promised to be an excellent soaring day, precipitated by a cold front moving through the middle of Europe on its way toward the eastern Mediterranean. Thermal strengths up to three hundred meters per minute and cloud bases around two thousand above ground were predicted by the Institute of Meteorology. It was an exceptional forecast for this early in the season.

By late morning we were experiencing strong lift and gusty winds, and, as a result, cable breaks. When the cable breaks, the pilot of the glider has to make a split-second decision: is there enough speed and altitude to make an abbreviated pattern, or land straight ahead? After the second break, which nearly caused a glider to crash into the winch, I made the decision to replace both cables. The cables should probably have been changed the prior day anyway.

The pilot in command during the second cable break had just started his extreme angle climb and barely had enough altitude to recover. Being too high for a straight ahead landing and rollout, but not high enough to make a turn and clear the hills, he had to groundloop the glider to avoid hitting the winch and ripped out the glider's undercarriage in the process.

Knowing it would take some time to remove the damaged plane, I decided to take an early lunch and headed toward the hangars. After leisurely consuming my bread and pork lard sandwich and getting my fill of raw milk, I started walking back toward the winch, taking the longer trail under the trees to stay out of the sun.

As I passed the main hangar, I spotted Géza busily working in the cockpit of a Pilis, a medium-performance single-seater known for its excellent climbing ability.

"Hello, Géza! I haven't seen you in some time." I pointed to the tools spread out next to the cockpit. "What's happening?"

He smiled. "Good to see you too! I'm installing a bracket to hold a barograph behind the seat."

"Yeah! Today would have been a great day to get my Silver

altitude, but alas, I'm stuck on the winch."

"If I cannot get this damned barograph installed, I'll be in the same fix myself," he responded, with uncharacteristic frustration.

"Where's Veronika? I haven't seen her for a while."

Géza picked up the screwdriver from the ground. "I don't know. She was to meet me here and help with installing the barograph, but she hasn't shown," he said.

I detected a bit of darkness in his voice. "That's not like Veronika," I said. "Something must have held her up. I would love to help you myself, but I must get back to the winch. We're replacing the old cables, and the work should be about done."

He nodded and reached for a bolt. "I should have this wrapped up shortly. Thanks. Hopefully we can celebrate a Gold Altitude tonight."

"See ya," I replied, "and good luck!"

An hour or so after operations resumed, I saw the Pilis being pushed tail first toward the flightline. It was one of those gorgeous soaring days with fluffy, billowing cumulus clouds pasted against an azure sky. The clouds' dark, flat bottoms attested to the strength of the thermals. Between tows, I gazed wistfully at the sky, watching the gliders circle overhead in vertically spread gaggles, their steeply banked wings marking the limits of the rising cylinders of warm air. At times, the sunlight reflected from their shiny wings like a flash off a signal mirror, beckoning me.

The flagman pulled me back to reality. The next plane on the flightline was ready to be towed, and judging by its low wings, it was one of the medium-performance breeds, promising a tricky tow. The flagman at the flightline indicated readiness. We replied in kind, signaling that the tow would commence. I started to add power and began to reel the cable in. In a few seconds the glider was airborne, holding level to the ground. When he began climbing I recognized the Pilis from the shape of the wings, one of several we had towed that day. The pilot reached the transition point and started into his extreme angle climb. Textbook! I slowly eased off power, giving him a chance to steepen his climb yet some more.

As he reached zenith, I backed off in anticipation of the slight pushover that reduced cable stress on release. He was nearly overhead now, still attached.

I throttled back, still giving him support, but letting him know it was time. Finally, the pilot lowered the nose.

"*Release,*" I commanded under my breath. The glider was now in a shallow dive. "Release now!" I spoke the words aloud.

"Your mother's sainthood!" I yelled, knowing full well he could not hear me. "It's time to get off!"

The glider continued to lower its nose and entered a vertical dive. In a moment, I heard the rush of air created by his growing speed as he continued unwaveringly toward the ground.

I jerked on the lever to activate the guillotine, severing the cable in an instant. "Pull out, damn you!" I pleaded, but he was now beyond recovery.

"Please, pull out," I screamed, but he continued into the ground.

I was already off the winch and running when the sound of the crash reached my ears like a muffled explosion, the air having been compressed in the fuselage during impact. A small cloud of dust obscured the wreckage as I was nearing it in a full sprint. *Please, God, let him be alive!* I prayed, knowing full well that he couldn't be.

I reached the wreckage a couple of seconds ahead of the cable puller coming from the flightline with several hangers-on. In the area where the cockpit should have been laid the motionless pilot, fuselage fragments covering most of his body. I stood there, panting, paralyzed. I saw Opitz hurdle the shattered wing of the Pilis.

He knelt down next to the body, paused for a moment, then gently turned it over. It was Géza. His head was flattened to the size of a large serving plate and fragments of his mirrored sunglasses were imbedded around the circles that once were his eyes.

I could not look any longer and ran off the field, retching.

Opitz found me at the clubhouse window, staring into space. "We have all the planes back on the ground, and we need everyone's help to put them away," he said quietly. When I didn't move,

891902

CUSTOMER'S ORDER NO.				DATE	Nov 2008	
NAME						
ADDRESS						
CITY, STATE, ZIP						
SOLD BY	CASH	C.O.D.	CHARGE	ON ACCT.	MDSE. RETD.	PAID OUT

QUAN.	DESCRIPTION	PRICE	AMOUNT
1	Caged Metal		17 95
2	Feathers		19 16
3			
4			
5			
6			
7			
8			
9			
10			
11			
12			

RECEIVED BY

adams 4705 **KEEP THIS SLIP FOR REFERENCE**

he put his arm around my shoulder and added, "Géza was my friend also!"

I nodded, and we walked out to the gliders silently. There were several vehicles, including an ambulance, at the crash site. Once the planes were all put away, Opitz got the jeep and drove us to the Top to give our report to Commander Pálinkás.

BITTERSWEET

Wolf Mountain Cemetery, the site of Géza's funeral, was only a couple of kilometers from our neighborhood. For some reason I had always thought Géza was from ÓBuda, from below Fishermen's Bastion on the shores of the Danube. I believed this because we usually met in that area, the location of Bathhouse Café. Now, the choice of the cemetery tells me we might have been living nearer to each other without realizing it.

The cemetery, centuries old, was the site of intense fighting between the Russians and the Germans toward the waning days of the Second World War. Why this earthly portal of the netherworld would be so hotly contested, no one knows. Possibly, one side or the other was trapped here, and the only way out was mortal combat, or maybe holding the area was part of a greater strategy. Certainly, whoever controlled the Hills of Buda would also control all that lay below.

The evidence of hand-to-hand, gravestone-to-gravestone fighting scars these now-silent grounds. Writing the final moments and agonizing death of so many into a macabre diary are the bullet-chipped marble headstones and the patterns of spraying shrapnel etched into hard granite. Here, in the city of the dead, filed among the shattered monuments with their obliterated inscriptions and maimed statues, are the records of the wages of war. They tell the story of a vicious contest that spilled the blood of the living and swelled the ranks of the interred.

By the time I arrived at the cemetery, a large crowd of mourners had gathered in front of the small, sandstone chapel where Géza's coffin was on display. The ornate chapel was created in the style of the baroque; its tall, arched windows of leaded glass depicted the ascent of Jesus and the agony of the Blessed Mother. The building's gray stone was entwined with thick, green ivy, its fingers exploring every angle, every spire, stubbornly growing new shoots where the caretaker's shears had attempted to trim it into submission.

The chapel was too small to accommodate all who came to pay their last respects. From a pool of mourners, a single line formed and slowly advanced toward the ornate door of the chapel, to be swallowed up by the waiting semi-darkness. Spilling from within, a strong smell of incense mixed with the morose sounds of a requiem.

When I stepped through the doorway and my eyes grew accustomed to the subdued light, I saw Géza's coffin on a platform at the head of the nave. A single bouquet of white flowers adorned the shellacked, black coffin, its golden sash draped over the side. Wreaths of white flowers accented with red roses and purple ribbons covered the rest of the platform. Sitting to the right were Géza's mother and only sibling, an older sister, both dressed in the formal black required by the occasion. Missing was his father who like so many other fathers had never returned from the Russian Front. Behind the grieving family stood a group of more distant relatives, none of whom I knew.

Toward my left, at the foot of the coffin, stood a solitary figure, head bowed, hands clenched in prayer, also dressed in black. As the somber procession advanced, I saw her gloved hand reach under her veil with a white, lace-edged handkerchief. Her body convulsed with waves of sobs. I recognized her and a feeling of deep sadness flooded my heart. Veronika!

Near the coffin the incense became overpowering. An irrational fear of being trapped in this house of the dead played on me. I looked around the sad assembly, feeling faint. In the background the sorrowful sounds of the requiem were reduced to the throbbing pulse of the bases and the agonized voice of a solo violin. This was not a place of comfort for me.

I placed my small bouquet at the base of the platform near the flickering eternal flame and walked out of the doleful place into the sunshine. Here, the dark body of the silent throng grew, even as I fled from it. I could not stay for the burial.

Twenty years from the solemn occasion of Géza's funeral, my father, the Whistling Horvath, would be buried in these hallowed grounds, and twenty years after him, my mother.

Now that I was cleared to fly again, my focus turned to earning my Silver Badge. To this end, I made an agreement with Opitz to fly whenever the weather made getting one of the badge requirements possible, instead of spending time with new cadets.

In March, I had earned the first leg of my Silver by staying aloft for five continuous hours after release. This one flight nearly doubled my total flying time. Achieving the other two requirements, a distance flight of fifty kilometers to a new landing point and a net altitude gain of one thousand meters, proved to be more difficult. But I had high hopes for the coming summer. With school out, I wouldn't be limited to weekends and could take advantage of good weather whenever it came, unless, of course, I took a job.

When Opitz asked me to assist him during the coming Summer Flying Camp, I eagerly agreed. Spending two weeks at the mountain without resources would be difficult. My parents were not in a position to help; if anything, they were counting on me to get a job and contribute to the family purse. At times, life gives us few choices.

I showed up for Summer Camp with about two kilos of dry salami and a loaf of bread of similar weight. The bunkhouse was clean, and the farmer who grazed cattle on gliderport property was obliged to deliver twenty-five liters of milk every day, of which I could have as much as I wanted. I would survive.

The morning after checking in, I met Veronika on the trail to the washrooms. This was the first time I had seen her following

Géza's burial, and I was completely unprepared for it. If there had been a way to avoid her, I would have. She had on the same red dress with white polka dots she wore on the occasion of Géza's cross-country seminar. My heart pounded as we approached each other without changing strides.

When we met up, we hugged silently. In the cool morning, I could feel the warmth of her embrace, and I pleaded with my body not to respond. When we stepped back, our hands still holding the other's, I saw infinite sadness in her eyes.

"Veronika, I'm so sorry," I managed.

"How have you been, Istvan?" She responded with a subdued, but even voice. "It's good to see you," she said, looking into my eyes. Her faint smile eased my anxiousness.

"I am here for Summer Camp. How about you?"

"I wish," she said uncertainly. "Alas, I'll have to leave tonight. Perhaps I'll see you again next weekend."

"I'll look forward to it." I nodded stiffly, not knowing what else to say. We exchanged small talk about the camp, carefully staying away from anything of substance. When the day was done, I was surprised to see her approaching the campfire. I was sitting by myself; the new cadets were doing assignments in the bunkhouse. She walked up and asked, "May I join you? The boys said you were out here. I had a change of plans and decided to stay for a couple of days longer." She crossed her arms in front of her and edged closer to the fire.

The evenings were still cool this time of year, so I covered her shoulders with my jacket and put more wood on the fire. We sat silently for a while. As the renewed flames rose toward the sky, she turned to me and in her usual simple way she said, "You know it was all my fault, don't you?" Her face glowed in the light, her eyes hidden by shadows.

"What was your fault?"

"They didn't find anything wrong with the Pilis' controls. That leaves just one other possibility." Her voice lost its measure, and I saw a teardrop wet her cheek.

"And what is that?" I asked, knowing what she meant. "He may have had trouble with his heart or possibly a stroke," I added.

"No!" Veronika shook her head. "He was in good health, young and strong!" She put both her hands on my arm and continued barely audibly.

"Everyone says it was suicide!" She turned toward me, her lovely eyes edged with glistening tears. "… And it was my fault!" she sobbed, gripping my arm hard enough to hurt. Veronika buried her face against my chest. I freed my arm and hugged her. I could feel deep spasms running through her body. After a long pause I broke the silence, trying to sound reassuring.

"That's crazy! Unless I am completely unaware of something, I can't believe that about Géza! And what could you possibly have to do with it? I know he was disappointed when you didn't show to help him install the barograph, but he knew something must have held you up."

"I saw him after you did," Veronika said between sobs, "… just for a few minutes." She turned to face the fire again.

"What happened?"

"It all started the night before," Veronika whispered. "We were to meet at the Top and spend the night in the guest room of the clubhouse. When I arrived, Géza wasn't there. He apparently telephoned my work trying to let me know that he was held up and for us to meet at the Lower Deck the next morning."

"So, what happened?" I repeated.

"I left work early and did not get his message. One of my friends who knew about our arrangements for the weekend called the Top to let me know about the change in plans."

I nodded.

"The clubhouse was full of people having a party when I arrived.

"Pálinkás gave me the message, so I tried to call Géza at work, but no one answered. Since I was not going to fly the next day, I dropped my bag in the guestroom and joined the party. It was the usual thing, you know, we sang songs, danced, and just had a good time."

She stopped to wipe away her tears before going on. I stroked her back reassuringly.

"It was getting late and the party was thinning out when

Pálinkás came up to me. 'Veronika', he said. 'I have to talk to you.' I said, 'Go ahead,' but he wanted to talk in private. I was reluctant because he had obviously been drinking, but he insisted. We went into his office where he started to tell me about his troubles with Éva. I knew he was having marital problems, so I listened and tried to be a friend.

"He said that Éva hated me and asked me to avoid her. I was really bothered. I hadn't done anything to Éva, why would she hate me? Pálinkás said he didn't know the reason and that he did not understand women. He became incoherent. Then he said that he had been admiring me for a long time, and as long as Éva was going to hate us anyway, we might as well give her a reason."

"You left, of course!" I said imploringly, looking into her eyes.

"I tried," Veronika whispered, starting to sob again, "... but he wouldn't let me."

I held her head against me and stroked her hair to calm her.

"He said if I gave him a kiss he would let me go." Veronika was unable to continue. She covered her face with her hands.

"Go on," I said.

"I kissed him, but he wouldn't let go. I yelled, but he just laughed. 'Everyone is gone,' he said. He started groping me. 'It's just you and me, Veronika. You might as well relax.' I fought him off, but he just laughed and held me down, and ... ." Veronika shook off my arms and walked away from the fire, crying.

I was stunned! "That son of a whore!" I yelled in helpless anger, and smacked my fist into my palm. I ran after her. "Stop, Veronika. He will pay for this," I growled, feeling full of hate and rage.

"No!" Veronika screamed. "Pálinkás swore to destroy Géza when Géza confronted him. You must promise you'll do nothing!" Veronika's voice became clear and firm. "Promise!" she repeated.

I would not, could not, promise her anything. Pálinkás was a pig, and somehow I would make him pay!

Slowly the rage in me subsided, and I led Veronika back toward the fire. "How did Géza find out?" I asked finally, wanting to know all of it. "When I saw him just before noon, he knew none of this!"

Veronika finished the sad tale. "After Géza got the Pilis to the flightline, someone who was at the party the night before must have told him something because he drove the jeep to the Top to find me. I was waiting for the shuttle in front of the clubhouse to bring me down when he spotted me. I must have looked awful because he instantly knew something was wrong.

"I didn't want to tell him what happened, but somehow he got it out of me. He acted like a wounded animal. He told me to stay with the jeep and walked angrily to Pálinkás' office. I ran after him fearing what he might do, but when I got there, the door to the clubroom was locked. I could hear them yelling at one another, but couldn't make out what was being said. When Géza came out, I heard Pálinkás scream after him. 'You bastard, you'll pay for this. If she didn't want it, it wouldn't have happened!' "

"And then?" I asked, my voice trembling against my will.

"Géza shoved me aside and walked to the jeep. I pleaded with him, but he kept pushing me away as we walked. 'I've got to think,' he said. Then he jumped into the jeep and drove off."

Veronika stared blindly into the fire and finally added with heart-wrenching agony, "That's the last time I saw him. I asked Pepe to take me down to the Electric and went home. I didn't learn about his death until Monday, when I got to work."

"My dearest Veronika!" I held her tight against me, her head in my hands, kissing her hair and teary face. "My dearest, I wish I could ease your pain." She nestled in my embrace, and we stood pressed against one another for the longest time.

After getting to bed that night I stayed awake plotting various ways to kill Pálinkás. Fortunately for him, or perhaps me, he was on vacation at Lake Balaton and did not return before Summer Camp closed.

★ ★ ★

Veronika did not stay for another day. The next time I saw her was about a month later when she joined me to help prepare about a dozen young pilots for their A test. We worked well as a team; she ran the retrieve crew while I coached piloting skills. By mid-afternoon they were ready for Opitz.

Veronika and I walked through the woods to Cool Valley at the end of the day. We had ice cream and coffee in the little shop near the Electric's end station.

"How are you doing, Veronika? I mean, how are you really doing?" I asked her, holding her free hand between mine on top of the table.

She sipped her espresso and looked at me thoughtfully. "I'm well," she said, then corrected herself. "No! I am better." She smiled a brave smile. "There are days when I am not thinking of him, but life is, … well, life isn't the same. How are you doing?"

"Everything is going well for me, school, flying, everything." I said without conviction.

"So, why the long face? You haven't smiled all day."

When she saw me shrug, she continued, "Come on, whatever it is, you can tell me." She squeezed my hand and smiled her special smile I hadn't seen for a long time.

"I'm doing well," I protested, staring at the bottom of my cup.

"Have you got a girl?"

"No, and I don't need one! They're just a heartbreak," I said, looking away, hoping my voice didn't give me away.

"We all need someone, István. Believe me, loving and being loved is the sweetest thing in life."

"It's not sweet at all, only painful," I blurted out.

"So, you do have someone." Veronika stood up. "Come on, let's walk and we can talk if you want to." Still holding my hand, she led me out. "What's her name?"

"She, … I mean, I don't really have anyone." I asserted. We walked side-by-side, her arm around my waist.

"Come on, István, it's okay to tell me." Veronika stopped walking and stepped in front of me. Her eyes bore into mine.

"I cannot," I said, turning away.

She gently moved my head back to face her. I remained silent.

"Are you in love with me?" She finally asked, holding her gaze.

"I … well, I am, … if you must know," I said softly and tried to pull away. She wouldn't let me. I stopped resisting and pulled her toward me, kissing her roughly, my body trembling.

She kissed me back lightly and pushed me away. "I am not the girl for you, István," she said. "You must find someone your age when you are ready."

"I don't want anyone else!" I blurted out, "I've loved you since we rode on the Electric."

Veronika hugged me. "I guessed it," she said tenderly. "And I love you too, but not that special way. You're a very dear friend."

I finally broke out of her embrace and started up on the trail. Veronika caught up with me after a few steps.

"Stop, István; let's talk. Sometimes, when we are young we become infatuated with—"

I interrupted her. "I can't help myself," I said, not understanding why I felt anger. "No matter how hard I try, I can't stop thinking about you. I promised myself not to tell you any of this, but you asked."

I wanted to turn away, but Veronika once again held my head in her hands and looked deeply into my eyes. "István, hush!" she whispered. The moonlight made her hair sparkle. Without averting her gaze, she kissed me on the mouth in a deliberate way. This time her kiss was not for a friend. I trembled against my will. She took my hand and led me away from the trail. We walked deep into the woods without speaking, stopping occasionally for an embrace and to kiss.

In a clearing of the woods at the base of Three Borders Mountain and in the light of a nearly full moon, she undressed for me. This was the last time I saw her.

The Operations Office was not much different from what I remembered: two desks, a file cabinet and pictures on the wall. The only apparent new addition was a two-way radio, complete with a microphone clipped to its side, connected by coiled wire.

The young woman behind the desk looked up when I entered. "Can I help you?" she asked in the manner all receptionists ask the same question the world over.

"I'm here to meet Commander Fehér. My name is Horváth István," I said in Hungarian.

"Yes, Mr. Horváth, the commander has been expecting you."

She got up from the desk, knocked on the door behind her, and opened it without waiting for an answer.

"Commander Fehér, Mr. Horváth is here to see you."

A man dressed in slacks and a shirt with an open collar emerged from the back office. He was of average height with a slightly receding hairline. He stepped toward me with an extended hand. His face displayed his best feature, a broad, unconditional smile.

"Welcome! I've been looking forward to meeting you. It is not often we have a chance to meet a Diamond Badge pilot around here, especially one who started his flying career at Three Borders Mountain." His voice was light and pleasant, and he sounded sincere.

"Thank you, Commander, for your courtesy," I said taking his extended hand. "I consider it a privilege to be here."

"Nothing, nothing." The commander continued. "As I said, it's a pleasure. After your call, I arranged for a brief check flight, and if you have no objections, I'd like to be the one flying with you. Regrettably, there are some formalities we must take care of first."

"Of course."

"Here are the papers, mostly formalities as I said, but you know, procedures. You must have some of the same bureaucratic obstacles in the United States too, no?" Still smiling, he picked up a couple of forms from his desk.

"Possibly more," I laughed, "and as you requested, here are my passport and pilot's license."

With the formalities taken care of, we were on our way to the north end of the field, where a line of gliders waited to be towed aloft by the winch.

Commander Fehér was thorough. The aluminum two-seater was checked from wingtip to wingtip before we strapped in for takeoff.

"Your controls," the commander said.

I reset the altimeter to a thousand meters above sea level.

"Thank you! I'm ready!" I reached over, closed the canopy, and latched it. After a last check of the controls for freedom of movement, I gave thumbs up to the young cadet at the wingtip to level the wing. The flagman on the opposite side twirled his flag to confirm our readiness to the winch operator.

We started rolling moments after the return signal, rapidly picking up speed. At about thirty-five kilometers per hour, I pulled on the stick and coaxed the glider into the air. We climbed gradually to fifty meters above the ground, at which point I raised the nose of the glider more and more steeply. On this portion of the tow we were in a sitting position on our backs, our feet slightly above our heads.

I felt the winch throttle-off, and I pulled back on the stick even more. From the corner of my eye I saw the commander reach for the controls, pause, then relax. The winch reduced power as I leveled off at the top. I pushed the nose down and released. We were much higher than needed for a landing pattern.

"Commander, we have plenty of altitude, would you like me to perform some maneuvers?" I asked.

"Thanks to your excellent tow, we are high enough to do what we need for the check-out. How about some seven-twenty turns and a few stalls?" he said with a smile.

After landing we walked back to the office.

"You're a fine pilot," the commander said, "hope you'll have fun this afternoon. The only thing I must ask you is to stay in the area. A cross-country flight has not been authorized."

"Thank you, Commander, for your time and courtesy. I'll stay in the immediate vicinity, that is, if I can stay up at all," I responded.

"I am sure you will. Please stop by and visit after you land. Thank you for the flight." He turned toward the office.

"Commander," I called after him.

He stopped and turned around.

"Commander, if you would give me another minute," I said. "When I was a student here, the operations commander was a man by the name of Pálinkás. Did you know him?"

"No," Fehér shook his head, "I know of him. Why do you ask?"

"Would you by chance know what became of him?"

The commander's soft, blue eyes turned to the color of steel.

He looked at me quizzically, then pointed toward the mountain. "See that woodless area just this side of Must Land Peak? One day, in the late fifties," he said, "Pálinkás jumped into an old Russian biplane they used for towing gliders, and crashed. Rumor had it that he was drunk."

"I see."

"Was he a friend of yours?"

"No," I said, "just someone I remembered."

It was growing into a beautiful soaring day with white cumulus clouds popping from horizon to horizon. The glider assigned to me was modest by current standards, but it turned out to be surprisingly easy to fly. After release, I stumbled into an area of broad lift and climbed to cloud-base through a gaggle of school ships.

From three thousand meters the area looked unchanged, except for the brown smog that now covered the Danube basin. *Progress!*

As I headed toward another promising cloud, memories came flooding back. I remembered the incredible winter flight when I ferried a Vöcsök primary from the Top to the Lower Deck. It was early morning, just after sunrise. The Danube valley was covered under thick fog, and the fog was spilling over the pouting lower lip of the ridge, tumbling into the crystal-clear air of the southern basin like a giant waterfall.

Upon landing, the primary's skid drew a long, straight line on the frost-covered grass.

I remembered the glories and the heartbreaks, the nameless and those who changed my life. I remembered Opitz, now larger than life; Pepe, the mechanic who could make motors run without parts; Zoltán, who taught me how to be responsible.

Memories, images real enough to touch, flooded back. Here comes Commander Pálinkás, his white-scarf flapping in the breeze. May his soul forever burn in the fires of Hell! Here is the open, friendly face of Géza, his Silver Badge shining on the lapel of his flight suit. And how could one forget the bittersweet memory of the beautiful Veronika, the girl we both loved, smiling her special smile. Veronika, who first showed me the sweetness of a woman. Amidst the woods that now swam below me, I learned about love and pain.

From just below cloud-base, I coaxed the glider into a spin and rode it down to pattern altitude. As the plane spun around with its nose pointing at the ground, all I could think of was the past. I got what I came for; I thought of all of them and said my goodbyes. I made a gentle landing for the last time at Three Borders Mountain.

PART FIVE

FLAMES OF ANGER

On Tuesday morning, October 23, 1956, I walked through the gate at Csepel Metal Works, on my way home. Weary from the rigors of the graveyard shift and having had little sleep the night before, I was ready to call it a day. Later that afternoon I would have a couple of classes at the university, and then the cycle would repeat itself: work, sleep, school. A seemingly endless succession.

In spite of my physical state, I was preoccupied with the recent political events sweeping Hungary. Pressure for reforms had been mounting on the government from many quarters, resulting in a grudging relaxation of the iron-fisted control over the printed media. For the first time in a decade, newspapers and magazines began printing truths about conditions in Hungary.

Our group, the Hungarian Indians, did its share of pressuring. We bombarded the capitol with leaflets demanding, among other things, the departure of the occupying Russian military from Hungarian soil. A couple of months back, we had formed an alliance with the prestigious Petőfi Circle that took its name from Hungary's beloved poet, Petőfi Sándor, an unimpeachable patriot and a much loved icon of liberty who led the 1848 War of Independence to free Hungary from the Hapsburg yoke. This group of intellectuals understood the perils of socialism and worked tirelessly to find legal means to force reforms.

Convenient to my streetcar transfer point, Lajo's fencepost mail drop was only a half-block out of my way. This day there was a message waiting in its hold. Lajos invited me to join a demonstration in front of the Radio Budapest Building, a stronghold of the government's propaganda machine. I was to bring a placard demanding freedom of speech, a right guaranteed by the Hungarian Constitution, but denied by those in power.

Even before the bus reached Brody Sándor Street, on which the radio building stood, huge crowds blocked the way. People numbering in the tens of thousands crammed the streets and neighboring plazas. The demonstrators waved Hungarian flags with the communist symbol cut from their middle, and strident, antigovernment placards. When a bus or trolley became stranded, the crowd would chant in unison, "If you're Hungarian, join us!"

I got off the bus and began making my way on foot. The scene I came upon a block from the radio station astounded me; a group of young people surrounded a small contingent of city police, demanding their weapons.

"We're here to keep order," the police pleaded, "we're not ÁVO."

The crowd would have none of that. "Give us your guns, or we will take them from you," they shouted.

The trapped policemen hesitated. When the circle around them drew tighter, the ranking officer stepped forward, holding his weapon at ready. "We are here to keep order!" he said. "Don't make us use force."

A young man sporting a university pin on his lapel stepped in front of the officer. "You're not our protectors; you're the servants of our enemies," he said, staring into the man's eyes, ignoring the leveled weapon. The crowd shouted epithets and spat toward the cornered men. The young man took the gun from the officer's hands and ordered the others to give up theirs. Visibly shaken, they laid their weapons on the sidewalk.

A block away, heavily armed members of the hated ÁVO protected the radio station. Similar in organization to the Soviet KGB, the ÁVO were the tool with which the state kept its citizens at bay.

The unruly crowd upended granite blocks from the streets and hurled them at the station's massive doors. In a short time the once impregnable gates of the fortress-like building were in danger of being breached. I scaled a wall and watched with terrified fascination.

Suddenly, the blare of megaphones overpowered the angry chants of the multitude. "Cease your assault, or be responsible for the consequences!"

When repeated warnings went unheeded, the ÁVO fired into the crowd. The demonstrators became incensed and intensified their attack. Cries for help, medical assistance, and for weapons to fight the ÁVO spread through the gathering.

From my perch on top of the wall, I saw bodies and injured being carried away despite the sporadic fire. The pressure of the crowd prevented me from getting closer, but I found myself caught up in the heat of the moment, joining in the shouting: "No more! No more! No more! No more!" The cry, thousands strong, drowned out the guns.

Armed with weapons confiscated from police around the capital, the crowd breached the doors and entered the building. Savage smallarms fire greeted them. Dozens fell. Cries for revenge spread through the crowd. One by one, the ÁVO men were either killed or forced to surrender. I later learned that angry mobs hunted down known members of ÁVO, summarily hanging them by the neck from light poles.

Fearing the worst, I fled the area and found myself among another large crowd marching on the parliament.

★ ★ ★

The hard won victory in the fight for the radio station paid instant dividends. The radio began airing news of the uprising the rest of the day. Radio Budapest, the way of informing the country simultaneously, was now in the hands of the Resistance.

For four days and nights the station was free of government control. Then, suddenly, in the middle of a newscast, it fell silent.

Radio Budapest resumed broadcasting from a secret location the following day. The populace was advised that Soviet units stationed in Hungary were petitioned by the "lawful" government to protect it from the belligerent West and its puppet counterrevolutionary elements. It urged citizens to stay at home and promised that as soon as order was reestablished, the Russian military would return to their bases. "The counterrevolution against the people has been crushed," the broadcast claimed.

In truth, the government was in hiding. Many of the top leaders fled to the Soviet Union. The Hungarian military, called upon to put down the rebellion, did nothing, and in some cases fought alongside the Resistance. The occupying Russian forces were badly mauled by people fighting with their bare hands and in a span of five short days were pushed out of Hungary.

Early morning on Sunday, November 4, 1956, mechanized armored divisions of the Soviet Red Army reentered Hungary and raced toward the capital under the cover of MiG-17 fighter jets. In a matter of twenty-four hours, Hungary was once again trampled, while the nations of Europe and the West focused their attention on the crisis at the Suez Canal.

★ ★ ★

Flame and smoke belched from the business end of the tank's cannon as it recoiled, ready for the next round. The wall of the building across the square erupted in dust and flames. The sound of the shot ricocheted through the square and rattled the windows. Bits of the building fell to the ground, adding to the growing pile of debris strewn across the sidewalk. By the time the gaping hole emerged from behind the dust cloud, the turret moved a couple of clicks and the barrel elevated. The heavy gun fired again. The new hole was over the third balcony below the fourth floor. A few more shots and the upper floors of the building would collapse onto the rest. *Unless—*

I sprang away from the wall at the far corner of the stricken building and ran for the gate across the street. My two companions stayed behind. If the gate were locked, I would probably not have enough time to get out of the line of fire. Still, I had to try.

I hit the gate with full force, shielding the benzene-filled bottle with my body. The lever gave. The door, inset into the portal, was not locked. The muffled sound of the next volley reached me just as the door slammed shut behind me.

In the courtyard I slipped on the dew soaked cobblestones and nearly broke the bottle. I slid on one knee and braced myself with my forearm. The precious bottle was our only chance to stop the Russian madmen from shooting the square apart. Béla's rifle was only good for annoying them and perhaps to confine the tank's gunner, keeping him from using the top mounted machine gun.

I sprinted across the courtyard, praying that the door at the far end was also open, so I could make it out to the next street and into the house behind the tank. *Hope, hope, hope!*

My throat hurt, and my lungs screamed for air as I flew up the stairs, two at a time, rounding the corners with my shoulder banging against the walls. First level, second, third, and fourth. *High enough.*

The door of the flat above the tank was locked. It was a heavy door, from a time before the Second World War when things were still made well. I frantically looked around for something to help me break in, and spotted a cast-iron mailbox on a steel stand near the elevator. Property of the post office, *too heavy, but it would have to do.* I set the bottle near the door, then dragged the mailbox to the apartment. Almost there, I heard steps pounding up the stairway. *One person.*

I slipped around the corner, ready for anything. From my position I could see a body in full stride make the turn, holding onto the rail. *Relief!* One of the companions I had left behind on the street.

"Gergely, come back," I yelled after him. The sound of the heavy steps momentarily stopped, then resumed.

When he reached me, he was completely out of breath. His chest heaved as he gulped in and exhaled air. White saliva caked in the corners of his mouth.

"We have to break into this flat," I explained. "The tank should be below the balcony."

Gergely, still gasping, reached for the mailbox. We swung the heavy iron box, hitting the door with force. There was a deafening sound in the corridor, followed by the blast of yet another shot from the tank's cannon. We struck again, splintering the wood, and the door burst open.

I handed the bottle to Gergely and rushed to the balcony. "Find a piece of rag for the bottle. Hurry!"

While he disappeared into the next room, I opened the balcony door and fell to the floor. Crawling on my belly, I edged near the gap under the glass half-wall of the balcony. The glass was textured for privacy, preventing me from seeing the street. I slid a patio chair in front of me for cover and peered over the top. The tank let loose again, and I heard the sickening sound of impact across the square, followed by a muted rumble. The corner of the building collapsed.

Bastards!

The tank was farther than I had hoped. Reaching it with the bottle would be a miracle.

"Here," Gergely said, handing me the bottle with the wick already stuffed in it.

"Get down! If they spot us it's all over," I said, as much to myself as to Gergely as I fished for my lighter in my topcoat pocket. "We only have this one shot. If we get separated, meet me at Kálmán Square at the underground's entrance. Let Béla know if you see him."

Gergely nodded. I raised myself to a crouching position and looked over the backrest of the chair one more time. The tank hadn't moved, but the turret was in motion again. The gunner's hatch on the top of the turret was propped open. I lit the benzine soaked rag and grabbed the rail on the top of the glass wall with my left hand.

"Here it goes, with the help of God!" I yelled and tossed the bottle toward the tank just as it fired again.

The bottle arched toward its target, barely wobbling, trailing smoke as it flew. It hit the tank at the junction of the turret and the hatch, just above the five-pointed red star. The benzine burned with heavy, black smoke, some of it dripping off the tank onto the ground. For several seconds nothing happened.

A gloved hand appeared. Before the hatch fully opened, a pillar of flame filled the opening and thrust toward the sky. In a moment, a huge explosion rocked the square, sending parts of the tank into the air and blowing the turret off its mount. When it was over, the turret rested on the tank's body at an awkward angle, the barrel pointing toward the ground. The tank was on fire.

Gergely and I hugged silently.

"Take that, you Russian sons of Hungarian whores!" I yelled triumphantly, but without joy.

I hid in the gate tunnel of a house similar to the one behind the burning tank. Gergely was gone, he ran off in the opposite direction when he saw a Russian unit close off the boulevard. We would have a better chance getting to the Buda side of the Danube alone. I explored the street toward Kálmán Square, slipping into one doorway after another, but upon hearing sporadic small arms fire and the sound of heavy armor, I returned to hide again. It seemed the Russians had gotten reinforcements and now controlled the major intersections. I heard sirens. The sky over the city was heavy with smoke. *Have to find better shelter and try again after dark,* I thought.

Finally, I screwed up enough courage to get within a few blocks of Chain Bridge. Here I ran into an approaching Russian patrol and was forced to back away. *What would I tell them if they captured me?* I speculated feverishly. *I would tell them that I was prevented from going home by the fighting.* As flimsy as this sounded, it would probably be the only excuse the Russians would accept. I attempted translating this into Russian as I sprinted from doorway to doorway, vocalizing the words.

I held up in front of a locked courtyard gate, temporarily out of sight. After catching my breath, I peered out and saw armed men spilling out of a truck, fanning out in all directions. Three soldiers were coming toward me in the center of the street and two on each side. *I'm done for!* I thought, fighting off panic. Then out of nowhere, a single shot rang out and ricocheted off the pavement.

The soldiers scattered and opened fire, shooting at shadows. I waited until the firing stopped then ran.

"*Stoy!*" came the faraway command, but I pretended not to hear it.

"*Stoy!*" The command to stop was louder now, accompanied by the sound of booted steps running on the pavement.

I glanced over my shoulder. They were still some distance away, and I was near another portal. My heart pounded as I made a break for it, only to find myself trapped in a small courtyard, separated from the street behind it by a high wrought-iron fence. I scaled the fence and fell headfirst onto the sidewalk on the other side, suffering a gash just above my left knee inflicted by the fence's lance-like spikes. *No time for pain.* I ran down the street and saw yet another truck with the hated red star on its door deploying troops. I turned and ran the other way.

I was at full speed when a large man stepped in front of me, grabbing me. He pinned me to the wall. "The Russians are everywhere," he said, "Follow me!"

I nodded and stopped struggling.

He led me swiftly to a stairway and we started climbing the steps two at a time in a dead run. Inside a well-furnished flat, the man introduced himself, his wife, and his teenage daughter. I told them my name and the cover story I cooked up, being trapped on the wrong side of the Danube by the fighting.

My host smiled. "We have been watching you from the time you fell onto the street, fearful you would be captured," he said. "The Russians are rounding up everyone found outside."

The lady of the house left and returned with a washbowl. She started cleaning my bleeding scrapes with a soapy cloth. I felt self-conscious about my sweaty, dirty state, but sat gratefully while she attended to one wound after another. A few minutes later, the daughter brought in a plate of bread, slices of pork, and peppers. I didn't realize how famished I was until the first bite. I hadn't eaten anything in the last twenty-four hours.

I spent the first hours of the night sleeping on the divan, sharing the sitting room with a piano. Sometime after midnight, the lady of the house awakened me.

"István," she said with urgency, "the Russians are going door to door, searching through the houses on both sides of the street."

I jumped up and pulled on my trousers.

"Quickly, please, follow me."

She led me to her daughter's room and had me slide under the bed.

"If the Russians come, she will pretend to be asleep. Please don't make any noise."

I waited for what seemed eternity under the bed, at times nearly overcome by fear-induced nausea. The poor girl above me quivered spasmodically. The motion set off by her tremors made the headboard rattle against the wall. She would whisper, "Sorry," each time it happened. I tried calming her. "Should I be discovered," I told her soothingly, "I will tell the Russians that I broke into your flat and hid here without anyone knowing." This seemed to quiet her. About an hour later, my rescuers sounded the all clear. The Russians had moved on without entering the building when they found the front gate locked.

I awoke mid-morning and the lady fed me breakfast. Her husband came home a few minutes later from a foray to a nearby store.

"The fighting has stopped," he said. "A lot of people are stranded on both sides of the river, wanting to get home. The Russians are allowing foot traffic across the bridges for those who have papers showing that they are on the wrong side."

"Is the Electric running?"

"Nothing is running; you'll have to walk."

"What else have you heard?"

"Not much else. The talk is that the United Nations is closely monitoring events in Hungary."

I thanked them for their warm, courageous hospitality and set out toward Chain Bridge. Without doubt, I owed my freedom and possibly my life to these kind, brave people.

On the way to Chain Bridge, I flagged down a truck loaded with older workers. They turned out to be members of a work brigade, summoned to clear away the barricades blocking the Palace Hill Tunnel. One of the men in the truck held the Socialist flag of Hungary. We were waved through the Russian checkpoint without inspection.

Neither Gergely nor Béla showed at the café in ÓBuda. I waited the better part of the day for them. Apparently, the café was one of only a few places open in the whole city. While there, I heard rumors of people being shot on sight by the ÁVO and the

Russians if they suspected them of any role in the uprising. I wondered how much one could trust word-of-mouth information; still, my spirits were lifted when Jenö, the afternoon waiter, brought me up to date. There were new pockets of resistance flaring up in the city and for the first time, around the country, he said. "The Security Council voted on a resolution denouncing Soviet aggression, but the Russians vetoed it. The Voice of America is broadcasting that NATO forces are massing on the Austrian border, ready to intervene."

I shook my head. "Don't believe it! They wouldn't risk World War Three for little Hungary!"

Jenö also said that according to Radio Free Europe, some of the Hungarian military had turned against the state, and incredibly, a Russian unit was fighting on our side in the city of Debrecen. The Voice of America was urging the "freedom fighters" to hang on, UN intervention was only hours away.

Two hours later I was home.

I spent the evening doing my best to play down the events of the last twenty-four hours to keep the family from being unduly concerned. We listened to the radio and heard that a provisional government had been sworn in and everything was returning to normal. This meant that the rebellion had been put down.

Father and Laci left in the morning, hoping to reach the plant where they both worked. After they departed, I told mother that I, too, needed to check in with my school and my work. This was a total fabrication as I never intended to do either, but the truth would have frightened her. Once out on the street, I headed for Gyuszi's well. After making sure I was unobserved, I climbed down the well to retrieve the German Luger I had hidden there a couple of years earlier. I had found the pistol in a metal ammunition box, packed in grease, on one of my hikes into the forest on Wolf Mountain. The box was sticking out of the dirt in an erosion-scarred runoff area. There were no extra bullets, but the clip in the gun was full. Since owning any weapon was strictly forbidden, I had hidden the box and its contents in the well without specific plans for what to do with it. *Now,* I thought, *it would come in* handy. *Even a handgun was better than bare hands.*

With the gun tucked away under my shirt in the front of my trousers, I tried to decide what to do. *First,* I thought, *I have to learn the fate of my friends. If the brick mailbox is empty, I'll try to get back to the café in ÓBuda. Someone should know something.*

As I neared the crossing at the bronze statue of the Russian Soldier, erected to honor the "liberators" of Hungary from Hitler's Third Reich, I saw a roadblock. The Russians were inspecting all pedestrian and vehicular traffic leaving the city. When I got there they waved me through. Relieved, I credited my good fortune to the fact that I was going the opposite direction. Still, the Luger weighed heavily in my belt. Coming around a slight curve in the road, I was struck by the sight of Russian armor: tanks, personnel carriers, and jeeps, all pointing toward the city. I was trapped!

I couldn't turn around; the roadblock behind me would be just as deadly because the Red officers who saw me go by minutes ago would know I had turned around and would want to know why. There was no choice; I had to continue straight ahead. *Maybe I could toss away the Luger without them noticing,* I thought. Alas, I realized I was being watched.

Slowly, but not too slowly, I approached the blockade. By the time I finally reached the point between the two military vehicles where a group of soldiers and officers were checking papers, I had reconciled myself to what was surely to come.

"Good day, officers," I managed in broken Russian, forcing a broad smile. "Glad to see you keeping order."

My friendly smile was not reciprocated. "Your papers," came the curt demand, also in Russian.

I silently handed the officer my identification book.

He looked at me, looked at my picture, then looked at me again.

"Where are you going?"

"I'm looking for an open store. The stores near here are all closed because of the trouble, and we need food. I have a sick, five year old sister waiting for some milk."

The officer fingered the slim, wooden box hanging from his belt and looked at me suspiciously. I knew that the box contained a long barreled side arm, standard issue for the officers of the Soviet Army. He motioned to one of the soldiers standing by with a submachine gun slung over his shoulder. "Search him!"

A million thoughts raced through my mind. *I shall not die as a coward!* I resolved. *Someone, someday, will remember me with pride!*

The soldier stepped in front of me and patted down my overcoat. He then turned me by my shoulders and shoved me against the side of the truck. He continued his search from behind. I had an uncontrollable urge to turn and run, but stood motionless. He scurried his hands down my legs and around my waist.

I will go for his weapon and take some of these bastards to the grave with me! I pulled in my stomach as far as I could, hoping to make the gun inconspicuous. I felt his hands pass over it, continuing the search. My forehead was wet at the hairline with perspiration.

He turned me to face him again. "*Menj!*" he said in Hungarian, pointing down the road.

His mother's sainthood, he missed the Luger, I thought, *or maybe he'll shoot me from behind.* I didn't move. The soldier shoved me away. I ignored him and extended my hand toward my identification papers, still in the hands of the officer. "Have a good day, Comrade!" I said.

His intensely blue eyes stayed cold and piercing. I tried to keep my hand from trembling. "Move on!" he grunted finally, handing me the papers with a disdainful look.

Somehow, I managed to say *dosvidanya* and turned to go, feeling the gun drop lower in my trousers with every step. As soon as I was out of sight, I tossed the Luger into the roadside bushes.

There was a message under the brick from Lajos; I recognized the writing. "We will try to regroup at South Station. The Russians are not in control there." The note wasn't dated.

South Station was at least an hour away on foot, much longer when one needed to avoid Russian patrols. I cautiously worked my way toward Palace Hill and headed out in the direction of the rail station. Except for a few people peering out from doorways, I saw no one about.

As I neared South Station on Krisztina Boulevard, several Russian personnel carriers sped by me while I hid behind a row of shrubs after jumping over a low fence. Soon I heard small arms fire. *Should I continue toward the hostilities,* I wondered, *or turn around and go home?* I decided on staying the course.

I approached South Station from between a row of beautiful old townhouses that lined Palotai Street at the base of Palace Hill. Many of the rococo-style buildings still bore the savage reminders of World War II, bullet holes and plasterless repairs scarring the walls. Still, these very buildings gave the flavor and character to this beautiful, romantic area of the city known as the Palace District.

As I slipped from one doorway to the next, the sounds of intense fighting grew. In a small park at the eastern boundary of South Station's giant square, the smoldering hulk of a Russian armored vehicle told the tale of the recent past. Gentle rain began falling as I continued cautiously forward. Suddenly, the gunfire stopped.

My momentary relief gave way to horror when I came upon several bodies lying on the sidewalk. *Civilians.* Steam rose from the bodies as the rain pelted them, attesting to their recent death. These poor people had probably been caught in crossfire.

I regained my composure and pressed on. At the confluence of Némtvölgyi Street and Krisztina Boulevard, I had an unobstructed view of the rail yard below. A Russian tank occupied this depressed part of the square. The tank commander had chosen his location well, having all approaches vulnerable to his heavy cannon.

Before me were several armed civilians, shielded by a cement retaining wall that prevented traffic from plunging off the five-meter-high embankment. I approached them with my hands in plain view. "I am with the Resistance," I shouted, "hold your fire!"

Without answering, a man dressed in a gray, mid-length topcoat motioned me closer.

"We're about to flank the tank," Graycoat explained, jabbing toward the station with a length of sausage. "We could use help carrying the ammunition."

"What's the plan?"

He took a bite from the sausage and pointed to the railroad tracks that appeared only as dark lines in the fading light. The tracks were depressed into the ground so that the passengers could walk right into the cars from the platform without having to climb or descend steps.

"The depression is nearly a meter deep and should give us all the cover we need to get close to the tank."

"Except for the fact that the tank could fire into it until the very end," I said and took the sausage from his hand.

He looked at me with steady eyes without changing expression.

"You got it summed up. So, what will it be; can we count you in?"

I broke the sausage in half and handed him the longer piece.

"Where's the ammunition?" I asked, taking a bite. "We should be helped by the dark."

Loaded down with clips of ammunition, benzene, and several bottles suitable for making Molotov cocktails, the four of us crawled toward the tank along the edge of the depression. It was slow going. The men we left behind the retaining wall fired on the tank from time to time. We could hear the bullets ricochet off the tank and the concrete. The tank would rotate its turret every few minutes, pinning us down. When we thought that the gunner's sight was obstructed, we sprang up and advanced a few meters. The track gradually sloped into a deepening pool of rainwater. We continued sloshing through it on our bellies.

We were now behind the tank and off to the side, about twenty meters away. The leader motioned for the bottles. I filled several with the help of my nearest companion, backs against the wall of the platform, feet against the rail. We installed the wicks.

"When I say *now*, light the wick," Graycoat said, "on my count of three we will get up and run a few steps to get off a good throw. The men on Krisztina will keep the Russians in check." He peered over the edge and waited. Satisfied, he turned toward us. "Ready?"

We nodded solemnly.

"Now!"

We lit the fuses. The leader counted. On three we stood up, ran toward the tank, and tossed the firebombs in near unison.

Moments after the bottles impacted the hatch flew open and soldiers wearing the leather headgear and dark uniforms of the Soviet Armored Division piled out of the tank. The burning benzene illuminated the area and the fighters on Krisztina Boulevard opened fire. We added our volleys from our shielded position. The Russians cowered behind the burning tank and returned fire with handguns.

This went on for about a minute. The tank, though burning, did not explode. One of the Russians made an attempt to reach the heavy machine gun mounted on top. He was summarily cut down.

Just as we were gaining the upper hand, new players entered the fight. From a perch high on the south rim surrounding the station, we began receiving small arms fire. Our flank was completely exposed, and we did not have weapons capable of reaching our new attackers. Bullets whizzed through our position, bouncing off the cement wall that until now had provided us with a safe haven.

We stood and ran to get out of the line of fire. One of our companions was hit several times and collapsed. I felt a bullet strike metal in the rucksack on my back and ran with renewed strength. The young man ahead of me stumbled and fell between the tracks. He lay there motionless as I ran by him.

Graycoat and I made it up to the boulevard and got momentarily out of range. Far on the other side of the station an armored personnel carrier rounded the plaza toward us. Several men to our right, men I did not know were there until this moment, opened fire at the armored vehicle. We dropped to the ground. I shed the rucksack and rolled toward the curb for protection.

The Russians continued toward us, and the firing intensified. I made myself as small a target as I could against the curb. The leader got up and shouted toward the men across the street, "I'm coming over; cover me!" He grabbed the rucksack and ran toward them. I saw him reach safety behind a pillar of a portal.

The armored vehicle screeched to a halt about three hundred meters away and started to disgorge soldiers. In seconds, a hail of bullets were exchanged between them and our men. I was fully exposed, but not yet noticed. Slowly, I crawled toward a bus pull-out inset a few meters ahead of me. *If I could reach it*, I thought, *I would be shielded from the Russians.* A pool of rainwater started to build in front of me, dammed up by my body against the curb.

The exchange of fire continued as I reached the inset. Bullets slammed into the granite pavers around me, and I felt sharp pain on the inside of my right shin. I had been hit! My exploring fingers found the wound and returned bloody. I felt intense pain, but I could move my leg, ankle, and toes. Every time I moved, new shots would impact around me. They had me pinned down. I felt exhausted. All I could do was wait.

I woke up and felt the rainwater trickle past my face. It was still dark, but very quiet. I was shivering. I raised myself to look around and was instantly jabbed by sharp pain. I sat up in the water and checked the tear in my pant leg, hoping not to find sharp edges. There were none. Possibly, a spent bullet or a piece of dislodged granite had slammed into my shin without breaking the bone. *Just a flesh wound,* I rejoiced, and clambered onto my feet.

James A. Michener's 'A Bridge at Andau,' first published by the Ballantine Publishing Group in 1957, gives a more detailed historical account of the 1956 Hungarian uprising.

ANYU

I walked up the stone-paved path from the front gate to the porch with apprehension. Without telephones it was impossible to communicate with my parents, and I could guess how much worry I had probably caused. I hadn't been home for days, and I was wearing battle-soiled clothes; my right pant leg torn and bloody.

Mother was sitting on the porch, peeling potatoes for the evening meal. She had a pan nearly full of lengthwise quartered potatoes in her lap, and a basket of the unpeeled stock and rinds at her feet.

"*Jóreggelt, Anyu,*" I said, greeting her, taking care to sound calm and unconcerned. She finished removing the last piece of skin from the potato before looking up. She looked me over while I waited respectfully for her greeting.

"Hello, son," she said, holding eye contact. "We've been worried."

I didn't like it when she was this calm. I would rather have her nag. Her usually dancing, golden-brown eyes were deep-set and looked tired. She got to her feet and lifted the pan to her hip. With her other hand she pointed to the basket still on the ground and walked into the kitchen. I gathered up the basket and followed her.

She put the pan on the table and sprinkled salt on the contents. I stood behind her, waiting for her to tell me what to do with the basket. She spoke without turning around, emphasizing every word. "Where have you been?" Her voice had a mixture of concern and disapproval as she turned to face me. She pointed to a spot near the stove where she wanted me to place the basket. She continued, "In troubled times like these, people need to stay close to one another."

"I know, Anyukám; I wish I could have let you—"

She raised her hand to silence me. "Look, son." Her eyes rested on me again, "I know you're mostly grown, but I worry. So does the rest of the family." She ladled warm water into the washbasin from the stove's hot water tank and motioned for me to take off my clothes. I undressed to my shorts while her eyes inspected me from head to toe. She picked a rag from the line above the stove, wet it, and started sponging the blood off my leg. She slowly worked her way toward the open wound just as she had always done when we hurt ourselves. The wound started to bleed again, and at one point I flinched and pulled away.

"Oww!"

"Nasty! Suppose you got this at work?" The tone of her voice carried her disbelief. "And how about these?" She pointed to the scrapes on my knees and shoulder.

"Mom—"

"Don't! I really don't need to know," she said. She took a spool of gauze from the credenza drawer and bandaged the wound. I watched her rinse the rag then disappear into the bedroom.

"Here, put these on," she said, returning with fresh clothes draped over her arm.

I dressed silently. By the time I finished, she was back to preparing supper.

"Your brothers have been here every day, and so has your father." She put the pan on the stove and brushed down her apron. "I can't tell you how worried we've been, wondering if you were dead or alive. I thought when you came home two days ago you would be here to stay." With expert hands she peeled an onion and started dicing it.

"Yesterday, two men came around asking for you."

"Two men?" My stomach muscles contracted. "What'd they want?"

"They didn't say. They asked a lot of questions. I guess I'd better make more food, now that you're home," she added, offering forgiveness, but maintaining the same inflection. She finished dicing the onion and dumped the cuttings on top of the potatoes. My eyes started to water. She put the lid on and moved the pan to a hotter area on the stove.

"They asked where you were. I told them I sent you to your grandparents for some food. I don't think they believed me. Would you know anything about this?"

"I can't imagine who they could've been. Maybe the university or the steel mill sent them out, wanting to know when I'll be back," I suggested, desiring to allay her concerns. But my mouth was dry.

"Son, I don't think so. They had a way about them I didn't like.

"They said they would be back in a day or two, but when I asked where you could contact them, they just went on asking more questions."

"What kind of questions, Mom? What did they look like?"

She gathered the potato peels into the now empty basket and put it into my hands. "Why don't you toss the peels over the fence for the neighbor's chickens," she said, then continued about the men as if she were still talking about feeding the chickens. "They were older, in their thirties. They wanted to know when I saw you last, and if you were home when the trouble started." Anyu put her hands behind her and leaned back against the edge of the table. "They scared me to death." She sounded childlike now, her voice small and scared. Her eyes were shiny, and I didn't think it was the onions.

I hugged her without saying anything.

On my way to the backyard, I thought about the likely explanation for the men's visit and who they might have been. I couldn't come up with anything reassuring.

Mother was putting fresh wood on the fire when I got back.

"Where is everybody?" I asked.

"Your father and Laci went to the plant to see if it reopened. They left about an hour ago, and Dodi walked your sister to the neighbors to ask about school."

"Mom, I'm sorry to have worried you, but now I must get some sleep. Except for a couple of hours, I haven't slept in days."

"Go ahead, but first, you need to know this. Pista, I'm afraid for you." She turned away from the stove and took my hands into hers, her eyes resting on mine with sadness. "I don't know what you've been doing, but I know you; enough to know that you'd be in the thick of what has been going on." Her voice broke a bit, but she straightened her body and continued.

"I think those men came here to take you away. There are people, some of them children, being shot for taking part in the uprising. Maybe someone said something they shouldn't have, or saw you do something. I don't know." Her eyes filled with tears. She let go of my hands and hugged me. "You said nothing about those days you were gone."

"Mom, I don't think anyone knows anything. These people are cannibals, turning on their own kind. And as far as the Russians are concerned, I only did what anyone would—"

"I don't want to know what you did, but even if you were only at the demonstrations that started all this, and I know you were, you're in grave danger."

I stepped back, holding her by the shoulders at arm's length. Her face was contorted with pain. I swallowed. "It'll be all right, Mom."

Her hands slipped along my arms until they met mine. She lifted them and pulled them against her bosom. "Son, you should think about fleeing the country. I heard the minefields at the Austrian border have been cleared, and the border guards are letting people out.

"It breaks my heart to tell you this, but I would rather have you out of my life than dead." She could no longer control her tears and put her head back on my chest. I locked my arms around her, and we rocked back-and-forth without speaking.

"Anyukám, I don't deserve you."

I slept soundly and woke around five PM, just minutes before my brother László came back from work.

"Pista, where have you been? The world is upside down and you disappear. And on top of everything, I got this!" he said, shoving a piece of paper into my hands.

I didn't look at it. "What is it?"

"My draft notice. I have to report to the induction office in three days. Two weeks from next Monday I'll be in training camp."

I glanced at the official *Notice to Report* and handed it back. "That's nuts! With the regime's fate very much in doubt, how can they expect anyone to report? There's still fighting going on, and some of the military is on our side."

"No, there isn't! The uprising has been put down! People connected with the opposition are being systematically rounded up." László tossed the induction papers on the table with disgust. "It's over!"

"I can't believe how quickly things can change," I said, "just yesterday it looked like we had a chance; they were on the run. And what about the UN and NATO?"

"Pista, you know as well as I, they can't do anything without risking war. It's over! No sense in hoping otherwise."

"Their whoring mothers!" I said turning away, choking down tears. *All those lives lost for nothing.* "So, what are you going to do?

Anyu said I should leave the country."

László pointed at the conscription document. "I must report in, or be treated like a deserter. But I'm not going in! I'm leaving for Ács tomorrow; then, somehow, cross the border to Austria."

"You may have heard from Anyu. A couple of men were here looking for me. I can't imagine how anyone could know anything about my activities, but I guess somehow they must. So, it looks like I'll be joining you. Before leaving, I want to find Feri to see if he would like to come. If they have kept me under some sort of surveillance, who knows what they may do to him if he stays."

Laci seemed deep in thought. "I don't see an alternative for either of us. Dodi is too young to have repercussions, and our parents cannot be held legally accountable for what you and I do; we're both adults. Not that the bastards would be concerned about the law!"

"All right then, I'll find Feri and, with or without him, I'll meet up with you in Ács at Uncle Anti's." I extended my hand. "Good luck to us both."

Anyu entered and heard the last few words. She had our sister, Gizi, with her. Gizi ran across the room and jumped into my embrace.

"My sons," Anyu said, "I will get together whatever I can for each of you. You do not have time to waste; the border may not be open for much longer. Once the curtain slams shut, it'll take a miracle to get out. Just like before."

László and I looked at each other, and my guess is, his thoughts were similar to mine: this small woman, our mother, was a lioness. She would cut off a part of herself so we could live. I understood her pain and was awed by her strength and courage.

"Anyukám," we said in near unison and showered her with kisses.

László left for Ács the next morning on his bicycle. He said his goodbyes in private, spending time with each member of the family. I admired his calmness and wondered if I would do as well when my turn came. He agreed to wait for me at Uncle Anti's house where he and Aunt Aranka, the youngest sister of our mother, had their photo studio. He said if I didn't get there in a couple of days, he would attempt to cross the border on his own.

We watched him pedal slowly away, down our street. He stopped, still in sight, looked around, and waved. Then he was gone. Father and I tried to comfort my sobbing mother and my siblings, but I, too, was overcome by grief, knowing tomorrow it would be my turn.

I did not have to look for my friend Feri. He showed up in the middle of the day, looking slightly nervous and reserved.

"Pista, I was hoping to find you home. What do you make of what's happening?"

"Hi! I was about to come and look for you. László left this morning for Ács, on his way to Austria. I'm leaving tomorrow to do the same, but first, I wanted to find out what your plans were."

Feri nodded. "I haven't been thinking about anything else, but I am undecided. Leaving would break my mother's heart.

As usual, he left the matter open. One of these days, Feri will surprise me by saying something with no room for interpretation. But before I could make my expected snide remarks, Feri continued, "If I'm not here by seven tomorrow morning, leave without me."

I understood his dilemma. Feri was the focus of his widowed mother's life. "Feri," I said, "you and I have not been together these last few days. I don't think people could connect us, so you're probably safe, but these are crazy times. I'll wait until tomorrow, but then I must leave. Two men were looking for me the day before yesterday, and that's not a good sign."

He looked down at his shoes and pulled on the threads hanging from the frayed sleeves of his raincoat. Feri often fidgeted when he was pressed. "All right, then," he finally said, "maybe I'll see you tomorrow." His hawkish face remained serious as he extended his hand, and we shook without words.

I watched him go through the front gate with unhurried steps. The vertical slats of our wooden fence blurred my view of him, except for his motion. I wondered if I would ever see him again.

I spent the rest of the day saying goodbye. My father did not have much to say, making my sad task with him easier.

"We've taught you all we know. Remember, the world isn't kind to idealists so be careful." His blue eyes glistened. "Pista, we want to hear from you as soon as possible, don't keep us in suspense."

"Father, listen for our message on Radio Free Europe. 'The Three Musketeers are safe' will be the signal we made it, even if Feri doesn't join us tomorrow."

"All right, son. God keep you safe! Now go say goodbye to Dodi and Gizi. I don't need to tell you to keep it under control."

"Thank you for everything, Father; God be with you!" We hugged, patting each other's back and letting our tears show.

★ ★ ★

My five-year-old sister Gizi and I shared a very special relationship. The bond between us was unspoken, but clearly felt. It was as though we communicated our deep love for one another telepathically. Years later, on my visits to Hungary, Gizi and I talked about this unique connection between us. All we had to do was look at one another and time and space evaporated; we were as one.

Now, on the precipice of a chasm I feared unbridgeable, we spoke to each other with great tenderness.

"Pista, Mom says you are leaving, just like Laci." She smiled through her tears, her face tilted upward. "I don't want you to go!"

I reached for her, then thought better of it and kneeled down in front of her. My hands slipped under her golden hair and cradled her lovely face. "Gizikém, even though you are little, I think you understand how much I love you. Believe me, this is not a forever goodbye. We will see each other again. I promise. And, even if we have to wait for a long time, I'll think of you every day." I pulled her to me, knowing my tears would betray my brave-sounding words.

She patted me on the back. "I love you, Pista. I will pray every night for you and Laci."

My mother hugged her and picked her up. "You will see Pista tomorrow morning, and you can say goodbye again. Okay?"

Gizi started to cry. "Okay, bye Pista, see you in the morning."

"Good night, honey, see you in the morning," I said, smiling while my insides were being ripped apart. "Don't let the Turks get you!"

I found my brother Dodi working on his bicycle behind the house. He inherited our father's special gifts when it came to something technical. He could fix anything from a toaster to the most intricate engine. He looked up as I approached.

"How goes it, Dodi?" I said, nodding toward the disassembled bicycle. I wanted to stay with as light a subject as I could, not wanting to add to an already difficult situation. "Looks like your bike is on its last leg."

"Naw! It's in better shape than it has been for some time. I traded for a new bottom bracket with a friend. It didn't fit his, so I got it cheap. All I have to do now is to get it installed, and the bike is ready to go." He brushed a strand of blond hair from his eyes with the back of his hand.

I watched him pack lubricating grease into the bearings with expert motions while I deliberated about how to continue. Dodi saved me from my predicament.

"I know you're leaving," he said simply, as if he knew the pain I felt. "Anyu is right, I don't think you have a choice. These bastards are rounding up people, and I'm afraid it will only get worse." He straightened his back and continued with a grin. "At last I am going to get your racing bike and all your tools."

"Dodikám, they are yours. Anything I have—all yours to keep." My voice broke slightly, and I started to slip out of control.

"Thank you, Pista, but I would rather all this weren't going on. Please let us know as soon as you can when you are safe." His face was still smiling, but I saw a teardrop run down from the corner of his eye and hang suspended on the tip of his nose. "I know you and Laci worked out some code with Father, using the Radio Free Europe broadcasts. We'll be listening, and will tell the rest of the family when we know."

The dam burst, and he started mopping his face with the greasy rag he had been using for his hands. I consoled him the best I could. "We're counting on the Red Cross to eventually be able to write."

"Is Feri going with you?"

"I don't know, but it's not likely. He's not in any trouble, so he might stay."

"I wish I could be going."

"Dodikám, don't even say it. You'll be the family's only son. Anyu needs you; Gizi needs you. You'll have to be all three of us for them.

"I'm sorry we're leaving you with this, but we have no choice. And even though it seems impossible now, I know we will reunite someday."

"God be with you, Pista," Dodi's freckled face broadened into a brave smile, and his tears started to stream. He kept wiping the grease off his fingers with the soiled rag, even though they were clean. I took my handkerchief and swabbed the bearing grease off his face.

"God be with you, Dodi," I said. We hugged in an awkward embrace. "Be strong for the sake of Anyu and Gizi. I'm counting on you."

THE JOURNEY WEST

"Hi!' Feri said, standing on our porch with a grin just as I opened the front door on my way to the toilet behind the house.

"This is a surprise! Yesterday you weren't sure about coming." Feri seemed older than I remembered. Or, I just hadn't been paying attention. We met in aviation class at our flying club and had been friends ever since. He stood two meters tall, a couple of centimeters shorter than me, weighing roughly the same.

Feri shrugged. "I wasn't sure myself until late last night, but here I am, ready to go." He dismounted the knapsack from his back. "My life all packed up," he said, pointing at the bulging pack.

I had been working on packing the essentials for the journey myself, but even after years of experience trekking through the mountains and forests, this time I was having difficulty anticipating my needs. What does one pack for leaving one's country?

"Feri, if you don't mind me asking, what did you pack?"

Feri shrugged. "Well, I knew I needed a toothbrush and paste, socks, clean underwear, a book or two—"

"You've got to be joking! You mean you're intending to read while we're fleeing the country?"

"Well, why not?" he grinned. "And if we do get out, there will be nothing available in Hungarian, so I thought—"

"Feri, you're hopeless. First of all, there's nothing 'if' about it; we're getting out! Here I am, trying to decide what to leave behind, not having enough space for everything I know we would need, and you're loaded down with books." I knew I sounded agitated, but couldn't help myself.

Feri fidgeted with his wristwatch, scratching to remove some imagined spot from the crystal with his fingernails. I was ready for our usual friendly battle, but he just stood there, preoccupied with the damned watch. Feri was frustrating at times, and I had to pee.

When I came back from the shed, Feri was in the kitchen eating breakfast, while Anyu was preparing sandwiches for the road.

"Feri," Anyu asked, "did you pack anything edible?"

"Well, Mrs. Horvath, actually, I didn't. But I have plenty of money to buy whatever," Feri said sheepishly. "I figured money would take up less space—" He trailed off into something incomprehensible, as he always did when answering would reflect poorly on him.

"That settles it. I'm making enough for the both of you." Anyu rolled the finished sandwich into a cloth napkin and started another.

"Ferikém, I'm glad you decided to accompany Pista. Between the two of you, you'll have a better chance. I'm sure your mother told you the same thing, but please don't take unnecessary chances. You know how Pista is; he doesn't know the meaning of caution."

"Anyu, you're not being fair. I give each situation—"

"Sure! Just like the time—" Anyu started, but I stopped her.

"Hush!" I said, embracing her. "And you," I turned to Feri, still holding on to my mother, "don't get me into trouble, keep your opinions to yourself." Finished with him for the moment, I kissed the top of my mother's head. "Anyu, we need to be on our way to have any chance of making Ács before Laci leaves. A hundred kilometers isn't bad on a bicycle, but on foot—"

We stood on the porch not knowing what to say. I think all of us knew whatever we could manage would be less than adequate. We just started hugging each other, going from one person to the next and back again. Soon our faces were shiny with tears. No one cared. Feri stood off to the side, but my mother pulled him into our circle.

"May God bless you both," she told us.
"God be with you, my dearests," I cried.
"And with you my son," said Anyu and Father.
"Goodbye, Pista, I love you!" Gizi sobbed.
"Goodbye, Dodikám. Goodbye, Gizikém. I love you both!"
We held on tightly. I tore myself away and dragged Feri with me. We walked down the steps to the stone-lined walkway, touching fingertips, except for Gizi whose arms were locked around my neck. Anyu pried her away.

We were raw with our sorrows. The family followed us to the gate and watched us take the first steps of a long journey. In front of Jani's house Feri and I turned around and waved.

"Be sure you write. We'll all be suffering until we know you're Okay!" Dodi yelled after us.

"Pista, Pista! …" I heard Gizi wail unstoppably. We picked up our steps, but her voice followed us down the street.

Mid morning found Feri and me on the far side of Wolf Mountain, trekking toward Cool Valley and Three Borders Mountain. We had a special reason for wanting to go this way, somewhat off the direct line of the Vienna Highway, which paralleled the Danube west of Budapest.

Somewhere along the climb to Wolf Mountain Cemetery we decided to detour, to see if we could steal the tow plane from the gliderport and fly it out of the country. By the time the Russians could scramble, we reasoned, we would be over Austrian territory.

Besides, with the slow-flying tow plane we could travel at treetop levels, making radar detection nearly impossible. Laci would go on as we agreed. Laci always did what he said he would; I knew I could count on that.

After the initial climb past the cemetery, the going became easier. We walked through neighborhoods along some of the streets where I had spent many a winter night shoveling snow. Hired by the city, one could make forty forints a night, about two U.S. dollars using comparable 1956 values. Sometimes we nearly doubled that, when the city did not have enough volunteers and had to pay a premium to get the job done. Most of the work was done overnight, with shifts starting at 10:00 P.M. and ending at six the following morning. There were students of both sexes, retired folk, and people who didn't do anything else. I found something very rewarding in doing this work, surpassing the value of the money I earned. Most of the nights were bitterly cold, but occasionally, when it snowed, the city transformed into a wonderland. Falling snow, streetlights, and, once in a while, a girl to flirt with; it was my kind of work.

"What's up?" Feri asked noticing my preoccupation.

"Just thinking," I said. "About life here and saying goodbye. I'm leaving everything and everyone I ever loved."

Feri nodded, and after a few moments of silence he said somberly, "I didn't tell my mother I was leaving."

"Feri!" I stopped in my tracks, stunned. "What in the hell were you thinking? Your mother has every right to know!" I looked at him with a mixture of disdain and disbelief.

"I left her a note. She won't see it until she gets home from work tonight. If I'd said anything to her last night about leaving, I wouldn't be here," he added quietly, looking down at his feet.

Knowing his mother, I understood. Still, I couldn't have walked away from my family without saying goodbye. Poor Feri. I knew how much he loved his mother; he would have to live with this decision for the rest of his life.

"We need to make sure we get word to her as soon as possible," I said, trying to lift a little bit of burden from his shoulders. "Starting with sending a letter from Ács," I added. Feri nodded, and we started walking with a faster pace.

We approached the gliderport with caution. Missing were the sounds of activity one would usually hear nearing the compound. No whooshing sound of gliders passing overhead, nor the throaty purr of Big Kadi powering a two-seater aloft. The area seemed deserted.

Of course Feri, an eternal conduit for bad expectations, thought the hangars might be guarded. "I'm sure guards are posted to protect the planes. They'd be stupid not to," he said.

Normally, I would have challenged him just on principle, but I was still preoccupied with my thoughts.

"This way." I put my arm out as we reached the small trail I had last traveled with Veronika. I knew the trail would lead to the large hangar, and if there were people at the compound, we would be afforded some cover. The tow plane, our ticket to freedom, would be tied down in front of the big hangar.

"Pista, let's say the tow plane is there, but we can't start it."

I just shook my head without saying a word. *Here comes doubting Feri and his worst-case scenario.*

Feri filled the void. "Okay, let's assume that somehow, we could start it. Neither you nor I are qualified to fly it." Feri continued in his dark "what if" voice.

"First of all, getting it started shouldn't be a big deal. If we have to, we'll break in and take the keys from the office. We've helped to get the engine started many times before.

"And as far as flying it goes, I flew it a couple of times with Pálinkás and feel pretty confident about it. I only worry about the takeoff and the landing. Pálinkás took off and landed both times and I thought it was a bit messy."

Feri stopped and put his hands on his hips. "Yeah! So, that's all, huh? No problem, except for taking off and landing! Minor details, but don't worry; Pista will take care of everything!"

I never knew how to respond to his sarcasm. It was always funny the way he voiced it, and made me want to laugh. But now, we had more serious things to do than banter. "Look, we are both accomplished pilots," I snapped back. "If you don't like my plan, you can always present yours."

Just as I finished, I spotted the big hangar through the trees. "Let's watch first and see if anyone is here."

We waited for a minute, then proceeded guardedly. As we rounded the corner of the hangar, we spotted the tow plane, tied to anchor rings at the apron's edge, its usual position. My spirits soared. We wouldn't have to break in to get the plane out; it was outside already. Just what I hoped for.

"We're lucky," I beamed at Feri. "Someone knew we needed it. I hope it's fueled to the top." *It should be*, I thought. *Pálinkás always insisted on having it filled to keep moisture from condensing in the tank and possibly fouling the ignition.* "It's looking good!"

By the time we reached the tail assembly, I was already doing the preflight inspection.

Feri walked past the right wings in front of me. "Yeah, it's great! Except for the fact that the propeller is gone," he said, with what sounded like a tone of relief.

"Their mother's sainthood, I can't believe this!" I said.

"Like I said," mocked Feri. "We were not qualified to fly the thing anyway. And someone knew it," he added triumphantly.

From Cool Valley, we turned toward Kőbánya, a small village mostly inhabited by Swabs. Germanic in origin, the Swabs settled the region in the sixteenth century at one of Hungary's king's pleasure, to spread their knowledge of winemaking. Swabs also lived in our neighborhood, and I spent a lot of time with a certain family when I was growing up. Like the Amish of North America, the Swabs kept to themselves and retained most of their customs. They spoke a Low-German dialect, and when I was little, I imitated their speech so accurately that my mother's friends actually thought I knew how to speak the language until Mother set them straight.

While walking toward Kőbánya, Feri and I stayed off the Vienna Highway to avoid the Russian patrols and roadblocks we knew would be there. We slogged from field to field, orchard to orchard, hiding in thickets when necessary, which was frequently. It was slow going, without the likelihood of improvement.

Sometime around 2:00 in the afternoon, we reached the outskirts of the village and decided to stop at a tavern to get food. We had long ago devoured the sandwiches packed by my mother.

Except for the man behind the counter, the tavern was empty. Feri and I settled into a corner near a wood-burning fireplace. The place smelled like a musty wine cellar. There were a couple of stuffed stag heads, complete with antlers and glass eyes, mounted over the bar.

"What can I do for you?" the burly man behind the worn cherry wood counter inquired, looking us over suspiciously.

"We'd like to order a meal, and some bread and sausage to take with us." I reached into my pocket and pulled out some bills.

"Sorry, we don't serve food here, only alcohol," the bartender said. The man seemed to enjoy saying no.

"Could you then please tell us where we might get a meal?" I pressed. "We're hungry."

"Are you coming from Budapest?" he asked without answering and stared at our muddy shoes.

I was about to make up a story, but Feri beat me to the punch.

"Yes, and we still have a long way to go," he said, smiling at the tavern keeper. "Where could we go in the village?"

"Everything is closed up around here. People are afraid of confiscation, so they are staying home. Perhaps you could find someplace open in Tata, on the way to Komárom, but I doubt it."

"But you're open!" Feri said, apparently determined to keep me out of the conversation.

The bartender shrugged. "Soldiers usually pay for alcohol." He came around the bar and sat on a stool facing us. "Except for a couple of the locals, no one has been here since yesterday. A truckload of Russians stopped, drank here for about an hour and moved on. How about you? Would you like something to drink? I have Hungarian schnapps, peach and apricot, red and white wine, and imported rum."

"Beer?" Feri asked.

"Sorry, beer was the first thing to go," he frowned. "Beer to chase the schnapps and brandy." We needed to get going, so I ordered a glass of rum. Feri followed suit. We started sipping the powerful drink, and soon I was feeling less weary.

"What is the situation between here and Komárom? We are on our way to my grandparents'."

The tavern keeper topped off our glasses. "There are roadblocks everywhere. I hear the Russians set up a temporary camp this side of Komárom. They're rounding up everyone without travel papers. You better have papers or stay off the highway."

Feri and I exchanged glances.

The bartender returned to the counter and poured himself a drink.

Feri leaned closer. "I think we better talk about this," he said, regressing into his "the world is a cold and dark place" routine.

I wasn't looking forward to traipsing through the muddy fields, either. An idea had been rattling around my head; one I knew would be rejected by Feri, but the buzz from the rum helped me stay optimistic. "Don't worry! We can avoid them in the fields, or, I have a better idea, one that would get us there faster."

"Afraid to hear it. One of these days your ideas will kill us!"

"Well then, before I tell you, we better get these glasses refilled." I motioned to our host. *Damn! Why hadn't I discovered rum before?* "Would you have rum available for us to take? We could use a couple of half-liter bottles filled with this great tasting stuff," I complimented him.

"Sure do," the man said, "I'll wrap it for you."

"Don't bother, we'll take care of that." I tapped on my backpack.

Feri paid the man and caught up with me on the path that led to the highway. "What in the hell are you doing? That's the Vienna Highway!" he said, grabbing the harness on my backpack.

"I think we have to do the unexpected," I said. I let that sink in. "I think we should stay out of the fields. Making headway there is way too hard. Let's walk on the pavement and flag down a vehicle that's going in the right direction." I jerked free from his hold and continued walking toward the highway.

Feri looked perplexed. "That's the most idiotic thing I've ever heard. We'll be in a work camp within minutes."

"You're not getting it. No one with something to hide would do what I'm suggesting. Trust me; I know people. Just keep quiet, and let me do the talking when someone stops."

Feri was having a hard time concentrating. "Whatever happens, it's on your head," he finally said, probably wondering whether or not he was crazy to trust my judgment. By this time we were walking in the middle of the highway toward Komárom. What had been drudgery until now suddenly became easy, even fun. No more sinking into the soft earth in the plowed fields or wading through muddy ditches. The highway beneath our feet was smooth and hard, making walking nearly effortless.

Feri and I bantered for several kilometers, taking an occasional swig from one of the bottles. Soon that bottle was empty. We walked arm-in-arm with the center divider between us. Lots of "remember when" was going on when a Russian staff car came up fast from behind. We jumped to the side of the road, but not completely off the pavement.

"*Stoy!*" I yelled, waving my arms, stepping in front of the approaching car. Feri joined me.

The shiny black car, with the sickle and hammer flag of the Soviet Union flying from the center of its hood ornament, halted next to us. The window of the back door slowly lowered and a face topped with an officer's hat emerged.

"What's the problem?" asked the officer in Russian, leaning slightly out of the window.

"Sir Officer, we are heading toward Komárom to get food from my grandparents," I answered him in Russian. "Our family is starving in the city; we must get some food. Could you please give us a lift, so we could get there before nightfall? Please, good Captain, please!"

The officer rolled up his window and conversed with his driver.

"Dummy, he's not a captain." Feri elbowed me. "He's at least a general, or a diplomat." Feri started to giggle.

Suddenly, I felt completely sober. *This may turn into an ugly end,* I thought, *and it would be entirely my fault*. We stood there for what seemed several minutes, then the driver got out and opened the door on our side. The officer looked us over with apprehension, apparently still deciding on what to do.

"Okay," he finally said, "but I am not going all the way to Komárom. I'll get you past Tatabánya; you're on your own from there."

"Thank you, Captain, thank you very much," I said. "We'll be that much closer. You are very kind."

So there we were, sitting in the shiny black limousine of a Russian officer, speeding toward our destination. We passed through roadblock after roadblock without being stopped. When the car rolled through, the soldiers manning the roadblocks stood at attention. Inside, I answered the officer's questions forthrightly, pleading ignorance only when the questions concerned current events.

Outside Tatabánya, the staff car halted in front of a modern building that stood just off the road. Our driver got out and approached the ranking officer. They talked briefly, with the driver pointing at us repeatedly. The officer and the driver came back to the limousine together, and after saluting our host, the officer motioned for Feri and me to get out.

"Thank you, Captain, for the lift," I said smiling, as if talking to a dear friend. We both waved as the limousine drove away.

"Come with me," said the officer curtly.

We followed him to the nearby building that must have been a regional headquarter for the Russian military, or so I judged by the number of vehicles, soldiers, and the activity. Once inside, we were ordered to the back of a short line of other Hungarians.

"Why are we here?" I asked the nearest man in the line.

"Shut your mouth!" A soldier said menacingly. "No talking!"

One by one, the people in front of us disappeared down a hall.

In a few minutes, it was our turn. Feri and I were escorted to a small office. The man sitting behind the desk wore a round-topped officer's hat circled with green, indicating his affiliation with the ideological section of the Soviet military. He was a political officer.

There were no decorations of any kind in the room, but there was what appeared to be a telegraph machine centered on the desk next to a short wave radio. Except for the officer's, there were no other seats. We stood in front of the desk with the armed soldier behind us.

The officer ignored us and kept writing on a form printed with Cyrillic letters, filling it out leisurely. He dropped the form on top of others next to the radio.

"Why are you here? Your papers say you are from Budapest," he said in fluent, but heavily accented, Hungarian.

"We are going to my grandparents for food. Our families are starving in the city; there is nothing available to eat there."

"What's the name of your grandparents?"

I answered him.

"Where do they live?"

I gave their address.

"What do you do in Budapest?"

The dispassionate, rapid-fire questioning continued. When he was finished, the officer said that an inquiry would be made to the authorities in Budapest, and if the information obtained disclosed nothing bad, we would be returned to the city. In the meantime, we would be placed in custody. When I asked how long this might take, he shrugged. "A few hours. Certainly no more than a few days."

He then motioned to the soldier.

"*Davaj!*" The soldier led us down the corridor.

We were herded behind the building into an uncovered enclosure that was separated from rows of military tents by a rope. The perimeter was secured with a three-meter-high barbed wire fence. We were allowed to keep our knapsacks and, surprisingly, we were not searched.

There were perhaps a hundred people inside the compound, standing in groups, milling around, or sitting on the ground. Except for a couple of middle-aged women, all the others were men, ranging in age from the late teens to graying, but mostly men in their twenties. The place smelled of unwashed bodies.

"You and your great ideas," Feri said as soon as we could talk. "Now look where we are! This is just the kindergarten of concentration camps." He frowned. "The worst is yet to come."

"You must admit we got here pretty fast." I said, forcing a

broad smile. My humor was lost on him. He looked so downhearted I felt compelled to cheer him. "And we're still a long way from Siberia. Let's check things out." Mentioning Siberia was probably a mistake, but I was in no mood for Feri's I-told-you-sos. I walked over to an older, bearded Russian who was pacing outside the fence. He walked with his forearms resting on the stock and barrel of his submachine gun slung around his neck in front of him. His long, woolen coat was unhemmed, some of the cloth's unravelings touching the ground. He reminded me of the soldier who had banged on our cellar door when the Russians "liberated" us at the end of World War Two.

"Officer, I have to go to the bathroom now. Where do I go?"

He seemed surprised by my Russian. "Come to the gate," he instructed me.

At the gate, he unlocked the chain securing it. He motioned to another guard to take his place and ordered me to follow. After taking care of business at the smelly, filthy urinal, I made an attempt at a conversation while he finished urinating. "My name is István," I said, "you seem like a seasoned soldier. What's your name?"

Again, he looked surprised. "Sergey," he said. "Where did you learn Russian?" He buttoned and wiped his wet fingers on the side of his coat.

"In school, and from my Russian friends. Where are you from?"

"We got here three days ago from Belarus. They told us we were going to the Suez Canal, but somehow we wound up here."

"Say!" I motioned him closer. "I have a proposition. If you let me and my friend go—"

He furled his brow and was about to speak when I quickly added, "To get food for our starving families. We're willing to be grateful."

"What are you suggesting?" Sergey put his hands on the gun, but I could see a flicker of interest in his eyes. "I could get into a lot of trouble," he continued.

"Listen, we have a bit of money and a bottle of rum. You can take us to the latrine, then just look the other way."

Sergey looked at me incredulously.

"I'll make it worth your while. Okay?" I pleaded. The seconds ticked away.

"No," he said, but he didn't move. He shifted his weapon and looked around.

His mother's sainthood, I thought, *I misfired on this one.* I nearly asked him to forget what I said, when Sergey spoke. "Come to the back of the fence, away from the lights. I'll meet you after I am relieved, if I can. And I want the rum now."

"I don't think that's a good idea," I said.

He shrugged and turned to go.

"I mean, somebody might see me handing you something," I quickly explained. "We will be there at ten. You'll get the rum plus all our money, and a watch."

He murmured, *"Dobre,"* and lumbered back toward the gate. I walked next to him, he didn't seem to care. He secured the chain behind me and walked away. In about a minute, I would know if I had misjudged him.

Feri was waiting. "I saw you talk to the Russian," he said hopefully. "What's up?"

I didn't feel up to teasing him. "We might have a chance to escape tonight. The Russian said he'd let us go."

Additional people were crowded into the compound all evening. On several occasions, a group would be called together by name, led through the gate, and boarded onto trucks. No one in camp knew where these people were taken.

Between bouts of calming Feri, I asked around to learn what I could about our predicament. Most of the interned had been picked up on nearby roads; many lived in the area. As the innkeeper at Köbánya said, without authorizations people were detained. I began to doubt we had much of a chance of getting out. Still, come ten o'clock, Feri and I were waiting at the designated spot.

Old Sergey was not to be seen. I had learned a long time ago, when one runs out of options, the least one can do is to keep faith. I must admit keeping the faith now was difficult. Feri was behaving admirably. It took him ten long minutes before his dark side surfaced. "I don't think I need to comment here," he said, more in the way of, "It's sad, but that's the way it is," than with reproach.

A small eternity later old Sergey materialized from the dark, right where he said he would be.

"Where have you been?" I hissed at him.

"I told you I would be here. Here I am." He grinned broadly.

Most of the camp's internees were asleep, curled up in whatever clothing they had. The tents were overflowing. Many were sleeping on layers of newspapers and on straw, the latter probably tossed into the compound for this purpose.

I silently motioned to Sergey to lift the bottom edge of the fence. He shook his head and pointed at our bags, indicating for me to pass those through first. I shook my head. "Him first." I pointed at Feri, "me second, then the knapsacks."

He shrugged and fished out a pair of pliers from his pocket, then cut the bottom wire. An unnervingly loud *pang* issued as the wire parted, but no one seemed to notice. Sergey lifted the bottom of the fence, creating a pass-through for Feri. I followed dragging the knapsacks by their straps behind me.

We were on the outside.

Sergey waved us along impatiently toward the adjacent field. *This could be a setup*, the thought flashed through my mind. If it was, it was too late to do anything about it.

Once in the dark, Sergey accepted the ransom greedily and walked quickly away. Feri and I ran through the open fields toward some distant shadows. The shadows turned out to be trees and bushes separating one field from the next. We ran until we could simply not continue. While resting, the exchange with the Russian kept coming to my mind. Finally, I remembered. "Feri," I laughed.

"What is it?"

"I forgot to give old Sergey my wristwatch."

We laughed and acknowledged that we were very lucky indeed. God willing, sometime before dawn we would be in Ács.

SEEDS ON THE WIND

Feri was on his last leg, and I was not far behind by the time we reached the outskirts of Ács. Walking through the fields was exhausting. Last night, during our mad dash to freedom my boots filled with dirt, and my feet were raw.

The sun had not yet broken the plane of the horizon, but there was enough light to see a fine layer of mist covering the fields. The mist hugged the ground and had that light blue quality I associated with cold. Our breaths trailed from our mouths, and steam rose from our bodies. For the last thirty or so minutes, we had been trekking through dew-laden pastures and our boots were soggy. On top of last night's injuries, my socks bunched up under the balls of my feet, and I was certain I had several blisters. *How much farther can I go?* I wondered, but pressed on. Feri, the chronic complainer, was quiet. *How could I complain with him bearing his troubles silently?*

A rooster called in the distance, followed by another. We walked between rows of haystacks along a stream that divided the community. At the outskirts, we held up to let a small group of milking cows lumber across a bridge that connected the two banks. Their hooves drummed a score without rhythm on the wood planks. It was a new day.

We approached the center of Ács from the west, along one of the dirt streets that I knew ended up at the church plaza in front of the townhouse, the seat of the local government.

The walls of the houses were washed in the obligatory white and a good many of them were still under thatched roofs, reminding me of our heritage. A century ago, that's all one would have found. Walking easier on the solid ground, I noticed the front yards' flowerbeds. The more elaborate they were, the clearer the message to the neighbors: "We're doing well, we can afford to be a little frivolous." *The essence of being Hungarian prevails even here,* I thought.

Behind the houses the backyards were planted with vegetables and fruit trees. Past them were equipment sheds and support buildings, and behind those, fields of barley and wheat, sugar beets, and corn. There appeared to be small variations on this theme, but people here were practical; they pursued whatever worked.

Feri, who had been quiet for some time, to my knowledge had no relatives in the country. "So," I asked, "what's your impression of this capital of the haystacks?"

He responded with uncharacteristic emotion; "This is the kind of place I see myself making a life. I love the peace and simplicity." Then, as if regretting this rare exposure of his inner self, he turned away and crossed to the other side of the street.

I followed wordlessly. I guess I didn't know him as well as I thought.

★ ★ ★

Many years later, Feri found his Ács in a faraway place called Pasco, in the state of Washington. Here he built a house in the high desert, converted to the Mormon faith, and had a large family. The fulfillment of his dreams.

★ ★ ★

Uncle Antal's place was one of several tradesmen's homes that housed businesses on the street level and family quarters above. He and Aunt Aranka, Mother's youngest sister, owned a photo studio that catered to the area's needs. Recording images of weddings, births, and other important events in the simple life of the people here provided them with a good livelihood.

As we neared their home, Feri and I briefly paused in front of the town center monument to clean our boots. Until recently, this tall, whitewashed obelisk had been topped with the Bolshevik's five-pointed red star. Now the star was gone. A feeling of elation washed over me as I looked at the defaced monument. That cursed red star didn't belong on the main square of any Hungarian community! We methodically scraped off the mud trapped at the base of the heels and wiped the uppers with handfuls of wet grass. Having clean shoes showed the host our respect.

The church bell pealed and on its signal cows from every direction invaded the street, all heading toward a new cement bridge that crossed the stream and led to the pastures. The pungent odor of fresh cow dung mixed with that of wet earth.

★ ★ ★

Aranka refilled our mugs and sliced another piece of *kalács*, a sweet Hungarian breakfast pastry, for each of us. We, Horváth boys, were allowed to address her without the respectful *néni*, (ma'am, in English,) because she was only eight years older than Laci, the oldest.

"So, Pista," Aranka said, "you are convinced that staying in Hungary is dangerous?" the inflection of her voice gave her question added significance.

"Anyu thought so, and I, too, believe there's no other choice," I replied sadly.

Uncle Anti winked at me across the table. "Pistikém," he said, using his favorite of the many diminutives of my Christian name, "would it be fair to say that at least in part, your decision to leave has to do with wanderlust? You and I had talked a lot about faraway places, and once outside the Iron Curtain, you can go wherever you want."

"I can't deny that," I said, feeling my cheeks turn red. "But I also think it's necessary!"

Sitting with his elbow on the table and chin on his fist, Laci raised his hand to interrupt. He spoke thoughtfully. "Considering my situation with the draft, Pista has even less of a choice; if he stays and I leave, he will most certainly be punished for not reporting me as a deserter. As is, I fear for Father and even Dodi, who should be too young for retribution. But this regime is out of control. Who knows what they might do." Laci turned to Feri. "What about you? You can still change your mind."

Feri made a disgusted swat at an imaginary fly. "And why would I stay? In two years I'd be graduating from trade school. Then, if I were a good boy and toed the party line, I could eventually become the head of a department in some run-down industrial plant? Someone hold me down!" Feri broke off a piece of his *kalács* and took a bite. "I'm going!"

I looked at him with surprise and admiration. It wasn't often that Feri made a decisive statement. All of a sudden I felt better about having him along.

"Anti-bácsi, what about you? And," I quickly added, "you, Aranka?"

"Well, Pistikém," Anti said speaking for both of them, "I've been elected to the post of Chairman of the Council. The council is made up of the same communists who ran Ács before the uprising and some new blood, mostly local merchants and a few of the smaller farmers." Anti paused for his characteristic belly laugh. "You would have loved to be a fly on the wall when I was nominated. The pigs were falling all over themselves to let the rest of us know how much they had disapproved of the heavy-handed governing they themselves perpetrated. The vote to have me head the council was unanimous."

Aranka interrupted. "Yes, but answer Pista's question: what happens now, now that the uprising has been quelled?" Aranka's voice betrayed her deep concern.

Anti spread his arms and once again treated us to his belly laugh. "What could they possibly do? The vote was legal, all the communists voted for me. They were the ones who elected me!" Anti's face showed mocked puzzlement as he raised his open palms toward the ceiling.

The way he explained it he had no repercussions coming, but all of us at the table knew that logic was not a strong suit of the People's Government; he was at great risk.

On Monday, November 19th, 1956, Feri and I borrowed bicycles from our hosts and joined Laci on a trek to the Tanya. Along the way I wondered if I would ever see this bucolic countryside again. So many memories of my childhood were created here, so much joy, learning, and, yes, some pain. Kneeling on corn facing a corner came to mind. I felt a sense of loss and, for the first time, homesickness.

Grandfather Lajos and Grandmother Etel were completely unaware of our decision to leave the country. Once past the obligatory "Dear me-s" I took a short walk to the orchard at the top of the hill with Grandfather, while Laci and Feri visited with Grandmother, who quickly regained her sense of balance and was already preparing a meal.

At the top, Grandfather, a man of few words, pointed to one of the peach trees. "This is one of the trees you grafted when you were just a kid," he said. "I had always hoped to see your children eat the fruit of this tree." He bent a now leafless young shoot toward me, holding it with his work-worn hands as if to say, "How can you leave this behind?"

Heavy silence hung in the air. I gently took the peach branch from his hand and gathered my thoughts. These were the questions, silent or uttered, for which I had no answers. It was difficult to speak with a lump in my throat. "Grandpapa, I don't know how or when, but my children will see this tree and eat from its fruit. Leaving you and this place is leaving part of myself behind." I hugged him. "Thank you for helping me become who I am!"

We stood in silent embrace. I remembered the times we had spent together and hugged him more tightly. "God bless you, Grandfather! Thank you for everything."

"God bless you, Grandson," he murmured and turned away. I think he understood better than I the nature of times ahead.

I followed him down the sandy path, among the plowed-over wheat fields and stubs of corn toward the thatch-covered house that would forever remain the essence of home for me.

The following morning, Aranka handed each of us carefully wrapped sandwiches. "I used the *kolbász* your grandmother gave you yesterday, to make these," she said, fighting back tears. "I won't go to the station with you, because I don't want to make a scene. God be with all of you. Let us know as soon as you are safe." She blew her nose and forced a cheerful smile, reminding me of my favorite picture of her. Anti took the photo while courting her; she was sixteen at the time. I was just a boy then, but I still remember being in love with her. I think all of us boys were; my aunt Aranka was the most beautiful woman we had ever seen. Even now, with tears running down her smiling face and her nose red, Aranka was a vision of great beauty. She waved one last time.

"Goodbye, Aranka, we'll write you soon," I said and turned to follow the others to hide my own tears.

★ ★ ★

We had said our goodbyes to uncle Anti the night before. Early that morning he left to attend an emergency meeting of the town council. I learned nearly a year later in a letter from my mother that on his arrival at the townhouse he was arrested by ÁVO, the Hungarian Secret Police, for unspecified crimes against the people.

★ ★ ★

On our way to the railway station Laci outlined his plan for crossing the border. "Anti said that he had talked with a man, a man he trusts, who worked near the border. The man said that the government's claim that all the minefields have been cleared is a lie. Large sections of the landmines along no-man's-land at the Austrian border have been uprooted, but there are still areas with intact minefields." Laci wiped his brow and continued. "After we reach Hegyeshalom, we should turn to the southwest toward Nickelsdorf, a small Austrian village just across the border. This is the area, according to the man, where the mine clearing operation has been completed." Laci paused as a locomotive positioning freight cars passed in front of us.

As soon as I could be heard, I interrupted. "Guys, I can't help thinking that the mine clearing was done by soldiers, and soldiers are notorious for shoddy work; just ask any farmer they had helped with the harvest. Feri, we should have looked for that damned prop for the towplane," I said jokingly.

Feri didn't seem amused. "Since when has crossing minefields been a laughing matter?" He spat on the pavement. "I don't exactly cherish being blown to bits."

Laci raised his hand. "Look, fellows, I don't believe the biggest danger will come from the mines. The ÁVO has regained control, and that includes the border areas. According to Anti, they are traveling on all the trains and are pulling off people who they believe are headed for the border. We'll have to be really careful once we pass Győr."

"Well, then," Feri interjected, "why are we even getting on the damned train?"

Laci frowned. "I wouldn't if you two weren't here. I planned on bicycling as far as I could, and then continue on foot. But we don't have much of a choice; the border is too far to walk."

We arrived at the station intending to purchase tickets to Hegyeshalom. Hegyeshalom is a small hamlet near the Austrian border, notorious for the vicious border guards whose job was to defend this part of Hungary from capitalist invasion. One had to laugh. In light of the fact that it was we, citizens of the Socialist Paradise, who risked life and limb to escape to the West, I wondered if any of them believed in what they were doing.

We walked up to the purser. The agent eyed us with suspicious scrutiny. "Due to security considerations, the train will terminate at Mosonmagyar-O'vár," he said in a tone used by officious bureaucrats when speaking to us ordinary people. I hated this kind of posturing and the fact that we were at his mercy.

The purser scowled. "I don't have all day, what'll it be?"

It's been said that given a chance, people in minor positions are the worst oppressors. I was about to give this little Napoleon a piece of my mind when Feri, fearing my predictable response, pulled us away.

"No point in antagonizing this mental midget," he said when we were out of earshot. "Let's get tickets to go as far as they let us, we'll figure out what to do on the train."

Laci, clearly our leader in these matters, agreed, and thirty minutes later we were on our way to Mosonmagyar-O'vár. Our hope was to blend in with the workers who rode the trains to the city from the surrounding rural areas. The three of us settled into a compartment and stowed our rucksacks.

A few minutes after leaving Ács, a boy about twelve knocked on the compartment's glass door, asking for admittance. Laci motioned him in. No sooner had he settled down the conductor came to inspect our tickets. Looking at the boy's he said, "Sorry, the train will terminate at Mosonmagyar-O'vár. You can get a refund of the unused portion. You should have been told this in Budapest when you bought your ticket."

The boy looked lost. We smiled at him to give him encouragement.

"Everything is upside down now," Laci said to him. "Were you visiting family in Hegyeshalom?"

"I was, but now I don't know what to do," the boy answered.

"I don't mean to interfere, but why don't you just turn around, and go back home?" I said.

"You seem to be quite young to be traveling alone in these troubled times," Laci said before the boy could answer me.

"I'm fourteen," the boy said defensively. "And I have been traveling alone for years." He extended his hand for a handshake to further prove his adulthood. "My name is Miklós."

"I'm László," said Laci, "and this is István and Ferenc."

Each of us shook hands with the boy. The train rolled on.

"So, what are you going to do?" Laci persisted. "Will you return to Budapest?"

Miklós' eyes clouded "I … I don't know what to do." He looked down at his bag and tightened the straps. "I have nothing to go back to." He spoke quietly, still looking at the floor.

When he looked back up, I thought I saw tears in the corner of his eyes. I felt compassion toward him, but there was nothing we could do.

Laci must have been affected in a similar way because he put his hand on the boy's shoulder. "You want to talk about it?"

The boy told his story haltingly. He had been orphaned during the war and was raised by his grandmother, who had recently died. The school for adolescent boys, where he was placed after his grandmother's death, burned down during the uprising, courtesy of the attacking Russian tanks, and he decided to find the only relative he knew he had, an uncle in the United States who had sent them packages from time to time. It seems the boy was on a quest similar to ours.

He knew that the border crossing would be difficult but figured he would have a better chance than most because experience had taught him that no one in authority paid attention to boys his age. The train's abbreviated route was a problem Miklós had not anticipated.

"Why don't you join us," Laci said upon hearing this. "We have similar plans."

Damn it! I thought. *Laci is taking a big chance inviting him, especially without discussion. Likeable or not, we don't know anything about this kid! Certainly not enough to take him into our confidence. For all we know, he could be a plant. It would be just like ÁVO to use a boy like Miklós. Or he could crack if we were caught.*

But the boy seemed genuinely relieved.

"Laci, could I talk to you?" I asked. I motioned my brother to follow me into the corridor that was jammed with workers. We went to the back of the Pullman, into the small enclosure used for boarding. Here the track noise was deafening, but we would be alone.

"We're taking a big chance inviting—"

Laci stopped me. "Look, Pista. We can't just abandon him! He's only a boy. I doubt he is fourteen as he says, but having him along may be a blessing. The authorities might not be as suspicious with him along. We can always change our minds, and he has just as much to lose if we are caught. What do you say?"

Leave it to László to present a convincing argument.

We were ready to return inside when Laci grabbed my arm. "Look! Those men in the dark windbreakers near our cabin. They look too well dressed to be workers."

"Their whoring mothers!" I said, stopping in my tracks. "I'll give you odds they're ÁVO!" I felt a rush of heat spread through my body and my skin puckered with goose bumps. The now all-too-familiar sick feeling of fear welled up in my stomach. We backed out of sight.

"What are we going to do?"

Laci edged around the frame to observe the men. "Looks like they're watching our cabin," Laci said. "This means we cannot stay on the train, the next time it slows, we have to jump."

"Let's get the others and wait out here," I said.

Lacy nodded.

We entered the corridor, and as we made our way toward our compartment, the ÁVO men turned to look out the window. *This confirms it. The bastards are ÁVO,* I thought.

Laci explained the situation to the others. As nonchalantly as we could muster, we moved out to the boarding area and waited. The ÁVO men didn't follow, but kept watching, presumably conversing about us. I glanced at our small band of would be dissidents. We looked as much out of place on this train as the ÁVO men. Our clothes, even our haircuts were of the city. No wonder we were spotted so easily. A few kilometers outside Mosonmagyar-O'vár, still in the flat expanse of farmlands, the train briefly stopped at a small station called Hedervár and took on a few more passengers. The ÁVO men inched closer to us, but stayed in the corridor. When the train got under way again, I saw them relax. At an opportune moment Feri quickly opened the door, and one by one we jumped off the accelerating train. My heart pounded crazily as I lay in the trackside weeds, waiting, thinking that the next few moments would be decisive.

The train picked up speed without anyone else jumping off of it.

★ ★ ★

We found ourselves in the open countryside. Just a few hundred meters to the north was the Vienna Highway, denied to us by frequent patrols and checkpoints. Stretching in all directions were fields plowed over for the winter, separated by tall acacia trees.

"Now what?" I asked my companions, still staring after the departed train.

"Just a minute," Laci said, unbuckling his belt and unzipping his trousers. He started fishing around the front of his shorts.

"You could at least turn away," I told him indignantly, but he just laughed. Finally, he pulled a piece of folded paper from his crotch and opened it up. It was a detailed map of Northwestern Hungary. Laci zipped up his trousers and pointed toward what he thought was west, then to an area on the map. "We have to find our way between Várbalog and Mosonszolnok. We should stay off all major roads and skirt around the settlements. We have to be extra careful until dark."

"Only one thing," I said when he finished. "That's not the right direction!"

"I don't think it is, either," Feri added, "let's align the map with the highway; we know that runs east and west."

There was nothing to add. We started out in the direction Feri had pointed under an overcast sky and a threat of rain. We walked across the soft, life-giving earth single file, stepping into each other's footprints to make the going easier.

The lead changed from time to time, Miklós, our young companion holding his own. With Laci setting the initial pace, I soon found plodding through the fields hard work. We pressed on through the morning, stopping finally at noon under a row of acacia trees for lunch. We ate heartily, and thanked Aranka and our grandparents for our bounty as if they were there.

Laci did not let us rest for long. "We have to move on if we want to cover the extra distance we did not plan on," he said. "My guess is that we've come about fifteen kilometers and are still twenty to thirty kilometers from the border."

We grumbled, but scampered to our feet and spread into the now familiar single file. *Like the cartoon characters in Snow White,* I thought, *on their way home from the mines. Only in our case it's to the mines*, I added wryly. Without realizing it, I started whistling their song, "Hi-ho, hi-ho, it's off to work we go—" The others joined in.

The day wore on. We passed village after village and the sky slowly turned dark. Soon the lights from the settlements became our guides. At times we could hear the yelping of dogs and the peal of distant bells. Sound carried surprisingly far over the fields.

"Hi-ho, hi-ho.," There was something insidious about this stupid tune I couldn't shake. The rhythmic melody interlocked with my steps.

"Knock it off!" Feri finally pleaded.

Around ten o'clock the sky began to clear, and there was a noticeable drop in the temperature. In spite of this, I was not cold; if anything, I felt overheated. I rummaged through my pack and found an apple. Feri turned to see what the new sound was and soon followed suit. His breath trailed him as he munched and dissolved by the time I reached the same spot from a meter behind.

In another hour the moon slid above the horizon, its huge, yellowish dish cast an eerie pall on the countryside. Laci and Miklós were carrying on a conversation behind me, but I could only pick out an isolated word here and there over the sound of the earth crunching under our feet.

I noticed that the sky to my right began to glow. I stopped and pointed. "Could that be Hegyeshalom?" No one answered. "Anyone?" I pleaded for an opinion.

No one knew. We pressed on through yet another field. Ditch, trees, field; ditch, trees, field. Village lights in the distance. My feet were raw from chafing, and my ankles felt sore from walking on the uneven ground. We marched on.

Shortly after midnight the ground once again changed under our feet. We were walking on harder soil, grasslands as opposed to plowed fields. The moon was now overhead. The frosted blades of grass crunched with every step. The illuminated corner of the sky where I thought Hegyeshalom might have been, had moved farther to our right in the last couple of hours and was now behind our field of vision.

Laci was back in the lead. "Let's take a break at those haystacks," he said, turning around. "We must be nearing the border."

"Good idea," I agreed, swinging my pack off my back. "We should talk about what to do next."

Feri and Miklós were only too happy to oblige.

The haystacks Laci had pointed out reminded me of Cervantes' *Don Quixote*. I kept the observation to myself. They stood in clusters of three, nearly white in the bright moonlight, and cast impenetrable shadows. *Were these my windmills to slay?* I wondered, laughing.

"What's funny?" Feri, ever vigilant about my quirks, asked. "Sounds like you're on one of your cerebral adventures."

"Doesn't this scene remind you of *Don Quixote?*"

"I don't see the comparison, but would it matter?"

"You guys, cut it out!" Laci weighed in.

We reached the nearest group of haystacks and settled down for a break with our backs against the straw. Laci halved his sandwich and offered it to Miklós. We ate hungrily.

We were nearly finished when Miklós pointed at something to our right. "I think we're in trouble," he said full of anxiety. I followed his finger and saw motion at the edge of the field. *Men! They could only be border guards,* I thought. I felt the skin on my back pucker.

"Maybe they haven't spotted us," Feri whispered.

In another minute, I could clearly make out two men coming toward us, their weapons glinting in the moonlight. "Don't do anything stupid." I said, "If they find us, let me do the talking." I didn't expect a challenge from any of my companions. Laci, though older and a better planner, never argued about who should do the talking. From early on he had learned when us kids were in trouble, which was often, it was better if I did the talking.

The guards were upon us. As they neared, one of them stepped into the shadow of an adjacent haystack, and I lost sight of him. The other continued straight ahead. The four of us were frozen to silent stillness in the shadows.

From a distance of about ten meters, the guard called out. "Step out of the shadows!" he said, emphasizing his words with a motion of his gun. "We know you are there!"

I stepped into the moonlight, keeping my hands in front of me. A bead of sweat formed on my forehead.

"Good evening, officer," I managed, desperately searching my mind for a plausible excuse for our presence.

"This is a prohibited area, what are you doing here?" he demanded.

"We're refugees from the city," I said. "The Russians are rounding up everyone under thirty, so here we are." Border guards were selected for their loyalty to the regime, but they were still Hungarians. I hoped I could kindle some sort of patriotic sentiment against our traditional enemies.

Somehow, I mustered a calm, deliberate voice and called to my companions. "Come out, fellas; these men are fellow countrymen," I said. As if they didn't know.

One by one they stepped forward into the moonlight, except Miklós. Panic gripped my insides as we stood side-by-side facing the guard.

"There were four of you," the guard said, advancing cautiously, elevating the barrel of his gun higher. "We've been watching you!"

Miklós appeared from the far side of the haystack, out of the guard's line of vision. "Here I am," he said with a little voice.

The guard swung his gun in his direction, clearly startled.

"That's only a boy," Laci said, stepping forward, moving between the guard and Miklós, holding his left arm high to indicate his good intentions. "Come, Miklós, these men don't mean us harm."

While this was going on the other guard reappeared and closed the distance. He stopped beside the other man, his gun hanging loosely from around his neck, pointing at the ground. I could see his eyes.

"Jóska, come back here for a minute," the newcomer addressed the other guard. He spoke with a heavily accented, rural dialect.

The guards retreated a few steps and talked in a quiet, but animated, manner. I could only make out the words *kids* and *money*, but their posture was not alarming. I motioned my companions to stay behind and took a step toward the guards.

"Friends, we consider ourselves very lucky to have run into you," I said tentatively. The guards stopped talking, and I continued. "We have been worried sick about the minefields. Could we ask you to assist us through them? We could give you a bit of money for your trouble; it won't do us any good on the other side, anyway!" I held my breath waiting for their response, hoping that I had done the right thing. I felt wetness under my arms, and my forehead was now drenched.

The guards moved farther away and exchanged a few words. The one with the rural accent stepped forward. "How much money do you have?"

A feeling of elation replaced my dread. "We have several thousands, maybe five or six," I answered. "And I have a beautiful wristwatch, completely refurbished only a couple of months ago." I moved toward them, unstrapping the watch from around my wrist.

The one called Jóska took the watch out of my hand and pointed to my companions. "Go stand with the others!" he commanded.

For a moment, I panicked. *They are going to shoot us down, after all! Who was going to stop them?* But the guard turned and walked back to his comrade. Once again they began talking among themselves. I could not make out the words.

"Let them be," Laci whispered. "When they come back, I want to state some conditions. Let me have all the money."

While we fished the money out of our pockets, I couldn't help admiring my brother. The guards had the upper hand and yet, Laci wanted to set conditions. *He has balls!* I could hear the guards laugh in the background. *Only cold blooded killers could laugh while gunning down people*, I thought. I saw the white of Feri's teeth flash in the moonlight. He was grinning. I guessed he had similar thoughts.

The guards returned.

"We will help you, but you must do as we say," spoke the guard from the country. "Any deviation, and we'll have to arrest you!" Then he added, as if his question was incidental, "Where's the money?"

Laci showed him a stack of bills, but did not hand it over. "It's nearly ten thousand," he said, "but we would like some assurances."

The guard looked aghast. "Assurances?"

"We want you to lead us through the minefields," Laci said, "one of you up front. This boy is terrified of the mines," he added. "Could you do that for us?"

The guard shrugged. "Okay, but you must be completely quiet. There are other patrols out here. We can't be detected, or it's all over."

Laci gave him about half of the cash. "You'll get the rest when we are safe!" he said.

Jóska swore, but the other held him back. "Let's go," he said.

We fell into single file, one of the guards in the lead, the other following. In a couple of minutes the grass under our feet gave way to a well-worn path. The dwarf miners' song popped back into my head, but I chased it away. We walked silently on the hard packed dirt. I noticed that the vegetation was completely gone on both sides. Other than the trail, the ground appeared to have been raked or finely graded.

Every so often the path took a ninety-degree turn to the left or right. At times, the guard in the lead hesitated before continuing.

He's lost, I thought. Then the trail split into two, and we stopped.

"Live minefields," the lead guard said, pointing to our immediate surroundings. "Stay on the path!"

After walking about twenty-five more minutes, I saw a machine gun tower loom out of the nearly black night. We passed under it without stopping. The last sliver of the moon dropped below the horizon, and we continued in nearly complete darkness.

Suddenly, I heard a whistle in the distance. The guard raised his hand and stopped so abruptly that I bumped into him. He grabbed my arm. "Be silent!"

We stood motionless for a few seconds. Finally, he resumed walking, then stopped again. "You are a hundred meters from the Austrian border," he said, stepping to the side, pointing toward a dark mass stretching across in front of us. "We can't go any farther."

"Just a minute," Laci said. He gathered us around him a few steps from the guards. "Fellas," he whispered in our tight huddle, "if they start shooting, everyone must scatter to the wind so they can't get all of us! Got it?"

We murmured our assent. There was no time to think, no time to even wish each other luck.

"I'll be the trailer," I offered.

"Okay, this is it," Laci said turning to the guards. "Are there any more mines?" he asked them.

"We passed them all," Jóska said. "The border is straight ahead."

"Thank you for helping us," I said, as the others began to leave.

"Just a minute!" Jóska said harshly. "What about the money?"

Laci turned around. "Sorry, I guess I'm a bit nervous," he told the guard and handed him the rest of the money.

They watched us silently as we turned to go. "Good luck, kids," the one with the country accent called softly after us.

We hurried off toward the dark mass ahead of us, stumbling as we rushed, but not running. There were no sounds of pursuit, and we broke into a run. In a few seconds we reached the dark wall, now towering over us. It was the edge of a forest. Hidden by the trees, we sprawled on our stomachs to be completely out of sight and rested for several minutes. None of us acknowledged relief.

It was Feri who spoke first. "I've heard rumors that the signs indicating the border had been deliberately moved to lull people into false security. They would be gunned down, still on Hungarian soil," Feri explained nervously, still gasping for breath.

Here comes Feri's dark side, I thought, and fought off an impulse to snap one of my well aimed barbs back at him. *Oh, what the hell!* "Just what we needed to hear right now," I said, but secretly I welcomed the return of his usual self. I got up and picked my way through the underbrush, deeper into the woods. The others followed.

After about ten minutes of stumbling through the dark, I spotted a light directly in our path. I cautioned the others and moved ahead with measured steps, eventually reaching the edge of a clearing from which I had an unobstructed view of the source of the light, a single bulb encased in a wire cage fastened above a doorway.

I moved cautiously into the clearing. From this better view, I noticed a sign hanging below the light, partly obscured by shadows. It was lettered in Gothic and read *Schoolhouse*. Remembering Feri's musings about a possible trap, I backed into the shadows and groped around for a stone. I found one suitably sized and hurled it at the door. The clang reverberated through the clearing. No response. I found another stone and this time aimed higher, right at the narrow band of windows above the massive doors. The rock crashed through the glass with a loud noise that was followed by the sound of falling glass.

A barrage of German expletives issued from within.

My spirits soared. I waved with my arms over my head and shouted. "Come, fellas, we're in Austria!"

We hugged. When the understandably grumpy watchman made his way through the door to see what the ruckus was, I explained: *"Ich bien eine Ungarischen froitlinger."* I kept repeating this in my limited German, telling him that I was a Hungarian refugee.

He said something in German. I told him I did not understand. He motioned us inside the door and left us there. He came back in short order with two policemen, who led us through the clearing to a large barn. Here a man speaking broken Hungarian asked us whether or not we were armed. We said no. Finally, we were escorted into the interior where, to our surprise, we saw men, women, and children bundled up on thick layers of straw. Refugees like us from the People's Paradise!

Exhausted as I was, sleep eluded me until nearly dawn. My mind raced from one random thought to the other, wondering what the future may bring. Slowly the realization of what we had done dawned on me, and I couldn't help second-guessing my decisions of the last few days. *Was the price of freedom too high? What now, alone in a world I knew little about? Dear God, please make this all come out right,* I prayed.

PART SIX

AN ODD DECISION

"Pista!" a distant, but familiar voice called my name. I was warm; my head partially buried under a soft, light cover. Even though I wasn't fully conscious, I felt wonderful, and somehow I knew that I was safe; the terrible monster of my dreams was nowhere in sight. I turned to my other side.

"Pista!" the voice was more insistent now. Someone pulled the warm cover off my face. "You have to get up now; we'll be going to another place soon, and we still have to talk with the Red Cross and eat."

The voice belonged to my brother. I opened my eyes and sat up. Last night's events came flooding back. The light, the schoolhouse, the barn. *That's right, we are safe—and free!*

"What time is it?" I finally managed, squinting from the light.

"Near ten," Laci said. "Come on, they're giving food to everyone."

I scrambled to my feet, still dazed, wrought with muscle aches. My bladder was screaming for relief. Laci strode away. "Hold up," I yelled after him, "I must get to a toilet! Where are the others?"

Laci pointed to the side. "W.C.," he said impatiently. "Feri and Miklós are standing in the food line, hurry up!"

When I emerged from the barn, I was surprised to see a different setting than I remembered from the night before. There were several smaller structures forming a semi-circle around the main building. I saw none of these when we were brought here. A well-worn roadway bisected the buildings, leading to plowed fields past a small thicket of woods. A scene not at all dissimilar to the ones we had left behind in Hungary. Farther out, the fields were covered in a layer of ground fog, and farther still, the tops of trees formed the horizon. My first view of a foreign landscape was nothing I had imagined.

Small groups of people stood off to the side, slowly advancing toward a table laden with large pots and pans, baskets of bread and, a luxury this time of year, all manner of fruit. Some of the pots were steaming hot; giving off a continuous stream of vapor that was quickly absorbed in the morning air. The tables formed a serving line with two warmly dressed women passing out food from behind.

I spotted Feri and Miklós near the first table, their plates already full of food, still piling on some more. Feri struggled with an apple, but managed to slip it into the pocket of his overcoat. Laci stood in line behind them, still a few steps and a half dozen people between him and the table. He turned and motioned for me to join him.

When we finally reached the table I picked up a ceramic bowl with my numb hands. The lady near us smiled and pointed to one of the steaming pots with a red-from-the-cold hand. I nodded. She reached for my bowl and filled it with gruel, then poured milk on top from an earthen pitcher with images of field flowers. Her smile warmed me.

"*Kakao?*" she asked.

I nodded again, returning her smile.

She spread the brown powder generously on top of the milk, then looked past me toward the next person in line.

"*Danke,*" I said, smiling broadly, remembering my small reservoir of German words. "*Danke schön, fraülein, guten morgen.*"

The woman turned back toward me and smiled. "*Bitte,*" she said, seemingly pleased. She quickly added several sentences, and I realized she might have thought that I understood more. I continued to smile, but shook my head to let her know that I was at a loss. I pocketed a couple of apples and moved along. More food, more smiles. Ham, cheese, an orange. My hands were full. Still, when I saw bunches of bananas, I had to examine them. I had never realized that bananas were connected at a stem. I had to have one, to see what they tasted like, having seen them only in pictures. The one I chose was attached to another, so I took both, looking around, feeling guilty about the excess.

Near the end of the line, her sleeves rolled above her elbows, a woman washed dishes in a large, metal container. She was partly obscured by the rising steam. Looking at her made me realize that there must have been many people laboring on our behalf. Someone had to heat this water and bring it out here; unseen people who had donated all we were now enjoying, unheralded, infinitely caring and generous.

The four of us sprawled out on the steps of one of the buildings and ate, our breath mixing with the steam from our bowls.

Feri, using a piece of bread, pointed toward the clearing behind the buildings.

I saw two busses idling there.

"Someone from the Red Cross told me that we'll be transported to somewhere in the mountains, possibly a village in the Alps," Feri said.

I was about to ask him if the man spoke Hungarian when Feri shook his head and continued. "It was funny: though I understood only a word here and there, we communicated without too much trouble. After we eat, we should go see him."

Laci scraped the last of his porridge out of his bowl. "What about sending our 'We're safe!' message?"

With all eyes on him, Feri finished chewing before he answered.

"As a matter of fact, I did, ask him," he said with a hint of a pride in his voice. "The man indicated that someone would be collecting messages."

"What about the radio?" I asked.

Feri took another bite. "The man kept repeating 'Red Cross, Red Cross' to all my questions, so I guess they'll let us know when it's time." Feri paused. "I only hope, whoever it is, he speaks Hungarian."

"Me, too," Laci added. "We must live up to our commitment!"

He sounded determined, and I took comfort in his resolve. When Laci decided on something, anything, it usually happened. I was ashamed to admit that this was not always the case with me.

Miklós, who had been quiet all this time, pointed to our surroundings. "Did you guys expect anything like this?"

"I didn't know what to expect," Laci answered. "Just look at the number of us being fed, housed, kept warm. And I don't see anyone official here; these are but simple village folk, helping out."

Feri, his mouth full once again, nodded. "Maybe we should think about staying here."

No one protested. We finished our meals in silence. My guess is, we were all thinking about home, the people we left behind. Then Laci, ever efficient about focusing on what was important, faced Feri. "Did the man say the name of the place where we're going?"

Feri shook his head. "I could only make out 'Alps,'" he said. He looked at his empty bowl and rose to his feet. "We should get going."

I nodded and broke the two bananas apart. I bit into the end of one of them and was surprised by the dry, acrid taste. I frowned.

Miklós doubled over and started laughing. Feri and Laci joined in when they saw my prune-faced expression and the tip of the banana sticking out of my mouth, about to be expelled. When Miklós could finally speak, he said, "That's what I did, too, but the lady at the table showed me what to do." Miklós took the banana from my hands and peeled back the skin. "I'm glad I wasn't the only one," he said. "Try it this way. With the skin off, it's not so bad."

Feri, ever alert for an occasion to see me make a fool of myself, couldn't stop laughing.

We ended up on the second bus, happy for the warmth. The seats on either side were on a higher platform than the passageway between them; quite different from the city busses we were accustomed to. The seats were covered with a soft, absorbent fabric and were quite comfortable. There was even a toilette on board. The bus was clearly intended for long-distance travel.

My interest in busses stemmed from the fact that Hungary produced almost all the busses for the communist world, something we as a country were very proud of. This gave me my first opportunity to see the differences between the products of two different ideologies, socialism, and the much-maligned capitalism. While I had to admit that Hungarian busses were excellently conceived, I was enjoying the obvious differences in quality.

In a couple of hours, the highway began crisscrossing a fast moving river. From the occasional signs placed at bridges, I gleaned that the name of the river was the Inn. As we progressed the mountain ranges on either side grew taller, more akin to what I thought the famed Alps should have been. The gentle motion, the warmth, and the rumble of the engine had lulled most of our group asleep. Feri, sitting with his head slumped to his shoulder, began to snore.

I wiped the steam off the glass and stared at the alien countryside. The sky darkened and snow began to fall in large flakes. The mountains closed the Inn into a narrow gulch, barely wide enough for the river, the highway, and the railroad tracks that ran parallel on the other side. Outside, the snow looked very deep, gradually nearing the tops of the red marker sticks along the side of the road.

I was taken by the pristine, bucolic setting. This was more like the foreign world I had imagined. The river looked like liquid ice, the color of the water bluer than it should have been, appearing surreal from the comfort of the bus. The tapestry of white, gray, and bluish-black shifted constantly in the curtain of falling snow. Entranced, I remembered a painting I had seen at the museum. It was a masterpiece by a Flemish artist whose name I could not recall. I had thought him a disturbed person; no other could have conceived that picture. His painting looked photographically accurate except for the nightmarish colors. The scene outside looked unreal, while I knew for certain that it was.

Slipping in and out of the mist were small villages clinging to the steep mountain slopes, perfect examples of Alpine architecture. High, peaked roofs, elaborately carved ornaments and balconies, the fairyland of Hansel and Gretel. Only after having been on the road for several hours did I realize that something was absent; missing from all the structures were the scars of war.

While Hungary had made a Herculean effort to repair the damage caused during World War II, we still had thousands of buildings showing bullet holes and bomb damage. How could Austria escape from such? Or, a better question might have been, how could they have recovered so completely? I knew Austria had been independent for only the past year, and yet it appeared to be untouched, peaceful, and prosperous.

At about six in the evening and in complete darkness, we arrived at our destination, a group of cabin-like structures near a small alpine village called Kematen. Here, members of the Red Cross assembled our group in a large hall. They made lists and assigned housing. Through interpreters we were able to arrange for our radio message to be included in a Voice of America broadcast as well as in Radio Free Europe programming. The Red Cross assured us that our message would be aired in a matter of days.

Soon the four of us were comfortably situated in a room, one of several in a barrack that straddled a mountain stream. Even though we could only see a few steps in any direction because of the dark, I was completely delighted with the dramatic setting. Alas, sleeping was difficult due to the ever-present sounds of the babbling, noisy brook.

We learned the genesis of our friendly compound the next day. The Germans had built a Messerschmitt factory into the mountain during the war; our rows of barracks housed the workers and technicians that ran the factory. Kematen served as the shipping center for the Luftwaffe's aircraft produced here. The factory was never discovered by the Allies and was in production to the very end. *At least now,* I thought, *the compound will be put to a more noble cause.*

Life at camp took on the undercurrents of routine mixed with expectations. Miklós got word through the Red Cross from his uncle and left on his journey to America within a week. Saying goodbye to him fanned the flames of an ongoing argument between Feri, Laci, and me, an argument about our intended destination. Feri turned out to be an unreasonable romantic, quite different from the pragmatic, brooding person I had known him to be. He wanted to settle in France.

"Why France?" I asked, hoping to sway with reason whatever answer he might give.

"I just like everything I've read about France. And I like the way the French countryside looks."

"Ah! And when did you ever see the France countryside?" I asked with mocked surprise.

"In the paintings of the Impressionists," he responded, not a bit defensively.

"You mean to say those are your reasons?"

"Yup," Ferenc concluded.

And that was that. There wasn't much to argue with. I didn't have a better reason for wanting to go to my country of choice, the United States, either. In a few days we would have to fill out petitions, choosing among the eighteen countries that offered us refuge.

"What about you, Laci?" I turned to my brother, who had been adamant about staying in Austria.

"I told you," he explained patiently. "I want to be close to Hungary. That means staying right here. I also admire the good-natured people we found here."

Succinct as usual, I thought, and chose not to fan the flames.

A couple of weeks later, Laci appeared to be ready to consider some other place. I think his change of heart was brought about by his construction worker's job, the job he had obtained after our first week at Kematen. All three of us started working together, but the job we were hired for was finished and the builder had ongoing work for only one of us. He chose Laci, obviously being a good judge of character. So while Feri and me, and the rest of the camp slept in and enjoyed the easy life, Laci worked like a dog on a construction site, the only work available for someone unable to communicate in German.

Laci traveled via bus every morning to nearby Innsbruck. He worked in bitter cold or rain, depending on the changeable weather, wheelbarrowing bricks and mortar, passing them up to the masons who stood on scantlings and built the walls.

I could see the work was extraordinarily hard. Laci had a sore back as a result of the constant bending and handling of the weighty bricks. In addition, the bricks wore through even the sturdy gloves he had been given and left his fingers bleeding at the tips by the end of the second day. Still, Laci persevered. In two weeks he had earned enough money to buy a camera, one of life's luxuries at the time, and clothes that actually fit him. All the photographs we have of those times were taken with this camera. Typical of his generous nature, Laci used the remainder of his hard-earned money to buy chocolates and items of necessity for the rest of us, including the stamps for our letters.

Monday, December 3, 1956. Feri and I were arguing the merits of the country of our choice when Laci stumbled through the door, dripping wet, sore from another hard day at the construction site. He peeled off his rain gear and hung it on a peg near the lone window. Then he sat wearily on his cot and fumbled with his laces. I watched him try to undo the tight knot without success.

I continued my discussion with Feri while I went down on one knee in front of Laci, gently pushing his hands aside and removing his boots. He did not protest. While I got a fresh, dry pair of socks on his icy feet, he rested his hands, palms up, on his lap. His fingertips were just short of bloody with most of the skin worn off by the bricks. When he rose and took a jar of Vaseline from the shelf to treat his wounds, I resumed my argument with Ferenc.

"And there is the Constitution. Where else in the world would you be protected from someone knocking on your door in the middle of—"

"So," Feri said, sounding exasperated. He finished shuffling the cards and started on the pattern for a game of solitaire. "Are you trying to say that the French constitution does not protect its citizens from unlawful search or arrest?"

"No, but they have an active communist party there, and—"

"Guys, what I want to know is this," Laci interrupted. "Does either of you intend to go to the country of your choice alone, or do you want us to stay together?" He let the question hang in the air while he dressed his raw fingertips.

"My preference is for us to stay together," I said passionately. "I think we will need each other's support, and if we wound up in different countries, that would be impossible."

"What about you, Feri?" Laci walked around the table to look him in the eye. "Is it France for you, regardless of what Pista and I do?"

Feri shoved the cards into a pile and turned away from Laci's unblinking gaze. "I guess," he said, still sorting the deck, "if there was a fair chance we would—"

"Look, guys," Laci screwed the cap back on the Vaseline jar and rubbed more ointment into his hands, "the deadline to give our answer to the Red Cross is the day after tomorrow. They can't petition a host country on our behalf unless we tell them where we want to go. I don't think we should wait until the last minute and wind up with a hasty decision."

Feri placed a row of seven cards next to one another to start another game. "So, what do you have in mind?" He sounded more reasonable than he had been with me all day. *What's Laci's secret?* I wondered. *All we do is argue.* The brook continued its noisy babble under our barrack.

Feri turned the queen of spades over to replace the ace of diamonds. "So, should we draw cards, or what?"

"I guess we could do that," Laci said agreeably.

"Oh, no," I feigned dread and bumped Laci with my elbow. "Feri is too slick with cards. If we let him cut or shuffle, we are as good as on our way to France."

We laughed. The laughter took the edge off the seriousness of the moment. Even Feri relaxed and smiled.

"If not cards, what?" Feri looked at me, pushing the cards into a stack once again.

"Tell you what, guys," I proposed lightheartedly, looking first at Feri, then Laci, touching each of them on the shoulder. "How about each of us flipping a coin? Then, the one who winds up with the odd side up chooses our destination?" I pulled them toward me with my arms around them. We were united at the shoulders. "Whatever method we choose, we need to stay together. What about it?"

"Okay!" Feri nodded hesitantly, pushing the cards aside.

"Okay with me, too," Laci said, and a nearly unnoticeable smile crossed his face. "Let me see if I have the coins," he continued and eased his sore hands into his pockets.

He fished our three one-shilling pieces. These were the basic units of Austrian currency, made of solid nickel and perhaps a bit larger than Hungarian Forints. The coins had the two-headed Austrian eagle on their flip side. Laci handed each of us our piece.

I hefted the coin and flipped it into the air with my thumb.

"Not yet," Feri said, snatching the spinning shilling out of the air. "Let's go through the rules once again."

"Okay," I said. "We each flip our coin into the air. Two of the coins, and possibly all three, will land on the same side. If all three show the same side, we toss again. But more likely we will only have two coins with the same side up." I looked at Laci, then Feri, to see if my proposal made sense to them. They both nodded, so I continued, "The person who winds up with his coin showing the odd side, will select the country for all three of us. Agreed?"

Laci nodded again.

"Feri, how about it?" I asked.

"Okay," Feri said solemnly.

We stood up and formed a triangle in front of the stove, the only space large enough in the cabin for all three of us to stand.

"Let's do it," Feri said.

We placed our shillings on top of our forefinger and thumb, ready to flick. We looked at each other, and without further discussion, flipped the coins into the air.

I watched my coin glint with each revolution as the light from the window bounced off it. Flash, flash, flash, it spun through the void skyward. I caught it and placed it on the back of my left hand. The coin was still covered with my right palm.

Laci had been laid off Friday. The construction was finished, and there was no other work. We celebrated the occasion by climbing into the Alps above our camp the following day. The weather was unexpectedly mild and the once thick blanket of snow that covered the road leading out of the village had melted away.

A short distance above our camp at the base of the mountain, we passed a massive wooden door that closed off the entrance to a cave. The door was fortified with thick iron bars and had *Verboten* written in large, red letters across it.

"This must be one of the entrances to the Messerschmitt factory they were talking about," Feri said. "I wouldn't mind exploring, but the place looks impenetrable."

"If we stayed here for a while, I bet we could find out who owns it, and maybe we could do something with it," I opined.

"You two are incurable dreamers," Laci sighed.

I shrugged. "So, what else is there?"

"Hear, hear," Feri echoed.

We climbed on. In about an hour, we came upon a hydroelectric plant along the trail. The stream that ran below our cabin floor came through this plant, which in turn used waters impounded in a small alpine valley. Several streams fed the reservoir, some plunging as thundering waterfalls down the face of the surrounding cliffs.

From our perch far above the valley floor, the majesty of the Inn valley had us agog. Across the river a nearly vertical rock wall reached toward the sky, disappearing finally in the capping clouds that shrouded the peaks. Below us, the hamlet Kematen, with its red roofs and church spires, looked like an artist's rendering on a post card. The river, white in places from small falls and rapids, wound its silver ribbon across this paradise. *No one*, I thought, *could look at this magnificence unmoved*.

"I wonder if we made the right decision," Laci said quietly. Feri and I didn't answer.

The big day came on Monday, December 17th, 1956. We hung around our cabin until nearly noon, getting nothing done. Feeling guilty, I finally washed the dishes and walked to the church with Laci to take pictures. In the afternoon we watched a film called *Two Lives*. All the girls cried. At the evening meal, Laci and I finally received our visas to enter the United States. Inexplicably, Feri did not get his. I don't know how the selection was made; we applied together. The next morning at eight-thirty, exactly one month after leaving Budapest, we boarded a train for a journey to Germany. We would go on from there either by plane or ship.

★   ★   ★

In 1999, forty-two years after the events described here, Laci graciously offered me a copy of his diary, the existence of which I was unaware of until then. "Here," he said. "I came across this the other day while rummaging through some boxes in the garage. I thought it might be useful to you."

The diary chronicled the day-to-day events of our journey out of Hungary and gave me much-needed information to authenticate my memory, thus helping me with the successful completion of this book. In addition to the events of the days in his diary, Laci described his struggles and, in my opinion, his extraordinary will to succeed. I found reading his diary a source of inspiration.

NIXON

Our departure for Germany was delayed due to the unavailability of accommodations at Bremerhaven. I celebrated my nineteenth birthday in Salzburg, at a place called Siezenheim, Camp Roeder. It was not as cozy as our barracks in Kematen, but the place was clean and much warmer. While the camp was well organized, I missed the babbles of our brook.

Laci and I spent considerable time walking around Salzburg, a quaint and lovely city. In spite of the cold, and at times, heavy snowfall, we slowly got to know the city. The parks featured statuary without political overtones, and romantic walks for lovers.

We visited the Mozart Museum. It was wonderful to see where this musical genius had lived. I tried to play a few notes on his piano, but was courteously prevented by a uniformed usher. I wondered what Mozart's life had been like here, in this city, among these objects that had become artifacts beyond price. I loved Salzburg. I could have been very happy living there. We found the people well dressed and friendly.

Our daily routine started at the camp office, asking about Feri. No one seemed to know what had become of him, but we were given assurances about finding him. *Better here in Austria*, I thought, *than somewhere in Germany or America*.

On a sloppy, rainy morning that made visiting the city uninviting, Feri came around the corner from the direction of the bathrooms. It had been at least two weeks since the last time we saw him in Kematen.

He was grinning from ear to ear. "You guys were asking about me?"

My heart skipped a beat, but I didn't want him to know how much I missed him. "Nah, must have been rumors," I said, hugging him. "We just wanted confirmation that your visa to the States had been denied."

We celebrated our reunion by counting our shillings and going to a typical Austrian tavern. Hung above the entrance was a gilded, wrought-iron-encased board with grape bunches framing *1698*, the year the tavern was established. As we descended a flight of stairs to a dimly lit room, I couldn't help wondering about the role this place might have played in Salzburg's history. Did Mozart or Beethoven ever drink here?

Below, people sat along a long bar, behind which was a beveled, smoke-colored mirror. Lamps with drop-shaped, multi-faceted crystal adorned every corner. Room after room, the place was crowded with patrons.

After having been seated, our waitress, an attractive young woman dressed in local folk attire, took our order. She leaned close to hear over the noisy chatter, and in so doing her breasts became fully exposed under the loosely cut blouse. Feri, who sat next to me and had the same view, elbowed me in the ribs. I ignored him. "*Baumglasser wein, bitte*," I said, struggling with my German pronunciation.

The waitress smiled. "*Sind sie Ungarische jungen?*" she asked and raised her eyebrows in anticipation.

I understood her to ask, 'Are you boys Hungarian?' so I answered, returning her smile, "*Ja.*"

She turned toward the room and said something loudly, which I couldn't understand. Suddenly, the noisy room became silent. In moments, merry people surrounded our table. Glasses of wine appeared; toasts were made. My limited German was useless. Questions flew at us in rapid succession, negating the need for our response. All we could do was smile. We smiled, shook hands, and raised our glasses.

"To Austria," we said.

"*Ungarische,*" they responded.

Our glasses could not be emptied; a fillup followed each sip. Someone in the room started a song. It must have been a drinking song, because the patrons held each other by the shoulder, swaying side to side, raising their steins. We were pulled to our feet. Every so often, to a refrain known only to them, we stomped our feet against the floor twice, and drank. Then, we hopped to our left to some disorganized rhythm and drank again.

I vaguely remember being dropped off in front of the compound sometime before dawn. My only clue to the time was the fact that it was still dark. Before making it to the gate, I vomited. The car full of merrymakers could be heard from a block away as they drove off.

Between bouts of nausea I said to my companions, "And we worried about the cost of a glass of wine!"

Word that the Vice President of the United States, Richard Nixon, would be visiting spread through Siezenheim. The next day the whole camp turned out and lined the roadway as his motorcade entered and pulled up in front of the main building. Laci snapped several pictures of him and his entourage as he made his way around the compound.

Franz, one of the interpreters, summoned me to the camp office after lunch.

"What's going on, Franz?" I asked.

"All I know is they are asking for people who went to school in Hungary," Franz said.

"That would be everyone here," I laughed. "You must have misunderstood."

Franz shrugged. "Just have a seat; someone will come and get you in a few minutes."

I was leafing through a magazine when a man in a dark suit appeared.

"Istvan Horvath?" he asked, pronouncing my name reasonably well.

"Yes?"

"Please come with me."

I followed him to a small office with a bit of anxiety. Without reason the circumstance reminded me of Tatabánya, being interrogated by the Soviet political officer. The man offered me a chair.

"Franz said you were a worker at the Csepel Metal Works. Is that correct?" He spoke halting Hungarian, but without an accent.

"Yes, I worked there on the graveyard shift and went to school during the day," I answered, wondering what this was all about.

"Vice President Nixon would like to meet with a representative group of freedom fighters this evening. Would you like to be there?"

I hesitated.

"The setting will be that of a dinner, hosted by the Vice President, and there will be interpreters to assist."

"I don't have anything suitable," I said, pointing at my attire.

"Please don't be concerned. The vice president understands the circumstances."

That evening, Vice President Nixon met with sixteen of us refugees, each representing a university or technicum, or, in my case, the Csepel Metal Works. We sat around a lavishly set dining table, answering questions posed by Mr. Nixon through his interpreters. The food served was Austrian; there was no alcohol, not even wine. The Vice President made remarks about America opening its borders to us refugees. "You will follow in the footsteps of millions," he said.

Except for a few words on BBC, this was the first time I had ever heard English spoken. After listening for a few minutes I wondered how humans could make sounds like these. At that moment, I seriously doubted I could ever learn this language.

After the Vice President's remarks, we were invited to ask him questions. A tall, young man sitting at the far end of the table asked, "What is the United States' position concerning the Russian invasion and occupation of Hungary?"

The Vice President listened carefully to his interpreter before answering. "The United States supports NATO in their efforts to preserve European security in the face of this Soviet aggression."

The young man mulled over Nixon's answer. "Mr. Vice President, will the United States or NATO act to support Hungarian independence?"

Again, Mr. Nixon listened carefully. "The United States, in concert with NATO, will do whatever is necessary to preserve European security," he said through the interpreter.

Several more questions were asked in an attempt to pin him down, but he sidestepped skillfully. While I hated this game of politics, I was impressed by the fact that a person of such importance would take the time to confer with us.

Much later, in the 1960s and 1970s, I saw Mr. Nixon on several more occasions. I worked for Western Airlines in California, and my job called for seeing to the needs of VIPs. He remembered me after I reminded him of our chance meeting in Salzburg. From that time on, whenever he came through the Los Angeles International Airport, we would visit. He would ask about conditions in Hungary and my family there. I knew him to be a courteous, immediate person. I voted for him twice when he ran for the Presidency.

Early in the morning on January fourth, we boarded a train for Germany in pouring rain. When the train made its first stop a couple of hours later, we were treated to a pleasant surprise, one that would be repeated time and again as we crossed Germany en route to Bremerhaven.

As the train pulled into the station, crowds of cheering people were waiting for us. When we lowered our windows, packages containing food, clothing, and personal items such as razors, toothpaste, soap, were tossed up to us. In a short time, we had more than we could possibly use. Still, we were happy to be so received.

As the train slowly advanced toward our final destination, Germany's, and perhaps Europe's, largest port, our progress slowed to that of a snail. We were halted at just about every sidebarb and sat for hours on remote pieces of track waiting for other, more important trains to pass, or for the loading and unloading of cargo. In spite of the jubilant receptions we had enjoyed passing through some of the towns, it was clear that getting us to Bremerhaven was not a priority.

At one point, during our third day on the train, we were halted for over five hours, freezing inside the compartment. The train sat idle a few kilometers outside an industrial city, perhaps Hannover. We could see smokestacks and cranes towering in the distance under gray skies. Then we began to move and the temperature in the cabin rose immediately as always once we were in motion.

Bremerhaven was a large, bustling port. It took us nearly four hours to traverse it, this of course with frequent stops. The skyline revealed distant skyscrapers, some of which appeared to be at least thirty stories high. The tracks now ran parallel to a narrow body of water, lined on both shores with cargo ships. From the size of the ships I knew they were ocean-going vessels, so this body of water must be part of the sea. My first sight of it. I had dreamt about the oceans, what they would be like, many times in my childhood. This was not what I had imagined.

With our faces pressed against the windows, we stared at the bustling activity. There were trucks, larger and longer than I had ever seen. Towering cranes lifted boxes trapped in giant nets onto ships' decks, and I saw a tugboat push a behemoth vessel toward the center of the waterway. The tugboat's screws were turning at full power, as evidenced by the waves behind the stern, and yet the giant freighter barely moved. The ship's depth marker showed *15m.* My own calculations surprised me. *That's four stories under water!* I thought, wondering about the ship we would be sailing on. "I hope ours will be at least that big," I said to my companions, pointing at the vessel.

"And I hope it's luxurious," Feri said.

COKE

The busses pulled up in front of a large vessel, unloaded, and left to pick up another load at the rail station. Feri, Laci, and I were among the first to arrive dockside. We immediately backed away some distance to look the ship over.

The ship's bulwarks arched proudly past the bow's waterline, at least two stories above the quay, and the flying bridge that spanned the beam rose another two levels above that. The communications mast was topped by the symbol communists the world over hated most: an American flag. The flag hung motionless in the absence of a breeze, nearly lost in the grayness of the sky. Three giant smokestacks completed the superstructure, each at least a meter in diameter and about five meters tall.

I slowly walked toward the bow with Laci and Feri in tow. I wanted to see her name. High above, suspended from the port bow, hung an anchor of such dimensions it must have weighed at least a metric ton. It was shackled to a chain whose links were the size of a man's leg from the knee down and as thick as his arm. Ropes, with diameters also that of an arm, stretched from nearby ballards to hold the ship in place. There, against the ship's naval gray penned in sparkling white was her name: *USS Marine Carp III.*

As the busses made their trips to and from the rail station, our crowd of hopefuls climbed the ship's stairs. The three of us lingered on the wharf, looking in amazement at the ship that was to take us to the New World.

"For all we know," Laci said with a measure of sadness, "these are our last few minutes in Europe."

If one didn't know him well, one would have thought his expression stoic, but I knew better. His face reflected deep feelings, carefully guarded from display. I put my arm around him. "I know America is far away, but right now any place on earth would be too far," I said to him softly. "I also know that when the time comes for our return, planes will make the journey reasonable." I hoped my understanding would give his spirits a lift.

The sky validated our mood. A gentle rain started falling out of the grayness and the fog thickened, obscuring our vision beyond a few hundred meters. Laci hastily took a couple of shots and put his camera back into his pocket.

We turned toward the ship's gangway and slowly walked our last few steps on European soil arm-in-arm. Then we joined the back of the throng and waited our turn to mount the stairs.

Our compartment was one of eight on our deck, each similar in size, holding about fifty berths suspended from the walls and bulkheads by chains, in sets of threes, one above the other. The deck below us had a similar layout. In all, *US Marine Carp III* accommodated a thousand of us refugees, none of whom had ever been at sea.

Once our meager belongings were stowed on our berths, which in my case consisted of a small canvas bag filled with two socks, a shirt, a pair of badly worn slacks, one spare pair of under shorts, a toothbrush, toothpaste, and a razor, we ran up to the deck to explore.

On each side of the ship, rows of lifeboats with canvas covers hung from their tethers. The bow, the triangular area enclosed by the bulwarks and the bridge tower, was loaded with winches and other equipment. These appeared to have been designed to handle the anchors and to lift supplies on and off the ship. There was a similarly equipped area amidships, minus the anchor-related machinery.

I was in the process of stepping off the length of the deck when the rain, which had slowed to nearly imperceptible for a while, began in earnest. The sudden downpour forced the refugees, who until now had crowded the rails two deep, to seek shelter. I stubbornly finished measuring, then joined Laci and Feri who, having more sense then I, stood out of the rain under the cover of the flying bridge.

The three of us huddled under the port side flying bridge and watched the sailors as they prepared the ship for departure. One by one the heavy ropes were winched onto the deck until only a single bow and stern line held us fast. Rain or not, the loading of goods continued through the gangway; the ship was not ready to depart.

We decided to go below and found our compartment filled with loud, boisterous laughter. A tall young man, whom I had met at the Nixon reception in Salzburg, stood on his cot, waving a piece of paper in each hand. He was dressed in ill-fitting, too-short slacks, and sky blue socks. Due to a slight hunch of his shoulders, he reminded me of a stork. He was reading alternating lines from the "official" schedule of meal times, mixed with lines from a paper in his other hand, a notice calling on us to appear on Boat Deck for emergency evacuation training at 1800 hours. The results were chaotic, and very funny.

The young man read with the serious, stereotypical voice of minor bureaucrats we knew so well, and while exploding laughter constantly interrupted him, he never cracked even a smile. This had us doubled over, howling out of control.

Someone handed us our copies of the notices. Both were written in Hungarian, but the letters lacked the dots and commas that characterize the Hungarian alphabet. Without these, Hungarian is nearly incomprehensible. Apparently it was this that gave birth to the much-needed hilarity.

At about the time the last drop of humor had been wrung from the notices and the laughter died away, a deep rumble reverberated through the ship. *The engines!* I thought.

"Hey, guys, what do you say, we skip our meals and ask permission to visit the engine room instead?" I said to my companions.

"I'm starving," Feri said, not really saying no, but indicating his preference.

Laci looked at his watch. "The next meal after this is three hours away, at noon. I vote with Feri. Let's eat."

We went to the stairway and descended two decks where, according to the ship's drawings on display in the hallway, the mess hall should have been. We followed the noise of clanking pots and dishes down a narrow hallway and found it without trouble. Here we had to wait. A small group of people stood in line in front of a large, oval-shaped door, the entry to the mess hall. I noticed the opening could be secured with a thick steel door of similar shape.

"In case of a torpedo attack," I smirked, pointing at the massive door.

"Never fear," Laci picked up on my mockery. "Russian torpedoes are designed to explode only upon impact. And that," he paused, "requires aim."

I guess our idle brains needed diversion. We were still roaring as we entered the mess hall and took a ceramic bowl from an ingenious device that thrust the next bowl up to the same level as the one just taken. Between chuckles I watched Feri put his bowl back, remove it, and put it back again. I guess he was similarly fascinated.

Following the example set by the fellow in front of me; I selected a paper box and opened it. The box was full of what appeared to be small, flat circles of baked dough, slightly browned near the edges, with a sprinkle of sugar encrusted on them. We dumped the contents into the bowl. The guy ahead of me poured milk on top of his from a spigot by pulling on a lever. Again, I followed his example. We joined a small group at a corner table.

The three of us were exchanging small talk when from the corner of my eye I spied something moving in my bowl. I turned and stared at it for a moment, but saw nothing. I shrugged and took a spoonful for a tentative taste.

Moments after my first, crunching bites, Feri jumped to his feet. "His mother's sainthood!" he said, staring at his bowl. Small black dots floated on top of the milk, several of them in motion. Just about then yells of disdain, only some of which would be worthy of translation, were heard throughout the dining room.

"This does it!" Feri snarled. "I am getting off of this ship and going to France. At least, I know the food there is edible!"

He sounded so serious; I was taken in for a moment. I spat my mouthful back into my bowl, which by now also had little wigglies floating on top.

"I'm with you, friend," I said grinning at him. "There, we could both look forward to eating gourmet snail dishes."

Feri shook his head from side to side, his face contorted in disgust. "I guess I can't win," he said with mock sadness.

We were en route to topsides when a deep, powerful blast sounded.

"We're leaving," Laci said needlessly. We doubled our pace.

From the rails, we saw two tugboats pulling our ship away from the wharf. Slowly, *Marine Carp III* separated from the quay and eased toward the center of the narrow waterway. The ship's horn blasted again and again, deafening us, the thousand hopefuls crowding her rails.

We stayed on deck, watching the ship negotiate the narrow channel and finally reach more open waters in the bay.

After the midday meal, Laci and I were relaxing on our cots when Feri showed up with a small bottle.

"Koka Kola," he said, and waited for some recognition. When none came, he repeated it. "Koka Kola. You know, the famous drink from America. I have been wanting to taste it for a long time, and here it is." He raised the bottle triumphantly. "I found a machine that gives you a bottle like this every time you put a five-cent piece into a small opening on its front. A crowd gathered, waiting their turn."

He said this as if he had just returned from a successful hunt, his trophy-sized prey in hand. I looked at the bottle. The base flared slightly and the faceted body had the words *Coca Cola* spelled on it with pretty, cursive letters.

"Well, let's open and taste it," Laci said. "I, too, have heard of this drink, and I'm curious about the fuss."

Feri fished a bottle opener out of his bag and popped off the cap. A small amount of dark liquid fizzed out and ran down the sides. Feri wiped it off with his sleeve and offered the bottle to Laci.

Laci shook his head. "No," he said. "It was your money."

Feri raised the bottle to his mouth and took a small swig. He swished the liquid around. "Oh," he said after swallowing, and handed the bottle to Laci with a quizzical expression on his face.

Laci cautiously sampled the fluid. "So, that's what Koka Kola is like," he murmured tentatively and passed the bottle to me.

Based on their response I was not about to attack the contents, as I would normally do. I raised the bottle toward the light. In the subdued light of our stateroom the color of the liquid appeared to be somewhere between darkish brown and purple. I put the opening to my nose. The smell reminded me of a childhood medicine I didn't like. I took a tiny sip. "Licorice," I said, and drank. In a moment, my throat closed down and my taste buds screamed foul. I spat the contents of my mouth onto the floor in an atomized spray. "This is terrible! The worst taste I've ever had!" I sputtered, and felt my face contort into a prune. "You mean to say people drink this for pleasure?"

I handed the bottle back to Feri, who shrugged and took another swallow. "I suppose one could get used to it," he said unconvincingly and offered the bottle to Laci again.

Laci shook his head with a bit more resolve this time and turned toward me.

"No more," I said, raising my palm to ward him off. I felt guilty. What had I gotten us into with my stubbornness about wanting to go to America? If this day foreshadowed what was to come, we were in for some trouble.

GREEN SKIES

USS Marine Carp III slipped through the calm waters of the English Channel, casting her bow waves toward the British Isles on the right and France on the left. The gray, dismal mist that had been our world for the last several weeks, lifted. Our throng of weary, America-bound refugees crowded the boat deck rails, enjoying the weather and taking in the sights none of us had ever dreamed of seeing.

Under a cloudless sky, we watched the afternoon sun reflect off the famed white cliffs of Dover. They looked deceptively close. France was clearly visible, also. Everywhere on deck one could hear excited voices and laughter. The feeble rays of the winter sun penetrated my parka and warmed my back. My first experience at sea was marvelous.

Feri found me, and we walked the steady-as-land deck to the

stern. A young woman tossed pieces of bread into the air, feeding the seagulls that followed the ship. We watched as the graceful gulls dove for the bread, their timing perfect. Not one piece of bread reached the water.

I bent over the rail and looked down at the boiling, white-blue water rushing out from under the ship, leaving a long trail. I guessed our speed at about twenty-five kilometers per hour.

Feri, in a rare display of curiosity, wasn't satisfied with just standing at the rail. He leaned far over to see the water immediately below us, so far, in fact, that I became concerned for his safety. The young woman who had been feeding the gulls exchanged worried glances with me. There was nothing to stop Feri from falling overboard if he lost his balance, except, of course, me.

I pulled him back. "If you should fall no one would hear your cries for help."

"And I doubt anyone could survive this cold, black water for more than a few minutes," said the young woman loud enough for us to hear, but seemingly to herself.

She was attractive, dressed in a smart ski parka the color of rust, and tight-fitting black slacks.

"I wasn't about to jump," Feri laughed. "If there were any danger of falling overboard, it would come from being pushed." He looked at me pointedly, still grinning. He turned back toward the woman. "Hi, I am Ferenc," he said playfully and with enviable charm.

"Zsuzsanna," replied the young woman, extending her hand in greeting. Then, she turned her attention to me.

"My name is István," I smiled and bowed my head.

She returned the smile. "Where are you from?" she asked.

I was about to answer, but Feri beat me to the punch.

"We're from Buda," he said. "And you?"

"I'm, oh, I,—" She looked past us and paused. "We are from New-Pest," she completed her words hurriedly.

I followed her gaze. A young man whom I had previously spotted, was approaching us.

"Zsuzsa," he said upon reaching us. "It's time for you to get out of this wind before you catch a cold." He pulled on her parka's collar and completely ignored Feri and me.

"These are Ferenc and István," she said, still smiling.

"Hi," the young man said absently, glancing at us only for the briefest moment. He pretended not to see Feri's extended hand and hooked his arm into hers. "Come on, it's time to eat," he said.

She shrugged and waved apologetically as he led her away.

We followed them with our eyes as they joined the rest of their group at the base of the superstructure. Feri sighed.

"Let's wake Laci," I consoled him. "We should get him up if he is still napping. As the man said, it's time for dinner."

The mess hall was crowded, and dinner did not look promising. We each took some bananas and apples, a piece of bread, and a tin of sardines, with a resolve to visit the engine room instead. On the way down, we quickly dropped our provisions on top of our bunks and hurried to the stairwell to begin our adventure of exploring the ship.

We descended several flights of twisting, stairs to the level of the engine room. In the few hours we had been aboard, the throb of the engines had nearly been erased from our consciousness, as had happened with the babbling brook in the Alps. Now, as we neared the engines, the rumble we could only feel before took on the dimension of a progressive loudness. The noise soon metamorphosed into a clanking, bone-shaking chatter of machinery. Even before reaching the engine room, I began feeling like a mouse trapped in the sound box of a piano with someone pounding on the keys. A placard hanging from a chain barred our entrance. I surmised the placard said *Authorized Personnel Only*.

"What do you guys think? Should we go on?" I asked rhetorically.

Laci motioned for us to stop and looked inside. "I see no-one," he mouthed, barely audible over the noise.

I unhooked the chain, stepped around him and through the oval opening. He and Feri followed. The interior was more cavernous than I had expected. Placed at inadequate intervals, light-bulbs caged in wire baskets cast pools of brightness here and there. When our eyes adjusted, pipes and machinery emerged from the gloom. The contradiction of the loud, body-invading noise and subdued light confused my senses.

We were walking on a steel mesh catwalk. Near the center, among more pipes and shiny, puzzling equipment, were two massive engines. They towered over us, twice again as tall as we stood. Along the length of each, a dozen set of rocker arms thundered up and down, blurringly fast. Their clatter resonated through every cell of my body.

"Their mother's sainthood!" shouted Feri, eyes wide.

I made a megaphone out of my hands and yelled, "Wow!" back to him. "Next to these, Big Kadi would look like a toy!"

"What?" Feri shouted back.

"No wonder the ship is so fast." I continued, stating the obvious, ignoring the fact that he had not heard what I had said before.

Laci just stood, transfixed.

Two glistening shafts extended from the engines toward the stern, each the diameter of my thighs. The shafts rotated with such speed as to appear motionless. I could imagine the size of the propellers they turned. As a child I read that the huge vessels that kept the arctic seaways open for shipping had propellers as large as nine meters across. That's about the length of two cars. I couldn't help wondering how our ship's propellers would compare.

I bent down to duck under yet another chain and take a closer look at a brass plate with engraving on it.

Feri held me back with a firm grip on my shoulder. "Someone is watching us," he shouted.

My eyes followed his outstretched arm as he pointed past the engines. Standing under a light halfway toward the ceiling on another catwalk stood a man in coveralls. He frantically gestured toward the exit. We turned our backs to the gargantuan engines and started to walk toward the exit where the man caught up with us. He pointed toward the tag on the chain, which was lying on the floor. "No," he said, shaking his finger while he looked at each of us, one face at a time.

We nodded our comprehension.

The man stepped back through the opening and hooked the chain to its former position. He was about to turn away when I stopped him by raising my arm.

"Thank you," I yelled in what I hoped was intelligible English.

He smiled and again pointed at the sign, which was now between us. "No," he said once more and stepped inside. The darkness swallowed him.

I awoke to a strange sensation, my body was pressing against the edge of my berth, first one side, then the other, then back again. The motion was soothing, but it woke me up. Eerie noises came from all around. Steel rubbing against steel, the sound of clothing slamming against a bulkhead. The air had the night smell of too many bodies in too small a space.

Our compartment was bathed in the red glow of nightlights. For a moment I thought I saw a man at the foot of my berth, but it was only my clothes, swaying back and forth, responding to the roll of the ship.

Cautiously, grabbing handholds with every chance, I reached the companionway. Outguessing the ship's motion was impossible. *Vertigo!* I recognized, sauntering from wall to wall like a drunk. I was happy to reach the boat deck.

A nearly full moon illuminated the deck and the water. Staggered by the roll of the ship, I walked loose-legged to the rails. Above me the subdued lights of the bridge were barely visible. Beyond, despite a bright moon, I saw a faint but familiar group of stars stare back at me as the ship rolled from side to side, responding to the swells that reached her starboard bow. The sea was dark, textured only with whitecaps and an occasional glint of the reflected moonlight. I peered into the night looking for land but saw none. I had realized one of my childhood dreams: we were at sea, out of sight of land.

By midmorning, most of the ship's company was turning green. I made the rounds up and down our deck. Compartment after compartment the story was the same: everywhere the onset of *mal de mer* showed on the chalky faces, and I could hear the moans and groans that went with it.

The sky gradually darkened, and the seas began to build.

Those of us who braved the cold and ventured onto deck were forced to hang onto anything securely fastened as our ship rolled.

On deck, the heretofore-unnoticeable crew began appearing in numbers. They were checking and securing all objects. A group of them inspected the lifeboats and tightened the ropes that held the canvas covers in place. They were preparing the ship for a blow.

I met up with my companions in the mess hall and found the place deserted. "Are we the only passengers who are not nauseated?" I asked. I selected a portion of bacon and scrambled eggs and place it on my tray next to a chunk of cheese.

"I'm afraid so," Laci said, scanning the empty hall.

"We aren't affected, because we're pilots." Feri said with a sense of pride as we sat down. "My guess is that by midday, unless the weather improves, the whole ship will stink of vomit."

"Stop! I'm eating breakfast," I said as I caught my sliding coffee cup and balanced it against the roll of the ship.

When we returned to the boat deck, we saw conditions had worsened. The sky was menacingly black and just ahead we saw low-hanging clouds. The waves had built some more, and once in a while the wind blew salt spray into our faces. I licked my lips. The water was as salty as I had read. In addition to rolling, the ship started pitching considerably as she mounted the oncoming waves. We followed Laci to the bow and huddled in the lee of the bulwarks, but finally the cold drove us below.

Even before we entered our compartment, the stench of regurgitated food assailed us. A sorry group of seasick people populated every corner, most holding lidless preserve cans and other containers at ready. The dignity of privacy was not afforded anyone.

I, too, came close to throwing up when I slipped on a puddle of a white-green, chunky discharge on the way to my bunk. Fortunately I caught myself; otherwise, I might have ended up sitting in it.

Feri didn't look good, either. "Let's go back to the mess hall and play cards," he suggested. "You look as if you need fresh air."

I was about to retort, but thought better of it. He was near tossing it up himself, and I didn't want to give him grief. "Must be the lights," I replied and tried to sound convincing. "I feel fine."

"You two might feel terrific, but I need to get out of here or lose my breakfast," Laci said, looking just as pale as Feri. "The smell is getting to me," he added.

"Let's take our coats so we can spend some time on deck," I suggested, hoping for takers. I wanted to see more of the storm.

"You're nuts. It's cold and wet out there." Feri looked unhappy. "Just my luck," he lamented, "instead of a luxury cruise, I'm trapped on 'USS Up-chuck.'"

I pressed hard against the steel door, and when it finally gave, I was rewarded with a blast of ice-cold air and a stream of seawater. "His mother's sainthood," I stepped back, letting the massive door slam shut with a bang.

"What's the matter?" asked Feri. "Let me help."

"It's nasty out there. I got a face full of water."

Laci stepped up to us. "Let's go. I'm ready."

The three of us pushed open the heavy door and stepped onto the deck. Nothing in my life, books, or imagination, could have prepared me for what I saw. As the door closed, the ship rose against us with the pressure of an accelerating elevator on its way up. The deck tilted to my left and sent us tumbling against the wall of the superstructure.

We watched a giant wave approach the ship. The wave towered above the deck, and as it neared, the ship rolled and rose to meet it. We continued to rise. The wave broadsided the ship and its cap boarded the deck we were on. Fortunately, the wind-driven top was mostly foam. Still, a tide of water rushed toward us, obscuring our view. We sprang away from the wall and sprinted toward the bridge tower where a steel wall formed a tunnel that shielded the door to the tower. The wall existed probably for just that purpose.

"The hell with this," exclaimed Laci. "If you guys want to stay, okay, I'm going below."

"I'm going to stay up here for a few more minutes," I said. "But I'll help you open the door."

"Me, too," added Feri.

I would have liked to explore the tower and perhaps find a way to the lee side, but Laci was ready to go below. When he left, Feri suggested we should go to the bow. Here the situation was much calmer. We leaned against the bulwark near the centerline of the ship where the rolling motion was minimal. I gazed through a small hole at the wild seascape. My brothers and I had often spent our summer days in the large pool of the Saint Gellért Hotel. The marble-lined pool had a wave-making machine, which created two-meter tall artificial waves every fifteen minutes to the delight of the bathing throng. But those waves were not even a ripple compared to these.

I watched as one giant after another approached. Not even in my dreams would I have believed such proportions. Everywhere I could see the ocean was a moving, erupting, living thing, ready to swallow the small, the wary, and the unprepared. First the water rose higher and higher, then the top curled forward and tumbled down into the trough, creating an avalanche that sounded like a thundering waterfall.

As the wave reached the ship, it detonated against the hull with a staggering blow. The ship shuddered and rose; the spray blasted into the air several stories above the bridge, falling as rain onto the deck. Then the ship rolled and slid into the void, and I could see the next giant that would mount a new assault. Our ship, which had been a man-made island, impervious to anything only hours earlier, had become a child's toy cast upon the angry ocean to be mauled at will.

I felt a tap on my shoulder, and when I turned I saw the grinning face of Laci. He must have had a change of heart and decided to join us. I was glad to have him near to share this experience.

"I think he means us," Feri pointed at the tower, where a small man dressed in the ship's uniform was waving frantically.

"Let's pretend he is just sending us a friendly hello," I suggested, and waved back with a broad smile.

The man clearly motioned for us to go toward him, but we pretended not to understand. A large wave sent a fountain of spray into the air, and the tower became obscured. When the cascading water cleared, the man was gone, and the door to the tower was closed.

"Look!" Laci screamed.

The next onslaught must have been a rogue wave because it impacted the ship nearly head-on and sent a wall of water over our heads. The wave continued in its path, slamming into the tower, sending a flood along its sides and white spray in all directions.

"Here comes the next one," Laci shrieked, and locked his arm around a piece of equipment. The deck dropped away from under our feet as the bow fell. We held on desperately. A savage vibration ran through the ship as the bow buried itself into the base of the wave and the ships propellers left the water. The sky above us became iridescent green. We sat down on the wet deck with our feet braced against the enormous links of the anchor chains and watched as tens of thousands of tons of water formed an emerald tunnel over us.

A communications mast carved a white path into the underside of the wave as the water passed over us with the speed of a locomotive. The liquid sky exploded against the bridge and sent a shock wave of white foam in all directions. I unbuckled my belt and looped it around the metal pole I had been hugging.

"Five, six, seven, eight—"

I became aware that Laci was counting. The bow dropped again, and again the savage vibration caused by the load-less propellers returned.

"Thirteen, fourteen, fifteen," Laci continued.

The bow submarined into the wall of water, rose abruptly, and the wall became our sky. Laci's face turned green. His coat turned green. I realized the absurdity of my thoughts but felt compelled to share them.

"Welcome to the Emerald City," I shouted with the booming voice of the wizard. "Oz, the wonder of wonders."

"I counted sixteen seconds between the waves," Laci yelled. "After the next wave passes, we should make a run for it." We only had a few seconds to discuss strategy before the next wave struck. Going for the door we had used to gain access to the deck was out of the question. The wave continued along the sides of the superstructure with the force of a dam break. The only chance we had was to gain entry to the tower through the forward door, the one used by the crewmember that tried to warn us.

"If it's locked, we're screwed," Feri said, probably thinking of his untimely death, seeing his broken body awash in the merciless, ice-cold waters of the North Atlantic.

"If we can't open it, we must get back to the protective shelter of the bow," Laci interrupted him. "We'll have just enough time."

Even before the wave was completely past, Laci and Feri sprinted past me on their way to the tower. I sprang up to run, but was firmly yanked back by my belt, which was still looped around the pole. With shaking hands, I unbuckled it. After what seemed an eternity, I took a couple of long strides toward the tower. My feet slid out from under me, and I slammed against a winch, hitting it hard with my shoulder and head. I saw the blackness of the open door and scrambled to my feet. I heard Laci's voice scream, "It's right behind you."

The deck started to fall away, and I felt the vibration of the exposed propellers run through the ship. I finished my run uphill. Feri and Laci pulled me through the door and dragged it closed behind me. The wave sent the sound of a giant mallet through our enclosure. I sat on the floor with my back against the wall and laughed. "Their mothers' sainthood! That was a ride!"

★ ★ ★

Little did we know that Liberty ships like ours were known to break up in rough seas. When, many years later on a sailing holiday in San Diego, California, I described my adventurous crossing to an old salt, he told me of his experiences.

During the Second World War, he had served as a first officer on a cargo carrier, which was also a Liberty-class ship. The ships had been built in the yards of Newport and Boston. During the height of the hostilities, a ship would be started every day and would be completed within thirty days from the time the keel was laid and it was commissioned. They were fast ships, designed to outrun the wolf-packs of the Third Reich, often traveling in convoys, escorted by even faster destroyers. Hundreds of Liberty ships plied the North Atlantic between the eastern seaboard of the United States and England, carrying men and war supplies. He estimated that, all told, German U-boats had sunk up to two hundred Liberty ships by the end of the war.

In addition to becoming prey to the wolfpacks, many Liberty ships were lost to the unpredictable storms of the North Atlantic. They became vulnerable in large seas, when the bow and stern were lifted by the waves, leaving the center unsupported. Given the right loading and circumstance, the ships would simply crack, fold amidships, and sink in a matter of minutes, usually taking entire crews with them.

His story finally explained our captain's decision to run from the storm and hide in the lee of the Canary Islands until the seas moderated. It was not his compassion for us, unseasoned refugees, that concerned him, but the safety of his ship. Well, maybe both. I am truly glad we were not informed of these dangers at the time of our journey.

★ ★ ★

The engines stopped. The sudden silence was startling. I wondered what had happened, but I was cozy under my blanket. Not only that, but both sets of my clothes were wet, hanging heavily at my feet. Feri and Laci were smarter; they had rinsed theirs with fresh water and hung them as soon as the storm abated. I, on the other hand, hadn't washed the saltwater out of mine, and they would not dry. By the time I realized this, it was too late into the night. Maybe the fellow above me would lend me a spare. Forget that! I saw him puke on his, and I doubt he washed it out.

"Guess what, Sleeping Beauty, we're at anchor." There was a rare element of excitement in Laci's voice. "We just had a briefing by one of the officers. The guy from across the hall translated, and even if he made some mistakes, it is clear that we are anchored at the Canary Islands off the coast of Africa. The captain ordered us here to get out of the storm. We'll stay here until the worst is over, maybe two or three days."

"His mother's sainthood! I thought the worst had passed, and we were in it," I mused. "Where's Feri?"

"He's on deck, supervising the crew," Laci laughed. "It's rain-ing and cold, but he has to make sure everything gets done right."

"Can you see the islands?"

"I came right here from the briefing and haven't been topside yet." He pulled something wrapped in paper out of his pocket. "Here, I got you a piece of cheese and an apple."

"Any chance you could get me dry clothes? I'll go crazy if I have to lie here for several more hours."

"I don't know, but I'll try. Guess what," Laci chuckled. "The officer in the mess hall talked about some foolish people who were nearly washed overboard in the storm last night—"

"That must've been us."

"He said that just when the captain ordered the ship to turn around and steam away from the storm, they spotted people trapped at the bow, but the ship was already turning, so he couldn't abort the maneuver, no matter what." Laci used his I-told-you-so voice to relay the story. I got the message.

"About the dry clothes—"

"Okay. I'll see what I can do."

While Laci was gone, Feri came below, soaking wet, and started to tell me the same story about the officer.

"I heard; Laci told me. What's happening topside? Can you see any of the islands?"

"I couldn't see islands, but we are about a kilometer off the shore. The land is obscured in fog, but seems to be very rocky."

Laci returned with some clothes, and I got to see a sliver of one of the Canary Islands between the low-hanging rain clouds and the dark waters. We anchored in calm waters for two more days, during which there was nothing to do or see. We ate and slept except for Feri, who read and re-read the two books he had brought from Hungary. Most of the passengers had recovered from the ravages of seasickness and, once again, enjoyed the voyage. At the end of the two days, the ship raised anchor and steamed out of safe harbor, making an elegant turn toward the west, throttling up to cruising speed. The skies never did clear, but the rain had stopped.

★ ★ ★

We spent the rest of the voyage in small huddles with various people. The whole ship was excited about the future and endless discussions raged concerning it. On the evening of the second day under cloudy skies and in thickening fog, we steamed into New York Harbor and docked at Ellis Island. We crowded the decks to catch a glimpse of the Statue of Liberty, but the famed lady was shrouded in fog. The date was January 17, 1957. It took me ten more years and a trip back to Europe before I had a chance to see her.

On this night, we said our goodbyes without fanfare. We were boarded onto busses and transported to a deactivated army base by the name of Camp Kilmer, in the state of New Jersey.

HELL IN PARADISE

Day by day, our numbers at camp shrank as the refugees were given employment. The ones with useful trades went first, followed by those who had some command of the English language. Of the three of us, Laci, who was a trained electrician, was taken first. He was hired as a handyman by an upstate New York sanitarium for the treatment of tuberculosis. Feri, who like me had no useful skills and couldn't speak English, came next, gaining employment as a laborer for a construction firm in Buffalo, New York. I was among the last to go.

Camp Kilmer was like a soccer field two hours after the big game, with only a fraction of the refugees still in residence. Except for the administration building and the commissary, most of the buildings had been re-closed. Even on this side, out of the twenty or so barracks, only six had occupants in them, including mine, soon to be closed due to lack of need. People were interviewed, hired, and gone. Gone, except for me, of course, and a few others like me: students without skills.

I'd had a chance the week before, but our interpreter caught influenza and couldn't make the interview. The people hiring, whoever they were, departed without taking anyone, and I was left to rot in this place for another week. It's not that the camp was bad, the buildings were warm and dry and there was plenty of food. Even movies every night. But the routine was boring, and I felt apprehensive.

At last, Tuesday brought some excitement. The dictionaries we begged for arrived, I received an English-Hungarian version. My initial enthusiasm waned when I realized its limited potential for learning; it was almost completely useless. How did they figure this would help? I wondered what an American would do if the situation were reversed and he was handed a Hungarian-English dictionary. How would he use it?

The big day finally came, and I found myself pacing nervously. Even reciting my small English vocabulary, "Hello, how are you? Good morning." didn't help pass the time. I kept glancing at the clock. Minutes to go before noon and my interview was not until one. I couldn't stay in my room any longer. I walked slowly around the sports field and headed for the administration building.

The woman shook my hand and sat down behind the desk, all smiles. The short, round-bellied man in a striped knit shirt who came with her made no attempt to be cordial. He moved his chair toward the door and sat, looking displeased.

The woman said something in a singsong voice and György, the interpreter, translated.

"She says she hopes you are comfortable here at camp. Her name is Dr. Baker."

I smiled. "Doctor, my name is Horváth, Horváth István," I said with a small bow. We both smiled.

"Have a seat," the interpreter said.

The woman riffled through papers on the desk in front of her. After finding what she was looking for, she read silently. I felt the small room close in on me; this woman had my future in her hands. Finally, she looked up and talked to the interpreter.

"I'm here representing a hospital in upstate New York," György explained for her. "We are interviewing for entry-level positions in patient care."

"Tell her I have no experience working in a hospital," I said apprehensively and smiled while the interpreter spoke.

"She says that's all right; the job she needs to fill requires no experience."

"What is the job?" I asked.

"They need people to clean up after patients and to supervise them, assisting the staff. They will pay minimum wages, but offer free housing and meals as part of the compensation package." György elevated the last syllable of *package*, hinting there was more. "Plus," he said, "free medical benefits."

"Sounds like a good deal," I said to him. "What do you think?"

György asked something of the woman, and she responded with a shrug of her shoulders before speaking. He translated. "This is the lowest job at the hospital. She does say there is a chance to move up after a year to a position called Attendant."

The fat man, who had been sitting quietly near the door, chimed in with a gruff, staccato voice. The Doctor responded with a bemused smile and dismissed him with a short wave of her hand. He fell silent.

"What is the title of the job she is offering?"

"Orderly."

The term meant nothing to me. I must have looked puzzled, because György repeated: "Or-der-ly." The Hungarian equivalent, *küldönc*, disclosed nothing.

"Please tell her I accept," I said and smiled at the doctor some more. I glanced at the man next to the door. His expression remained impassive.

György conveyed my assent and Dr. Baker nodded. She spoke briefly.

"She says she has two more people to interview. She would like to meet everyone selected in front of the administration building at three this afternoon. She wants to take everyone with her and asked if you could be ready."

I just about jumped with joy. I had been offered a great job in the state of New York. It was more than I could have hoped for.

"I'll meet her in front of this building at three," I said, still smiling. "And György, please let her know how much I am looking forward to working at the hospital."

The translator complied.

Dr. Baker smiled and nodded. "Good!" she said. She stood and offered her hand.

When she and the fat man were gone, I stopped György at the door.

"What kind of hospital did she say this was?"

"A state hospital. You know, a place for crazy people," he said and walked out.

I paused. What did I get myself into this time?

The station wagon was brand new, a 1957 Chevrolet with stylistic tailfins. I had never sat in an American car before, but I remembered admiring them in Budapest. In particular, there had been an all black DeSoto in front of the American embassy with chrome bumpers that had me agog. It had the most beautiful, green-tinted windows I had ever seen.

The elongated car we were about to ride in even had a windshield shade and, as I discovered later, a heater and a radio. The ultimate in luxury. Judging from what I could see, everyone drove shiny new cars. Perhaps, one day—

By ten after three, we were rolling through the main gate of Camp Kilmer on our way to Poughkeepsie. I remember asking Dr. Baker time and again to pronounce the name of the town, but I couldn't quite master it. She wrote it down in my notebook: *Pough-keep-sie*. Hard as I tried, I couldn't connect the sounds with the letters.

There were two other Hungarians traveling with us. They were, I learned, destined for a campus different from the one I had been assigned to. We sat on the seat behind our driver, the round-bellied man, and Doctor Baker.

The road was very wide, with two sections in each direction, separated in the middle by a drainage ditch. The drive was so smooth and quiet I could hardly believe we were traveling at breakneck speeds. We paralleled the Hudson River most of the time, and except for the strange architecture, the whole area looked very much like the countryside along the Danube.

After about an hour and a half, our driver pulled over to the side and stopped in front of a building that was brightly lit even in daylight. There were benzene pumps outside and bathrooms inside. Soon we were back on the road, our car fueled and we, refreshed.

Poughkeepsie was beautiful. Nestled on the north bank of the Hudson, the small city's lights sparkled under a forest of stately pines, illuminating orderly rows of houses. The grounds were landscaped with trees and ornamental shrubs.

Once across town, Dr. Baker pointed to an elaborately landscaped mound, which had an ornately lettered sign centered on it. The property was behind a wrought-iron fence of pointed lances and red brick posts.

"The hospital," she said.

I saw no sign of a hospital behind the fence, only undulating, grass covered hills and clusters of pine trees. I thought perhaps I had misunderstood. Finally our car pulled up in front of a massive gate, which slowly opened. A uniformed man stepped out of a pinnacled, sandstone guardhouse. Dr. Baker called out to him. Satisfied, he waved us through.

As the car rounded a small hill, a large, well-lit mansion came into view. It had tall pillars holding a peaked roof over an elaborately detailed, marble-floored entry. Judging by the rows of windows, it was three stories high, perched on a red brick foundation.

"Ithaca Hall," Dr. Baker said.

It was Greek to me.

In the next few minutes, we passed several similar buildings. We finally stopped at another three-story, imposing structure, and our driver motioned for me to get out. Dr. Baker also got out, and after a brief exchange between her and the driver, the others continued on their way. A scent of flowers drifted in the cool breeze.

Dr. Baker said something, and when I responded only with a smile and my shoulders pulled to my ears, she reached for my hand and led me to the entrance. She rang the bell. The well-lit portal became bathed in additional light. A male dressed in all white opened the door and motioned us in. He was a tall, husky man with the name Kowalski embroidered over his left chest. As Dr. Baker and I followed him, I noticed he carried a number of keys chained to his belt. The chain looped halfway to his knees and banged against his thigh as we walked.

We went through several doors, each requiring one of our escort's keys, before we stopped in front of a white door off a blue corridor. Dr. Baker spoke briefly with the man. He opened the door, and we stepped into a small, attractively furnished room with pale blue walls. There was a freshly made bed on a metal frame against the far wall; a white dresser; a small table, also white; and a couple of chairs.

The man turned toward me and pointed at his chest. "Kowalski," he said. He fished a small notebook out of his shirt pocket and wrote something on it. He handed it to me.

"Te-le-phone," he said slowly and loudly. "Telephone Kowalski," he repeated.

I looked for the phone and after spotting it, glanced at the paper. There were three numbers on it. "Thank you," I said and offered my hand to Dr. Baker, then to Kowalski. We were all smiles.

"Bye," Dr. Baker said, and she left the room.

Kowalski opened the wall and exposed a row of hangers. I nodded my understanding. He motioned for me to follow him. We walked a few steps down the corridor, where he pointed at a door with the silhouette of a man on it. We entered. There were several shower stalls, sinks, urinals, and commodes inside. Everything was sparkling clean. I used one of the urinals. Kowalski waited until I rinsed my hands.

"Good night," he said and walked out.

Back at my room I stood in the doorway. *This is paradise,* I thought, and strode to the bed to try its firmness. I had arrived.

I spent the next few days learning my way around the building.

There were three stories, if one counts the ground floor as such, and in Europe, we don't. The first level housed the staff's quarters, the cafeteria, and the administrative offices; the upper two each had a large dayroom for patients, bedrooms, toilet facilities, and isolation rooms. Every room required a special key to access. At this point, I was not considered staff, so someone, usually a nurse, always accompanied me. There were two women on staff, nurses, who spent only their working hours here and were housed in a separate building. I found both of them attractive.

The first time I was escorted to the upper floors, I had a lump in my throat. I wondered what I would see. Though this was the middle of the day, the patients were dressed in pajamas. Most of them were gathered around a television set, staring at the blank screen. As I walked through the dayroom, I had the impression of zombie-like movements among the interned. One of them sat on the hardwood floor rocking back and forth incessantly. He was about my age. He smiled a drooling smile when Kowalski called him by name. I felt pity for him and wondered what had happened to bring him here.

Another patient, an emaciated older male, was shooed off a hot, steam-heated radiator by Kowalski. With only a nightshirt covering his upper body, his buttocks were scarred with burn marks. I raised my eyebrows at Kowalski. He shrugged and circled his right temple with his pointing finger.

The man climbed back onto the hot radiator and stared at the floor in front of him. The attendant on duty, a well-muscled young man, walked up to him and hit him on the head with his paperback. The man squealed and raised his arms over his head. He slid off the radiator, walked a few steps, and sat on the floor. The attendant resumed reading his book. By the time Kowalski and I returned from the floor above, the patient was back atop the radiator. I felt relieved when we left.

The staff cafeteria was in a separate structure about an eighth of a mile from my building. Right from the start, a small group of nurses asked me to join them. They helped me learn new words and laughed when I massacred them. They also laughed at my choice of foodstuffs: bread, milk, and fruit. I had a difficult time eating any of the meals, except for breakfast. Even Americans couldn't spoil the taste of ham and eggs. The food looked good for the most part, but had no taste. I must have lost weight in the few days I had been there.

I loved walking the seemingly limitless grounds. Without doubt the most beautiful garden I had ever seen. Even though it was winter, the sun shone nearly every day, and I spend a lot of my free time outdoors, vocalizing English words and phrases. Everywhere, the walks led to gardens with gazeboes. There were at least a half dozen of these specially landscaped areas scattered throughout the hospital grounds.

The vine-covered enclosures had small, babbling waterworks, statuary, and comfortable benches. One could sit and read, or just listen to the water and the finches. I would come alone or with Lois, one of the nurses assigned to my ward, to study words. She helped me with pronunciation.

In the evenings, once I was off the clock, I wrote down the list of words I wanted to learn next. On average, I learned fifty or so words a day, including ones that came up in conversation or on TV. I quickly became familiar with all the new products and what they did. I loved the commercials because they showed through pictures what they were talking about.

Work did not go as well as I had hoped. My days started with a shower and shave, a quick breakfast at the cafeteria, and reporting in for duty. Someone would let me into the dayroom on the second floor a few minutes before the patients returned from their breakfast. I'd quickly mop the linoleum floor in the hallway and the parquet in the dayroom, usually finishing as the patients began milling about. Then I would turn on the TV and help dispense pills. Many of the patients refused their medication and had to be forced.

The rest of the day I watched the patients and kept them from doing harm to one another. If there was trouble, I called for help on the wall phone, which automatically rang the nurse's station.

My quest to speak English as quickly as possible took on increased importance with every passing day. In spite the lovely setting, I slowly realized fortune had landed me in a terrible place. Many of the patients frightened me, but none as much as the attendants. They were a sadistic bunch that got along well with everyone as long as they didn't have to do anything. As soon as a patient required attention, they would punish the person mercilessly, seemingly enjoying the process. Most of the patient's bruises and black eyes were not acquired by accidents or fights with one another as claimed by the attendants, but were inflicted by them. Despite the heavy sedation practices of the times, the patients were terrified of anyone wearing a white uniform.

One day on duty with Kowalski, we both joined the patients watching television. A patient walked up to Kowalski and muttered something in his ear. Kowalski was engrossed in the program, and when the patient insisted, he shoved him away. I watched the patient walk to a corner, pull off his pajamas, and defecate on the floor. I nudged Kowalski, not knowing what to do. He jumped to his feet, ran to the patient, and smacked him in the face with his fist. The man fell back into the smelly pile on the floor.

"You son of a bitch!" Kowalski screamed, "you better get this mess cleaned up." He then slapped the man who was struggling to get to his feet, and pushed him back onto the floor. The patient, attempting to gain his footing, grabbed Kowalski's arm with his soiled hands. Kowalski lost his mind. He started beating the patient with all his might. The poor man was bleeding from the mouth and nose. I ran to the wall phone and called the nurse's station.

"Help, please, help now, very now, please …" I pleaded.

When two other attendants rushed into the dayroom, they bulldozed their way through a ring of onlookers. The man was lying on the floor, and Kowalski was kicking him in the ribs, still spewing expletives. The patient was quickly straitjacketed and carried away. Kowalski changed his uniform and returned to finish watching the program.

The next day I was asked to report to Dr. Baker's office. She sat behind her desk and looked at me thoughtfully.

"The patient who attacked Kowalski in your ward yesterday is in serious condition at the infirmary," she said.

"I not understand," I said.

"Hurt! Badly hurt," she explained.

"Oh, Okay. Badly hurt," I nodded. The light came on; I finally understood. "Kowalski hurt," I said.

"The patient hurt Kowalski?"
"Yes."
"How?"
"He boxed the face."
"Why?"
"Every day, somebody hurt."
"Yesterday, Horváth, what happened yesterday?"
"Kowalski hurt patient."

Dr. Baker looked exasperated. "Before, you said the man punched Kowalski. Now, you say Kowalski hurt the patient. Which is it?"

"I not understand. Kowalski big fist patient. Patient blood from nose. Kowalski—"

I just couldn't explain. I took a pillow off the chair, dropped it on the ground and kicked it hard against the wall. I pointed at myself and said, "Kowalski."

Dr. Baker sighed, stood up and pointed at the pillow. "Patient?" she asked.

"Yes."

"Thank you, Horváth. You may go."

My heart was heavy when I left her office. The next day Kowalski sat next to me in the cafeteria.

"What did you say to Dr. Baker?"

"Sorry, I not understand."

He glared at me. "Did you tell her what happened?"

"Sorry, I not speak English. Sorry."

"Shit," Kowalski said and left.

★ ★ ★

I started devouring words at an increasingly rapid pace so I could get another job. I knew if I didn't get out of there, I would either lose my mind and become one of the patients, or be killed by the attendants. I had a run-in with them nearly every day, usually trying to protect a helpless patient from their brutality. They would go out of their way to make my life miserable. One morning when I about finished mopping, the young burly attendant who relieved Kowalski for the swing shift, kicked my mopping bucket, toppling it over.

"You stupid son of a bitch! Why did you place this underfoot?"

"I not place underfoot; you kick bucket," I said, not very happily.

He kicked the mop against the wall. "Clean up this mess," he growled with a vicious sneer, his fists on his hips.

He was big, about twice my weight, and he frightened me. I turned and walked to the wall phone to call for help. He shoved me aside and ripped the phone out of my hand.

"You little, brown-nosing shit. I said, clean it up!" he yelled, approaching menacingly.

"You stop!" I ordered him, but he kept advancing. I stepped behind the couch to evade him. We played ring-around-the-rosy for a few moments. Unexpectedly, a group of patients started to gather around me. When I had a moment to look up, I saw one of them speaking agitatedly on the telephone. The attendant was furious. In a few seconds, a nurse came into the dayroom, and the attendant backed down. I mopped up the mess while she was there and left with her. I walked straight to the administration building and into Dr. Baker's office.

"What is the matter, Horváth," she asked.

"You call nurse on my ward, please."

She picked up the phone and dialed. She spoke a few words. I watched her face change into a frown as she listened.

"You report to Pine Hall tomorrow," she said replacing the phone in its cradle. She pulled a key from her desk drawer and handed it to me. "I'll change your assignment."

I thanked her. *At least now, I wouldn't have to work with the bastards*, I thought. I now had a key to come and go as I pleased.

Lois the nurse remained the one bright spot in my life. She helped me with calling Laci and Feri, whose phone numbers I received in a letter from my mother. Lois was patient and understanding, herself in trouble with an abusive husband. She had filed for divorce, but he was relentless in his effort to make her suffer. We learned to lean on each other. When I told her my dream was to go to California, she said she would like nothing better than to come along. But she had family in Poughkeepsie and had to stay.

On a beautiful sunny day in March, Bruce, the black attendant I now worked with, got a phone call. When he hung up, his face was all smiles. "We're going to play baseball today," he said happily.
"Bés-ball?" I asked.
"Baseball," he repeated.
Bruce called the patients into a corner of the dayroom. They became very animated when he explained. He selected three of the patients by name and asked me to escort them to the ground floor.

At the nurses' station I was directed to a small room that had striped uniforms, shoes, hats, and other equipment stacked in lockers along the wall. The nurse quickly selected some of these and handed them to the patients. Once she left, the patients stripped and put on the uniforms without needing assistance.

We gathered outside Pine Hall, then walked with the still-excited patients to the sports field. Past the tennis courts there was a mostly grassy area that also had some of the same red surfaces as the tennis courts but only in places. On two sides, stadium style, there were rows of benches just like we had around our soccer fields. But here the comparison ended.

I escorted my patients to the benches, and we joined about fifty others who were already there. From high above, I had a good view of the field. It was shaped, more or less, like a slice of pie, with a metallic wire structure squeezed into the narrow end. This contraption looked like a man's hand; palm facing forward, with the fingers apart and slightly curled forward at the top. It was about three meters high.

In front of the structure there was what appeared to be a dirt strolling path cutting into the lawn, shaped like the diamonds on a playing card. I couldn't imagine the game that would be played on a field such as this.

Just about the time we got settled, men started running onto the field. They wore knickerbockers and had skull-fitting caps with bills that extended over the eyes. I had seen these caps around the hospital; many of the men wore them when they were not on duty. The shoes were cleated just like the ones we used for soccer.

The players tossed small white balls to one another. Some had strange, glove-like things on one hand; they used these to catch the white balls. The gloves looked like frog feet, webbed and much larger than one would expect a glove to be.

Off to the side, a man was engaged in some wild gymnastics. He tossed his ball to another about ten meters away, but every time he would throw the ball, he would lean back, raise one leg high into the air so his toes were well over his head. He did this time and again. Some people used round, oddly shaped sticks of wood to stretch, raise it over the head and lower it down behind the shoulders. Others grabbed the narrow end with both hands and swung it through the air in an arc.

Strangest of all was the man who came onto the field last and crouched in front of the wire contraption. He wore a cage on his head that turned into a grotesque mask in front of his face, with horizontal slats and openings. He had black armor covering the front of his torso and kneepads similar to the ones used by flat-track motorcycle racers who dragged these on the ground to help them corner at high speeds.

Completing the weird ensemble were shin guards; not like those used by soccer players, but big and clumsy, held in place by heavy straps. He reminded me of the divers in Jules Verne's *20,000 Leagues Under The Sea*.

Someone blew a whistle, and the field was cleared. One by one, people wearing red-striped uniforms took positions around the walk. Three others spread out in the grassy area farthest from the wire structure. Captain Nemo's "diver" reappeared in front of the wire cage. A man I had only noticed now, also wearing head-gear and body shield but dressed in black from head to toe, stood closely behind him. Two others, also in black but without the mask and armor, stationed themselves along the sidelines.

To the applause of our crowd of crazies, a tall young man, whom I recognized as one of the patients, walked onto the field and took position on top of a small sandy hill. Someone in the crowd yelled a few words that sounded like encouragement in his direction. The people in the stands laughed.

The last player to take the field was wearing a blue-striped uniform. He walked without haste and carried one of the wooden sticks on his shoulder. A few steps from the diver, he stopped, reached down with his gloved hand, and picked up some of the red dirt from the walk.

He rubbed the dirt into the handle of the stick.

"Play ball," yelled the man dressed in black.

The stick-man stepped in front of the diver and swung his stick wildly several times, then froze with the stick just above his right shoulder. He leaned slightly forward with his feet spread far apart.

One of the white balls was tossed to the young man on the sandy hill by the man in black. He caught it with his frog-foot glove, put the glove between his legs, and started kneading the ball with his bare hands. The diver pushed his mask onto the top of his head and used his cupped hands to yell something to the man on the hill. Then he crouched down, sitting on his heels, and using the fingers of his ungloved hand, he pointed at the ground between his legs. The other grabbed his left ear, slid his fingers along the brim of his hat, and nodded.

He looked to his left, then to his right. He stepped back, holding the ball with both hands, and kicked his left leg high above his head. The next movement was a blur. Lurching forward, he hurled the ball toward the three men positioned in front of the wire cage. The stick-man swung. There was a hard, slapping sound, but I saw nothing.

"Strike," yelled the man in black, jerking his right elbow toward his body and stepping away from the others. The word *strike* must have had a different meaning from what I knew because no one left the game.

The diver stood, retrieved the ball from his frog-gloved hand and tossed it back to the man on the hill. Several of the players yelled to each other, using their hands as megaphones. The one on the hill rudely scratched his privates and spat on the ground, a behavior I thought very ungentlemanly in the company of the ladies in the stands.

This same scenario was played out several times, but without anything else happening. One time the stick-man couldn't get his stick out of the ball's path in time and the ball careened wildly against the wires of the cage. Finally, I understood the purpose of it. I was glad to have Lois join me in the stands; she was someone who might know about this strange game.

"What is it they are trying to do?" I asked.

She smiled. "See the one holding the bat? He's trying to hit the ball so that it flies over the heads of the other players."

"Bat? I haven't seen a bat. And where is the man holding it?" I said perplexed.

She pointed to a new player walking onto the field with the wooden stick.

"That's Kowalski," I said.

"He's carrying a bat," she said. "The club on his shoulder."

"Oh, I was looking for a little winged animal. You mean the stick?"

"Yes. He'll try to hit the ball out of the playing field with the bat, to get on base and score," she explained.

"Uh-ha," I said, but I didn't have the foggiest of what she was talking about. Still, at least I learned that the bat-man was trying to hit the ball.

Responding to some rule I couldn't discern, the teams changed positions several times. Some of the players walked on the path, some ran. At times, the ball was hit and caught, other times, it would just roll on the ground amid much shouting, but no action.

"Bye, I have to go," said Lois. She got up and left with her friends.

"Hey, what about the game?" I yelled after her.

"It's over," she yelled back waving.

"Bye," I said in a tone audible only to myself, and waved back.

Bruce bought a new car, at least new to him, a 1948 Buick. It was black, just like he, and he was anxious to show it off. On our next day off, we drove on the turnpike to Albany, the capital city of New York. He had family there. They were personable, warm-hearted people, and made me feel welcome. We had fried chicken prepared similarly to how Hungarians do it, but with a slightly different taste. I had two helpings; it was delicious. Afterwards, I told Bruce how much I enjoyed his family and our meal.

"Southern hospitality," Bruce explained. "The best people anywhere."

On the way back, Bruce let me try my hand at driving. Until now, the only motor vehicles I had driven were the cable-retriever at Three Borders Mountain, and for a few minutes, a jeep. Never had I driven on the open road and never at such breakneck speeds. Bruce laughed when he saw my white knuckles.

"Step on it," he said. "The turnpike has no speed limit, and 35 is slow even for a sidewalk."

I was glad when I could pull over and he took the wheel.

When we got back to the hospital a message from Feri was waiting for me. He would be visiting Laci in Lockport, New York in a couple of weeks, and he would like to meet me there. I went to see Dr. Baker and asked her if I could take the weekend off instead of the Monday and Tuesday I would normally get. She said she would work on it. Bruce offered to drive me; I gladly accepted.

Laci and Feri saw each other regularly because they had landed near each other. They made friends with a second-generation Hungarian family, the Fehérs, and usually met at their house. When Bruce and I arrived, Mrs. Fehér had a big party for us. One of her daughters played jazz on the piano, the other sang. Bruce used a chair as a drum. We had a great time and I got to talk to Laci and Feri about California.

"I'm staying here," Laci said. "I have a great job, and I met someone I really like."

"Where is she?" I asked. "What's her name?"

"Her name is Betty, but she couldn't get the time off to be here."

"What about you, Feri? Are you happy with your job?"

"I hate it. I'm working for a real idiot, but he's the boss, and I have to do what he says. In a month, I'll be ready to join you and go to California. I know someone who has a friend out there, and he will try to arrange jobs for us."

"That's what I wanted to hear. Every day I spend in Poughkeepsie is torture. When you are ready, I am."

Back at the hospital things remained the same. But Lois said she would leave town too, whenever. I bought my Greyhound ticket for Los Angeles the following week. Feri and I would meet up in Buffalo and travel to California together the rest of the way.

When the big day came, I dropped a letter explaining what I was doing into Dr. Baker's mailbox and walked to the hospital's Hudson gate where I was to meet Lois. Lois did not show up. I waited for an hour past our meeting time, but eventually I had to accept that she was not coming. I called her from the gatehouse and got her husband. I hung up the phone and ran for the Greyhound terminal with my bag in hand, already thinking about California and a better life.